SECOND EDITION

Case Approach to Counseling and Psychotherapy

ABOUT THE AUTHOR

Gerald Corey is Professor and Coordinator of the Human Services Program at California State University at Fullerton. A licensed psychologist and a National Certified Counselor (NCC), he received his doctorate in counseling psychology from the University of Southern California.

Jerry is a Diplomate in Counseling Psychology, American Board of Professional Psychology; is registered as a National Health Service Provider in Psychology; and is a Fellow of the American Psychological Association (Counseling Psychology). He is a member of the American Association for Counseling and Development, the American Group Psychotherapy Association, the Association for Humanistic Psychology, the Association for Specialists in Group Work, the Western Association for Counselor Education and Supervision, the Western Psychological Association, and the National Association of Human Services Educators.

Jerry and his wife, Marianne, and other colleagues regularly give presentations at state, regional, and national conventions. They also conduct in-service training workshops, weeklong residential personal-growth groups, and a variety of special courses and workshops at universities in various parts of the United States and in Mexico, China, and Europe. Jerry's special interest is in teaching theories of counseling and courses in group counseling.

Jerry was the recipient of the Association for Specialists in Group Work's 1984 Professional Career Award for Distinguished Service in the Field of Group Work. In that year he also received the Distinguished Faculty Member Award from the School of Human Development and Community Service of California State University at Fullerton.

Recent publications by Gerald Corey—all with Brooks/Cole Publishing Company—are:

- *I Never Knew I Had a Choice*, Third Edition (1986, in collaboration with Marianne Schneider Corey)
- *Theory and Practice of Counseling and Psychotherapy*, Third Edition (and *Manual*) (1986)
- *Theory and Practice of Group Counseling*, Second Edition (and *Manual*) (1985)
- *Issues and Ethics in the Helping Professions*, Second Edition (1984, with Marianne Schneider Corey and Patrick Callanan)
- *Casebook of Ethical Guidelines for Group Leaders* (1982, with Marianne Schneider Corey and Patrick Callanan)
- *Groups: Process and Practice*, Second Edition (1982, with Marianne Schneider Corey)
- *Group Techniques* (1982, with Marianne Schneider Corey, Patrick Callanan, and J. Michael Russell)

SECOND EDITION

Case Approach to Counseling and Psychotherapy

Gerald Corey
California State University at Fullerton
Diplomate in Counseling Psychology,
American Board of Professional Psychology

Brooks/Cole Publishing Company
Pacific Grove, California

Brooks/Cole Publishing Company
A Division of Wadsworth, Inc.

Printed in the United States of America
10 9 8 7 6 5 4

Library of Congress Cataloging in Publication Data

Corey, Gerald F.
Case approach to counseling and psychotherapy.

Includes bibliographies.
1. Psychotherapy—Case studies. 2. Counseling—Case studies. 3. Case method. I. Title.
RC465.C67 1985 616.89'09 85-9683
ISBN 0-534-05262-2

Sponsoring Editor: *Claire Verduin*
Project Development Editor: *John Bergez*
Editorial Assistant: *Pat Carnahan*
Production Editor: *Fiorella Ljunggren*
Manuscript Editor: *William Waller*
Interior and Cover Design: *Katherine Minerva*
Typesetting: *Kachina Typesetting Inc., Tempe, Arizona*
Printing and Binding: R. R. *Donnelley & Sons Company, Crawfordsville, Indiana*

To my daughters, Cindy and Heidi,
whose enthusiasm for life is a delight,
and to Alexandria, our family cat,
who provides me with nothing but unconditional positive regard,
even though she thinks I am a "case"

PREFACE

Case Approach to Counseling and Psychotherapy (Second Edition) reflects my increasing emphasis on the use of demonstrations and the case-approach method to bridge the gap between the theory and practice of counseling. Students in the courses I teach have found that a demonstration in class often corrects their misconceptions about how a therapy actually works. This book is an attempt to stimulate some of the unique learning that can occur through seeing therapy in action. It also gives students a chance to work with cases from the vantage point of nine therapy approaches: psychoanalytic, Adlerian, existential, person-centered, Gestalt, transactional analysis, behavior, rational-emotive, and reality.

The format of this book gives students an opportunity to see how each of the various therapeutic approaches is applied to a single individual, *Ruth*, who is followed throughout the book. Each of the nine theory chapters presents the following common aspects of her therapy: (1) basic assumptions, (2) initial assessment of Ruth, (3) goals of the therapy, and (4) therapeutic procedures.

The *therapeutic process* is concretely illustrated by client/therapist dialogues, which are developed through process commentaries (or brief discussions pertaining to the course of therapy). These commentaries explain the rationale for the therapist's interventions as well as pointing to directions that each therapeutic orientation might take. *Questions for reflection* encourage students to apply the material to their personal life and offer guidelines for continuing to work with Ruth within each theoretical orientation.

For teaching purposes I take on the role of Ruth's therapist for each of the therapy systems. Although I have attempted to work with Ruth within the general parameters of the particular theory under discussion, I should make it clear that readers are getting my version of how these therapies might be practically applied. I find it difficult to present a "puristic" approach, because I believe that even within a theoretical camp there is great variability in translating theory into practice.

A *second case* is then presented in each theory chapter to further illustrate how the concepts of a particular theory may be applied, and students are again asked to work with the client within the framework of that orientation. The rationale for providing a second case is to focus on a different set of life themes and to show how the same theory can be applied to a person with problems different from Ruth's. Also, these second cases illustrate therapy techniques additional to those used with Ruth. Again, specific questions are provided to help students proceed.

After the nine theory chapters, Chapter Eleven is devoted to bringing the approaches together and providing assistance to students in developing their own therapeutic style. Key themes addressed in Ruth's therapy are dealt with from several contrasting therapeutic perspectives. Then I demonstrate how I would work with Ruth using my own approach. This consists of my integrated perspective, drawing upon all nine approaches for a conceptual framework as well as for techniques and procedures.

A final chapter contains supplementary cases for students to gain further practice. Cases 1–9 are *identified* by a specific theory. Thus, if a third case is desired for each approach, reference can be made to Chapter Twelve at the same time that each chapter is being studied. Cases 10–15 are *unidentified*, designed to give students practice in taking a situation without contextual clues and approaching it from the stance of determining which theory or combination of theories is most appropriate. These unanalyzed cases are intended to be discussed only after students have read the whole book. Students can then compare and contrast approaches, use a combination of concepts and techniques drawn from several theories, and attempt to apply their own personal therapeutic style to these six cases.

Case Approach to Counseling and Psychotherapy can be used as part of a *package* of Brooks/Cole books that I have written for courses in counseling theory and practice. In the textbook, *Theory and Practice of Counseling and Psychotherapy* (Third Edition, 1986), students are given an overview of the key concepts and the applications of techniques that flow from the nine contemporary therapy models. In the accompanying *Manual for Theory and Practice of Counseling and Psychotherapy* (Third Edition), there are many experiential activities and exercises designed to help students apply the theories to themselves personally and to connect theory with practice.

This casebook can also be used, however, in conjunction with any standard text on counseling theory, and references to several textbooks are noted at the end of the theory chapters. The present book assumes that the student has been exposed to the major theories. Unless students have had a course in counseling theory or have at least read a textbook covering the range of contemporary approaches, they will have trouble in working with the cases in this book, for it is not designed as a substitute for a survey text. At the end of each chapter are several annotated sources particular to each theory that can be used as background reading.

Acknowledgments

A number of professors and students have reviewed this book, and their useful suggestions have led to substantial revisions and the expansion of the original edition. Because of reviewers' reactions, I decided to greatly expand information on Ruth's case, as well as to provide a concise summary of key concepts of the therapies discussed. I am most appreciative of the student reactions, which helped bring more reality and clarity to the cases. The following students read the revised edition and offered suggestions that strengthened the book: Joanna Doland, Susan Gattis, Carl Johnson, Andrea Mark, and Donna Robbins.

I also appreciate the support and challenge given by those professors of counseling courses and clinicians who read the revised manuscript and provided direction for improving the effectiveness of the case presentations. In a real sense they served as collaborators on this project by providing rich detail to the cases. These people are Patrick Callanan; William Culp of Indiana University of Pennsylvania; Michael Dougherty of Western Carolina University; Mary Moline of Loma Linda University; Beverly Palmer of California State University at Dominguez Hills; Jorja J. M. Prover; and J. Michael Russell of California State University at Fullerton.

Recognition goes to the staff of Brooks/Cole Publishing Company, who have given extra time and attention to this revised edition, especially John Bergez, who provided a clear design for organizational changes, and Claire Verduin and Fiorella Ljunggren, both of whom offered valuable help, humor, and a sense of perspective when times became difficult. Bill Waller, manuscript editor, has helped make this a more readable book.

Special appreciation is extended to Marianne Schneider Corey, my wife and colleague, for her support, time, and contribution to this revision. Drawing on her clinical experience as a marriage and family therapist, she painstakingly went over each case, challenging me to pay attention to important nuances. She also collaborated with me on this project by assisting in the creation of many of the client/therapist dialogues.

Finally, I want to acknowledge the special clients I have worked with in groups and workshops. Over the years my contact with these people has taught me more than I ever learned from courses and textbooks. Indeed, through these encounters I have developed many of the themes that appear in this book. Many of these clients' struggles and life themes appear in disguised form in the cases presented in this book.

Gerald Corey

CONTENTS

SECOND EDITION

Case Approach to Counseling and Psychotherapy

CHAPTER ONE

Introduction and Overview

Structure of the Book

Students in my classes in counseling theory and practice have consistently told me that seeing a counseling session in action provides them with a concrete illustration of how a therapy works. At times, even after reading about a theory and discussing it in class, students still have unclear notions about its applications. I began to experiment by asking students to volunteer for a class demonstration in which they served as "clients." Seeing concepts in action gave them a clearer picture of how therapists from various approaches work.

This book is designed to show you nine therapies in action and to give you some experience in working with different cases. I advocate that you learn how to selectively borrow concepts and techniques from *all* of the major therapeutic approaches, and I encourage you to search for some basis for integrating techniques into a style that is an expression of who you are as a person. Before such a large task of developing a personalized approach can be hoped for, however, it is necessary to know the basics of each of the theories and to have some experience with these therapies. Toward this end I have written this book with some balance between describing the way therapists with a given orientation might proceed with a client *and* challenging you to try your hand at showing how you would proceed with the same client.

In this initial chapter I describe methods of conceptualizing a case, and I provide background material on the central figure in this book—Ruth. Her intake form and autobiography can be referred to frequently as you work with her in the nine theory chapters. Ruth is not an actual client. I have created her by putting together many of the common themes that I observe in my work with clients. Thus, in Ruth's case as in all of the other cases in this book, the clients have a basis in fact, but details have given them a new identity. In this way, I believe, the clients represent some of those you may meet.

Ruth appears in each of the chapters on individual theories (Chapters Two to Ten). Each chapter begins with a look at the approach's basic assumptions, an initial assessment of Ruth, and an examination of the theory's therapeutic goals and procedures. The therapeutic process is made concrete with samples of dialogues between Ruth and her various therapists, along with process commentaries to provide an explanation of the direction therapy is taking.

You are asked to become an active learner by evaluating the manner in which I work with Ruth from each of the nine theoretical perspectives. You are also asked to show how you would proceed with Ruth's counseling, using the particular approach being considered in the chapter. To guide you in thinking of ways to work with Ruth, I provide questions for your consideration. I strongly suggest that, besides reflecting on these questions by yourself, you arrange to work with fellow students in small discussion groups as you explore various alternatives. I am convinced that you will get more value from these cases if you are willing to exchange viewpoints on them.

In Chapters Two–Ten, following Ruth's case there is another case for additional practice. I decided to offer a second case to show you how the same therapy approach can be applied to a client with different life themes and issues. This second case also allows me to describe some other techniques for each therapy besides those employed with Ruth. As with the case of Ruth, you are invited to become an active participant and show how you would continue working with each of these second cases if the client were referred to you. You will learn the nine therapy systems best if you think and work within the general framework of each theory. You will also be able to determine what aspects of that approach you would most like to draw from as you begin putting together your own synthesis, your personal counseling style.

You can further enhance your learning by participating in a variety of role-playing exercises in which you "become" the client under discussion, and also by participating in small-group discussions based on the cases. Rather than merely reading about these cases, you can use them to stimulate reflection on ways that you have felt like the given client. Thus, as you read about Ruth, Walt, Sally, Manny, and so on, it will help if you reflect on the degree to which you see yourself in these people. I hope that you will use the themes that run through the various cases as catalysts that touch your own experience. In experiential practice sessions you can "become" the client by drawing on your own concerns, and you can also gain some valuable practice in "becoming" the counselor. Think of as many ways as possible to use these cases as a method of stimulating introspection and as a basis for providing lively class discussion.

In the final chapter I provide 15 additional cases. Nine of these cases correspond to the approaches discussed in this book. If you have the time and the interest, you can refer to these cases as you study each chapter. Of course, using Chapter Twelve as a review of all the theories is another option. The more practice you can get with different clients, the better sense you will have of each theory. I have decided to provide more cases than you might have time to discuss in class, so that you can select those that have the most meaning and interest to you. After each of the cases I raise a number of questions that I hope will serve as catalysts for your thinking. I suggest that you focus on those questions that seem to best put the cases into perspective for you.

I encourage you to consider the advantages of eventually developing your own counseling theory and style. Such an *eclectic perspective* of counseling entails selecting concepts and methods from various sources and theories. It does not necessarily refer to developing a new theory; rather, it emphasizes some systematic basis for integrating underlying principles and techniques of the various therapy systems. Those who call themselves eclectic range from practitioners who haphazardly pick and choose to those who seriously look for ways to validate their own personal perspective. I am not endorsing a sloppy eclecticism of grabbing at any technique that appears to work. Instead, I encourage you to strive to build a unified system that fits you and is appropriate for the particular setting in which you practice. It is also essential to be willing to challenge your basic assumptions, test your hypotheses as you practice, and revise your theory as you confirm or disconfirm your clinical hunches.

Of course, developing a personalized counseling stance is a long-term process that requires a good grasp of the theories and much experience in counseling. Although it may be unrealistic to expect you to complete the formulation of your personal perspective while reading this book, my hope is that you will begin this process. Toward this end I suggest that you develop your own reading program, emphasizing those theories that you find the most valuable in understanding and working with a diverse range of clients. After each theory chapter you will find reading suggestions. The *Recommended Supplementary Readings* are a few selected annotated readings that you might find most useful if you want to learn more about each theory. The next section, *Suggested Readings*, lists eight textbooks on counseling theory, with the specific chapters for the theory under discussion. If you feel a need to review some of these theories, any of these references could be of value. Because this book is not intended to be a substitute for a theory textbook, you will want to read selected chapters from such a text if you need a refresher on theories.

To get a general overview of the structure of this book and the best way to use it, I strongly recommend that you (1) read the Preface, (2) glance at the main headings of all the chapters, and (3) at least skim Chapter Eleven, so that you can begin to see how the nine theories can be used together in working with a single case.

Overview of the Therapeutic Perspectives

In the chapters to follow, the case of Ruth will be analyzed and discussed from nine therapeutic perspectives. For each of these perspectives we will consider (1) its basic assumptions, (2) its view of how to assess clients, (3) its goals for therapy, and (4) its therapeutic procedures. This section presents the essence of the various approaches. As a way of laying the foundation for developing an eclectic, integrative approach, we will look for common denominators of the nine perspectives and also differences among them.

Basic Assumptions

When you make initial contact with a client, your theoretical perspective determines what you look for and what you see. It largely determines the focus and course of therapy, and it influences your choice of therapeutic procedures and strategies. As you are developing your counseling stance, you will need to pay attention to the basic assumptions you hold as well as how these assumptions affect the way you view clients and work with them. Developing a counseling stance is more involved than merely accepting the tenets of a particular theory or combination of theories. The theoretical approach you use to guide you in your practice is an expression of your uniqueness as a person and an outgrowth of your life experience.

What is the influence of your theoretical assumptions on practice? The goals that you think are important in therapy, the techniques and strategies that you employ to reach these goals, the way in which you see the division of responsibility in the client/therapist relationship, your view of your role and functions as a counselor, and your view of the role of the assessment of clients are largely determined by your theoretical orientation.

Attempting to practice counseling without at least a general theoretical perspective is somewhat like flying a plane without a map and without instruments. A counseling stance is not a rigid structure that prescribes the specific steps of what to do in therapeutic work. Instead, a theoretical orientation is a set of general guidelines that you can use to make sense of what you are doing. One way to consider the basic assumptions underlying the major theoretical orientations is to consider three categories of theory under which most of the contemporary systems fall. These are (1) the *psychodynamic approaches*, which stress insight in therapy (psychoanalytic and Adlerian therapy); (2) the *experiential and relationship-oriented approaches*, which tend to stress feelings and subjective experiencing (existential, person-centered, and Gestalt therapy); and (3) the *cognitive and behavioral approaches*, which stress the role of thinking and doing and tend to be action oriented (transactional analysis, behavior therapy, rational-emotive and other cognitive therapies, and reality therapy). Actually, Adlerian therapy, which I classified above as a psychodynamic approach, could be placed in the cognitive/behavioral camp as well, for in some respects it foreshadowed the current interest in the cognitive therapies. What follows is a thumbnail sketch of the basic assumptions underlying each of these nine therapeutic systems.

Psychoanalytic therapy. The psychoanalytic approach embodies the assumptions of the medical model. Human nature is viewed from a deterministic framework. People are largely determined by unconscious motivation, irrational forces, sexual and aggressive impulses, and early childhood experiences. Because the dynamics of behavior are buried in the unconscious, treatment consists of a lengthy process of analyzing inner conflicts that are rooted in the past. Therapy is largely a process of the therapist's direction in restructuring the personality; therefore, clients must be willing to commit themselves to an intensive, long-term process. It should be noted that some of the extensions of psychoanalysis (such as the ego psychology of Erik Erikson and the theories of contemporary psychoanalytic writers) are not necessarily grounded in these basic assumptions of human nature.

Adlerian therapy. According to the Adlerian approach, people are primarily social beings, shaped and motivated by social forces. Human nature is viewed as creative, active, and decisional. Adler held that we are pushed by the need to overcome inherent feelings of inferiority and pulled by the striving for superiority. He asserted that we develop inferiority feelings, which stem from childhood, and that we then develop a style of life aimed at compensating for such feelings and becoming the master of our fate. The style of life consists of our views about ourselves and the world and distinctive behaviors we adopt in the pursuit of our life goals. We can shape our own future by actively and courageously taking risks and making decisions in the face of unknown consequences. Clients are not viewed as being "sick" and needing to be "cured"; rather, they are seen as discouraged and needing encouragement to correct mistaken self-perceptions. Counseling is not simply a matter of an expert therapist making prescriptions for change. It is viewed as a collaborative effort, with the client and the therapist actively working on mutually agreed-on goals.

Existential therapy. The existential perspective holds that we define ourselves by our choices. Although there are factors that restrict the range of our choices, we are ultimately the author of our life. Existential practitioners contend that clients often lead a "restricted existence," seeing few if any alternatives to limited ways of dealing with life situations and tending to feel trapped or helpless. The therapist's job is to confront these clients with the ways in which they are living a restricted life and to help them become aware of their own part in creating this condition. As an outgrowth of the therapeutic venture, clients are able to recognize outmoded patterns of living, and they begin to accept responsibility for changing their future.

Person-centered therapy. The person-centered approach rests on the assumption that we have the capacity to understand our problems and that we have the resources within us to effectively resolve them. Emphasis is placed on the basic trustworthiness of human beings. The implication is that clients can move forward toward growth and wholeness in the absence of a high degree of structure and direction from the therapist. Seeing people in this light means that the therapist focuses on the constructive side of human nature and on what is right with people. Therapy becomes something more than a process of objective assessment, diagnosis, and treatment. Clients are able to make progress without the therapist's interpretations, diagnoses, evaluations, and directions. Clients do need from the therapist understanding, acceptance, support, respect, caring, and positive regard.

Gestalt therapy. The Gestalt approach is based on the assumption that people must find their own way in life and accept personal responsibility if they hope to achieve maturity. The therapist's task is to provide a climate in which clients can fully experience their here-and-now awareness and can recognize how they are preventing themselves from living in the present. Clients carry on their own therapy as much as possible by doing experiments aimed at change and finding their own meanings. They are encouraged to experience their conflicts directly instead of merely talking about them, by which they gradually expand their own level of awareness and integrate the fragmented and unknown aspects of themselves.

Transactional analysis. TA acknowledges that we were influenced by the expectations and demands (injunctions) of significant others, because our early decisions were made when we were children and were highly dependent on others. We were not passively "scripted," however, for we did cooperate in making these early decisions. Thus, we can recognize how certain early decisions may be archaic or nonfunctional, and we can make new decisions that are more appropriate. Therapists play an active and directive role and function much like teachers and resource people in therapy. Clients are viewed as equal partners in the therapeutic endeavor. If therapy is to be effective, clients must carry out contracts that specify what they will change. The goal of therapy is to free clients from outdated early decisions and help them make new decisions about how they will live.

Behavior therapy. Although behavior therapy assumes that people are basically shaped by learning and sociocultural conditioning, this approach does focus on the client's ability to eliminate maladaptive behavior and acquire constructive behavior. Behavior therapy is a systematic approach that begins with a comprehensive assessment of the individual to determine the present level of functioning as a prelude to setting therapeutic goals. After clear and specific behavioral goals are established by the client, the therapist typically suggests strategies that are most appropriate for meeting these stated goals. The therapist's role is to teach clients how to recognize and alter maladaptive behavioral patterns, leading to permanent changes in behavior. It is assumed that clients will progress only if they are willing to practice new behaviors in real-life situations. A basic part of therapy is continual evaluation to determine how well the procedures and techniques are working for the client.

Rational-emotive therapy. From the perspective of RET our problems are caused by our perception of life situations and our thoughts, not by the situations themselves, not by others, and not by past events. Thus, it is our responsibility to recognize and change distorted thinking that leads to emotional and behavior disorders. RET also holds that people tend to incorporate irrational beliefs from external sources and then continue to indoctrinate themselves with this faulty thinking. To overcome irrational thinking, therapists use active and directive procedures, including teaching, suggestion, and assigning of homework. Therapists have the job of persuading clients to do what is necessary to make long-lasting and substantive changes. The goal of therapy is to substitute a rational belief system for an irrational one and to have the client eventually assume responsibility for solutions.

Other cognitive-behavioral therapies share some of the assumptions of RET. A basic assumption of many of these approaches is that people are prone to learning erroneous, self-defeating notions and that they are capable of unlearning or correcting them as well. By pinpointing fallacies in their thinking and correcting them, individuals can create a more self-fulfilling life. Cognitive restructuring plays a central role in these therapies. People are assumed to be able to make changes by learning to listen to their self-talk, by learning a new internal dialogue, and by learning new coping skills needed for behavioral changes.

Reality therapy. Like rational-emotive therapy, the reality approach is largely didactic. Therapists have the task of challenging clients to look at their current behavior, urging them to make a decision whether what they are doing is working effectively for them, and then teaching them better ways to meet their needs. It is clients' responsibility to decide for themselves if they want to change their behavior and, if they do, what aspects of it they want to modify. To do this, it is assumed that planning and making commitments to stick with these plans will be the core of the therapy process. Therapists do not accept any excuses for failing to follow through on commitments; rather, they challenge clients to reevaluate whether they really want to make changes.

Views of Assessment

Some therapy approaches stress the importance of conducting a comprehensive assessment of the client as the initial step in the therapy process. The rationale is that specific therapeutic goals cannot be formulated, nor can appropriate treatment strategies be designed, until this thorough picture of a client's past and current functioning is completed. In this section the various views of the role of assessment in the therapy process are described. Some ways of conceptualizing an individual case are also presented, with emphasis given to the types of information that it is helpful to gather during the initial stages of therapy.

Psychoanalytic therapy. Psychoanalysts assume that normal personality development is based on dealing successfully with successive psychosexual and psychosocial stages of development. Faulty personality development is the result of inadequate resolution at some specific stage. Therapists are interested in the client's early history as a way of understanding how past situations have contributed to a dysfunction. Projective testing (techniques designed to tap a client's unconscious processes) may be used as a way of identifying themes running through the client's life. Other forms of personality assessment are also used. Because psychoanalytic therapy is based on the medical model, focusing on psychological disorders and their treatment, it emphasizes the importance of comprehensive assessment techniques as a basis for understanding personality dynamics and the origin of emotional disorders.

Adlerian therapy. Assessment is a basic part of Adlerian therapy. After creating a relationship based on trust and cooperation, the therapist conducts a comprehensive interview to gather specific information about the client's family constellation and early recollections. Clients are often asked to complete a detailed life-style questionnaire. Interest is devoted to family relationships and how the family structure has influenced the client's development. Childhood experiences are connected up with the shaping of one's unique style of life, which includes one's views of self, others, and the world. All of these data are summarized, integrated, and interpreted in light of "basic mistakes" (faulty perceptions and assumptions about life) that the client originally made and has carried through into present functioning. This assessment, which is made early in therapy, provides a direction for the course of therapy.

Existential therapy. Therapists with an existential orientation maintain that the way to understand the client is by grasping the essence of the person's subjective world. They view assessment that is done objectively as missing the point, for it overlooks the reality of the inner person. Likewise, diagnosis of clients, which is an external measure done by others that results in some type of clinical classification, is not given weight. Every attempt is made to grasp the internal world of the client.

Person-centered therapy. In much the same spirit as the existential orientation, person-centered therapists maintain that assessment and diagnosis are detrimental because they are external ways of understanding the client. The reasons for this opposition to objective assessment procedures, leading to a diagnosis, are that (1) the best vantage point for understanding another person is through his or her subjective world; (2) the practitioner can become preoccupied with the client's history and thus neglect present attitudes and behavior; and (3) therapists could develop a judgmental attitude, with the responsibility being shifted too much in the direction of telling clients what they ought to do. Focusing on gathering information about a client can lead to an intellectualized conception *about* the client. The client is assumed to be the one who knows the dynamics of his or her behavior, and for change to occur the client must experience a perceptual change, not simply receive data.

Gestalt therapy. Like the previous two approaches, Gestalt therapy does not gather information about clients as a prerequisite to therapy. It does not use diagnostic labels, because they are seen as an escape from full participation in the client/therapist relationship. Assessment and diagnostic procedures might foster *talking about* a client's life, whereas the focus of this therapy is gaining awareness by *direct experiencing*. It is assumed that the salient points in a person's developmental history will surface as the client pays attention to where he or she is stuck in the present. Themes that run through a person's life will become evident during the therapy process itself.

Transactional analysis. A rather detailed life-script questionnaire may be used to collect significant information pertaining to parental messages that the client accepted, early decisions that were made based on such messages, and other relevant data that tie into the client's life script. Once clients have reviewed some of their decisions that are influencing the course of their life, they are able to select specific goals for therapy. This assessment process culminates with clients' developing a therapeutic contract that spells out what they will change.

Behavior therapy. The behavioral approach begins with a comprehensive assessment of the client's present functioning, with questions directed to past learning that is related to current behavior patterns. The purpose of the assessment is to gain sufficient knowledge of present behavior that a differential treatment plan can be tailored to the client. An objective appraisal of specific behaviors and the stimuli that are maintaining them is called for. After this assessment a treatment plan can be developed, and an evaluation can be made of the effects of the treatment. Some of the reasons for conducting a thorough assessment at the outset of therapy are that (1) it identifies behavioral deficiencies as well as assets, (2) it provides an objective means of appraising both a client's specific symptoms and the factors that have led up to the client's malfunctioning, (3) it facilitates the selection of the most suitable therapy techniques, (4) it specifies a new learning and shaping schedule, (5) it is useful in predicting the course and the outcome of a particular clinical disorder, and (6) it provides a framework for research into the effectiveness of the procedures employed.

Rational-emotive therapy. The assessment used in RET is based on getting a sense of the client's patterns of thinking. Attention is paid to various beliefs that the client has developed in relation to certain events. Concern is not merely with gathering data about past events; rather, the therapist looks for evidences of faulty thinking and irrational beliefs that the client has incorporated. Once rigid, unrealistic, absolutistic ideas have been identified, the therapy process consists of actively undermining these self-defeating beliefs and substituting constructive ones.

Other cognitive-behavioral therapies also emphasize the value of the assessment process. For example, clients discover their warped thinking and learn more realistic ways to formulate their experiences.

Reality therapy. Assessment of clients is typically not a formal process; psychological testing and diagnoses are not generally a part of the therapy process. There is little interest in the causes of an individual's current problems or in gathering information about the client's past experiences. Instead, the focus is on getting clients to take a critical look at what they are doing now and then to determine the degree to which their present behavior is effective. This informal assessment directs clients to pay attention to their successes, personal strengths, and assets. Therapy then builds on what is right with the client.

My own perspective on assessment. Now that we have surveyed the nine theories of assessment, let me present my ideas on this issue. I see assessment and diagnosis, broadly construed, as a legitimate part of therapy. The assessment process does not necessarily have to be completed during the intake interview, nor does it have to be a fixed judgment that the therapist makes about the client. It is a continuing process that focuses on understanding the client. Ideally, it is the result of a joint effort by the client and the therapist that flows out of an ongoing interaction between them. Both should be involved in discovering the nature of the client's presenting problem, a process that begins with the initial sessions and continues until therapy ends. The questions that are helpful for a therapist to consider during this early assessment phase are:

- What are my immediate and overall reactions to the client?
- What is going on in this client's life at this time?
- What are the client's main assets and liabilities?
- What are the client's resources for change?
- Is this a crisis situation, or is it a long-standing problem?
- What does the client primarily want from therapy, and how can it best be achieved?
- What should be the focus of the sessions?
- What are some of the major factors that appear to be contributing to the client's current problems, and what can be done to alleviate them?
- What are some significant past events that appear to be related to the client's present level of functioning?
- What specific family dynamics might be relevant to the client's present struggles and interpersonal relationships?
- What support systems can the client tap in making changes? Who are the significant others in the client's life?
- What are the prospects for meaningful change?

As a result of questions such as these, therapists will develop tentative hypotheses about their clients, and they can share them with the clients in an ongoing way. This process of assessment does not have to result in classifying the client under some clinical category. Instead, counselors can describe behavior as they observe it and encourage clients to think about its meaning. In this way, assessment becomes a process of *thinking about* the client *with* the client, rather than a mechanical procedure conducted by an expert therapist. From this perspective, assessment and diagnostic thinking are vital to the therapeutic procedures that are selected, and such a process helps practitioners conceptualize a case.

General guidelines for assessment. The intake interview typically centers on making the assessment described earlier and prescribing an appropriate course of treatment.

As we have seen, depending on the practitioner's orientation this assessment may take many forms. For example, Adlerians look for ways that the family structure has affected the client's development, whereas a psychoanalytic practitioner is interested in intrapsychic conflicts. This section will present a fairly comprehensive scheme for conceptualizing an individual case. After looking at several intake forms and case summary forms, I have pulled together some guidelines that might be helpful in thinking about ways of getting significant information and about where to proceed with a client after making an initial assessment. Below are ten areas that are a basic part of conceptualizing an individual case.

1. *Identifying data.* Get details such as name, age, birthdate, sex, appearance, ethnic background, socioeconomic status, marital status, religious identification, and referral source. (Who referred the client and for what purpose?)

2. *Presenting problem(s).* What is the chief complaint? This includes a brief description in the client's own words of immediate problems for which he or she is requesting therapy. The presenting situation includes a description of the problems, how long they have existed, what has been done to cope with them, and why the client is seeking therapy at this time. Other relevant factors are precipitating events, duration of the problem, progression, current status, and other central conflicts besides the presenting problem.

3. *Current living circumstances.* Information to collect here includes marital status and history, family data, recent moves, financial status, legal problems, basic conflicts or concerns in one's life-style, support systems, and evident problems in relationships with significant others.

4. *Psychological analysis and assessment.* What is the client's general psychological state? (For example, how does the client view his or her life situation, needs, and problems? What is the client's level of maturity? Is there evidence of detrimental influences in the client's life?) What are the client's dominant emotions? (Is the client sad, excited, anxious, ashamed, angry?) This phase of assessment entails describing the client's ego functioning, which includes self-concept, self-esteem, memory, orientation, fantasies, ability to tolerate frustration, insight, and motivation to change. The focus is on the client's view of self, including perceived strengths and weaknesses, the client's ideal self, and how the client believes that others view him or her. What is the client's level of security? What is the client's ability to see and cope with reality, capacity for decision making, degree of self-control and self-direction, and ability to deal with life changes and transitions? Standardized psychological tests of intelligence, personality, aptitudes, and interests may be used. Another assessment procedure is the *mental-status examination* (a structured interview leading to information about the client's psychological level of functioning).

This examination focuses on areas such as appearance, behavior, feeling, perception, and thinking. For example, under the *behavior* category the counselor making the assessment will notice specific dimensions of behavior, including posture, facial expressions, general body movements, quality of speech, and behavior in the interview situation. Under the *thinking* category it is important to assess factors such as the client's intellectual functioning, orientation, insight, judgment, memory, thought processes, and any disturbances in thinking.

5. *Psychosocial developmental history*. The focus here is on the developmental and etiological factors relating to the client's present difficulties. Five types can be considered here: (1) precipitating factors—for example, maturational or situational stress, school entry, divorce, or death of a parent; (2) predisposing factors—for example, parent/child relationships and other family patterns, personality structure, and hereditary or constitutional factors; (3) contributory factors—for example, current or related illness and problems of family members; (4) perpetuating factors—for example, secondary gains such as the sympathy that a sufferer from migraine headaches elicits; (5) sociocultural factors—that is, customs, traditions, family patterns, and cultural values. In thinking in a developmental perspective, the following questions could be asked: How well has the client mastered earlier developmental tasks? What are some evidences of conflicts and problems originating in childhood? What were some critical turning points in the individual's life? What were some major crises, and how were they handled? What key choices were made, and how are these past decisions related to present functioning? How did the client's relationships within the family influence development? What was it like for the client to be in the family? What are some past and current relationships that are of significance to the client? How are these relationships significant now? How are the client's cultural experiences related to the individual's personality? This section might conclude with a summary of developmental history, which could include birth and early development, toilet training, patterns of discipline, developmental delays, educational experiences, sexual development, social development, and influence of religious, cultural, and value orientations.

6. *Health and medical history*. What is the client's medical history? What was the date of the client's last consultation with a physician, and what were the results? Is there any noticeable evidence of recent physical trauma or neglect (for example, battering, welt marks, bruises, needle marks, sloppy clothing, sallow complexion)? What is the client's overall state of health? Included is an assessment of the client's mental health. Has the client been in previous treatment for the present problem? Has there been a prior hospitalization? Has the client been taking medications? What were the outcomes of previous treatments? Is there any history of emotional illness in the family? It is important to be alert to signs that may indicate an organic basis for a client's problem (such as headaches, sudden changes in personal habits or in personality, and other physical symptoms).

7. *Adjustment to work*. What does the client do or expect to do? How satisfied is the client with work? What is the meaning of work to the person? Does he or she have future plans? What are the benefits and drawbacks of work?

8. *Lethality*. Is the client a danger to self or others? Is he or she thinking about suicide or about hurting someone or something? Does the client have a specific plan either for committing suicide or for harming another person? Have there been prior attempts at self-destruction or violent behavior toward others?

9. *Present human relationships*. This would include a survey of information pertaining to marriage, siblings, parents, children, friends, work, school, and social life. Included are the level of sexual functioning, family beliefs and values, and satisfaction derived from relationships. What are the client's main problems and

conflicts with others? How does he or she deal with conflict? What support does the client get from others?

10. *Summary and case formulation.* Provide a summary of the client's psychodynamics, major defenses, and ego strengths, and make an assessment. What are the major recommendations? What is the suggested focus for therapeutic intervention? (This formulation might specify the frequency and duration of treatment, the preferred therapeutic orientation, and the mode of treatment.)

After the initial assessment of the client is completed, a decision is made whether to refer the client for alternative or additional treatment. If the client is accepted by the therapist, the results can be discussed with the person, and this information can be used in exploring his or her difficulties in thinking, feeling, and behaving and in setting treatment goals. Assessment can be linked directly to the therapy process, forming a basis for developing methods of evaluation of how well the therapeutic procedures are working toward the client's goals.

Because most mental-health agencies require interns and professionals alike to do intake interviews, familiarity with these assessment procedures is essential.

Goals of the Therapy

After the initial comprehensive assessment of a client, therapeutic goals need to be established. These goals will vary, depending in part upon the practitioner's theoretical orientation. For example, psychoanalytic therapy is primarily an insight approach that aims at regressing clients to very early levels of psychological development so they can acquire the self-understanding necessary for major character restructuring. Psychoanalytic therapy deals extensively with the past, with unconscious dynamics, with transference, and with techniques aimed at changing attitudes and feelings. At the other extreme is reality therapy, which focuses on evaluating current behavior in the hope that the client will develop a realistic plan leading to more effective ways of behaving. Reality therapy is not concerned with exploring the past, with unconscious motivation, with the transference clients might develop, or with attitudes and feelings. It asks the key question "What is the client doing now, and what does the client want to be doing differently?"

In surveying therapeutic goals we find a diverse group, including restructuring personality, finding meaning in life, creating an I/thou relationship between the client and the counselor, eliminating irrational beliefs, teaching clients how to rewrite their life script, helping them look within themselves to find the answers they are looking for, substituting effective behaviors for maladaptive behaviors, and correcting mistaken beliefs and assumptions. Given this wide range, it is obvious that the perspectives of the client and the therapist on goals will surely have an impact on the course of therapy. The goals specify what interventions will be made and how time will be spent in therapy.

Despite this diversity of goals, all of the therapies share some common denominators. All approaches aim at increasing the individual's autonomy—that is, at intervening to encourage the client to develop resources for making changes that will lead to self-reliance. To some degree, all of the approaches also have the goal of identifying what the client wants and then modifying the client's feelings, thoughts, and behaviors. It is simply that some therapies focus on a particular dimension as a route to changing other facets of personality. For example, both Adlerian and rational-emotive therapists focus on the client's cognitions under the assumption that, if they are successful in modifying a client's beliefs and thought processes, behavioral changes will follow, and from these changes feelings will eventually be modified. As you read the chapters, think of ways that you might integrate the various theoretical perspectives so that you are able to work on all three levels.

Goals of the nine approaches. Below is a summary chart showing the essence of each of the theoretical perspectives on the matter of goals. Consider how you might combine the concepts and techniques of several theories as a way to meet more than a singular goal in counseling clients.

- *Psychoanalytic therapy.* The main goal is to explore the unconscious. Other goals include assisting clients to relive earlier experiences and work through repressed conflicts toward the end of reconstructing their basic personality.
- *Adlerian therapy.* Therapists aim at helping clients develop social interest, to provide encouragement to discouraged individuals, to facilitate insight into mistaken ideas, and to show how these ideas are related to the development of one's unique style of life.
- *Existential therapy.* The principal goal is to challenge clients to recognize and accept the freedom they have to become the author of their life. Therapists confront them on ways that they are avoiding accepting their freedom and the responsibility that accompanies it.
- *Person-centered therapy.* The approach seeks to provide a climate of understanding and acceptance through the client/therapist relationship that will enable clients to nondefensively come to terms with aspects of themselves that they have denied or disowned. It aims to enable clients to move toward greater openness, increased sense of trust in themselves, a willingness to be a process rather than a finished product, and an increased sense of spontaneity.
- *Gestalt therapy.* The goal is to challenge clients to move from environmental support to self-support and to assist them in gaining awareness of moment-to-moment experiencing. Clients are encouraged to experience directly in the present their struggles with "unfinished business" from their past, which allows them to integrate fragmented parts of their personality.
- *Transactional analysis.* Therapists strive to help clients become script-free, game-free, autonomous people capable of choosing intimate relationships. They assist clients in examining the basis on which early decisions were made and in making more appropriate decisions based on new evidence.
- *Behavior therapy.* The main goal is to eliminate clients' maladaptive behavior patterns and help them learn constructive patterns. Therapists teach clients specific skills that they can use in developing a self-directed and self-managed behavioral change program. They identify patterns of thinking that lead to behavioral problems, and then teach new ways of thinking that are designed to change the clients' ways of acting.

· *Rational-emotive therapy.* The goal is to eliminate clients' self-defeating outlook on life and assist them in acquiring a more tolerant and rational view of life. This is done by teaching clients how they incorporated irrational beliefs, how they are now maintaining this faulty thinking, what they can do to undermine such thinking, and how they can teach themselves new ways of thinking that will lead to changes in their ways of behaving and feeling.

· *Reality therapy.* The approach challenges clients to make an assessment of their current behavior to determine if such ways of acting are getting them what they want from life. The therapist assists clients in making plans to change specific behaviors that they determine are not working for them.

My perspective on goals. As much as possible, I attempt to integrate goals from most of the major theories by paying attention to changes that clients want to make in the ways they typically feel, think, and behave. As much as possible, my early interventions are aimed at helping clients identify specific ways in which they want to be different. Once they have formulated concrete goals, we can then utilize a variety of techniques that foster modification of feelings, thinking processes, and ways they behave.

Therapeutic Procedures

Selecting techniques depends on whether a therapist's goals are oriented toward changing *feelings, thoughts,* or *behaviors.* Psychoanalytic therapists, for example, are primarily concerned that their clients acquire *insights* into the nature and causes of their personality problems. They employ techniques such as free association, analysis of dreams, interpretation of resistance, and analysis of transference as tools to uncover the unconscious and lead to the desired insight. Gestalt therapists are interested in helping clients fully experience what they are *feeling* moment to moment; they have a wide range of exercises and experiments designed to intensify this experiencing of feelings. Rational-emotive therapists have a primary concern with aiding clients to identify and demolish irrational *thinking,* and they have a variety of cognitive (as well as behavioral and emotive) techniques aimed at the modification of thinking. Behavior therapists are interested in helping clients decrease or eliminate unwanted *behaviors* and increase adaptive ones. Thus, they employ many procedures aimed at teaching clients new behaviors.

As a therapist, you would do well to think of ways to take techniques from all of the approaches so that you are able to work with a client on *all levels* of development. Take the case of Ruth, with whom you will become very familiar in this book. At the outset your interventions may be directed toward getting her to identify and express feelings that she has kept bottled up for much of her life. If you listen to her and provide a place where she can experience what she is *feeling,* she is likely to be able to give more expression to feelings that she has distorted and denied. As her therapy progresses, you may well direct interventions toward getting her to think about early decisions that continue to have an influence in her life. At this time in her therapy you are likely to shift the focus from exploration of feelings to exploration of her attitudes, her *thinking processes,* her values, and her basic beliefs. Still later your focus might be more on helping her to develop *action programs* in which she can experiment with new ways of *behaving*, both during the sessions and outside of them. It is not a matter of working with one aspect of Ruth's experiencing while forgetting about the other facets of her being; rather, it is a case of selecting a focus for a particular phase of her therapy. The challenge you will face as you encounter Ruth (and the other "clients" in this book) is how to utilize an *eclectic approach* as you draw on a variety of techniques to effectively help clients work through their struggles. The following list summarizes the highlights of some techniques commonly used by each of the nine therapeutic approaches considered in this book.

- *Psychoanalytic therapy*. All techniques are designed to help the client gain insight and surface repressed material so that it can be dealt with consciously. Major techniques include gathering of life-history data, dream analysis, and interpretation and analysis of resistance and transference. Such procedures are aimed at increasing awareness, gaining intellectual insight, and beginning a working-through process that will lead to the reorganization of personality.
- *Adlerian therapy*. Practitioners are not bound by any set of prescribed techniques, and they characteristically draw eclectically from a variety of methods that are suited to the unique needs of their clients. A few of these therapeutic procedures are attending, encouragement, confrontation, paradoxical intention, interpretation of the family constellation and early recollections, suggestions, homework assignments, and summarizing.
- *Existential therapy*. The approach places primary emphasis on understanding the client's current experience, *not* on using therapy techniques. Thus, therapists are not bound by any prescribed techniques, so they can use techniques from other schools of therapy. Interventions are used in the service of broadening the ways in which clients live in their world.
- *Person-centered therapy*. Therapists maximize active listening, reflection, and clarification. Current formulations of the theory stress full and active participation of the therapist as a person in the therapeutic relationship. Because this approach places primary emphasis on the client/therapist relationship, it specifies few techniques. Techniques are secondary to the therapist's attitudes. Procedures that are minimized include directive intervention, interpretation, questioning, probing for information, advice giving, collecting history, and diagnosis.
- *Gestalt therapy*. A wide range of techniques is designed to intensify experiencing and to integrate conflicting feelings. The approach stresses confrontation of discrepancies and the ways the client is avoiding responsibility for his or her feelings. The client engages in role playing by performing all of the various parts and polarities alone, thus gaining greater awareness of inner conflicts. Techniques commonly used are dialogue with polarities, exaggeration, focusing on body messages, staying with particular feelings, reexperiencing past unfinished situations in the here and now, and working with dreams. Interpretation is done by the client instead of by the therapist.
- *Transactional analysis*. A life-script questionnaire is useful in recognizing injunctions, games, life positions, and early decisions. Some type of diagnosis may be useful in making an assessment of the problem. Clients participate actively in the

diagnostic process. Contracts are an essential part of TA, specifying the topics to be explored in therapy. Other therapy procedures include questioning, teaching, family modeling, role playing, and analysis of games and life scripts.

- *Behavior therapy.* The main techniques are systematic desensitization, relaxation methods, reinforcement, modeling, cognitive restructuring, thought stopping, assertion training, self-management programs, behavioral rehearsal, coaching, and various multimodal therapy techniques. Assessment and diagnosis are done at the outset to determine a treatment plan. "What," "how," and "when" questions are used (but not "why" questions).
- *Rational-emotive therapy.* Typically, practitioners use a variety of cognitive, affective, and behavioral techniques. Procedures are designed to get the client to critically examine present beliefs and behavior. *Cognitive* methods include disputing irrational beliefs, carrying out cognitive homework, and changing one's language and thinking patterns. *Emotive* techniques include role playing, RET imagery, and shame-attacking exercises. A wide range of active and practical *behavioral* procedures are used to get clients to be specific and committed to doing the hard work required by therapy.
- *Reality therapy.* The approach is an active, directive, and didactic therapy. Behavioral methods are often used to encourage clients to evaluate what they are doing to see if they are willing to change. If clients decide their present behavior is not effective, they develop a specific plan for change and make a commitment to follow through. Contracts are typically used as a way to focus clients and as an accountability measure.

Having considered a survey of nine therapy perspectives from the vantage point of their basic assumptions, views of assessment, goals of therapy, and therapeutic procedures, we are now ready to consider a specific case. As you study Ruth's case, look for ways that you can apply what you have just read in gaining a fuller understanding of her.

The Case of Ruth

The themes in Ruth's life are characteristic of many of the clients I have worked with individually and, especially, in groups. In essence, I took typical struggles from a number of clients and based a clinical picture on them. Pulled together, these common themes form Ruth. Her intake form and autobiography will provide you with much of the information you need to understand and work with her. As you read the following chapters, I suggest that you refer back to this information about Ruth to refresh you on some of the details and themes in her life.

Ruth's Autobiography

As a part of the intake process, the counselor asked Ruth to bring the autobiography that she had written for her counseling class. Although most therapists do not make it a practice to ask their clients to write an autobiography, I think that doing so can be a

AGE	SEX	RACE	MARITAL STATUS
39	Female	Caucasian	Married
			SOCIOECONOMIC STATUS
			Middle class

APPEARANCE

Dresses meticulously, is overweight, fidgets constantly with her clothes, avoids eye contact, speaks rapidly.

LIVING SITUATION

Recently graduated from college as an elementary-education major, lives with husband (John, 45) and her children (Rob, 19, Jennifer, 18, Susan, 17, and Adam, 16).

PRESENTING PROBLEM

Client reports general dissatisfaction. She says her life is rather uneventful and predictable, and she feels some panic over reaching the age of 39, wondering where the years have gone. For two years she has been troubled with a range of psychosomatic complaints, including sleep disturbances, anxiety, dizziness, heart palpitations, and headaches. At times she has to push herself to leave the house. Client complains that she cries easily over trivial matters, often feels depressed, and has a weight problem.

HISTORY OF PRESENTING PROBLEM

Client made her major career as a housewife and mother until her children became adolescents. She then entered college part time and obtained a bachelor's degree. She has recently begun work toward a credential in elementary education. Through her contacts with others at the university she became aware of how she has limited herself, how she has fostered her family's dependence on her, and how frightened she is of branching out from her roles as mother and wife.

Ruth completed a course in introduction to counseling that encouraged her to look at the direction of her own life. As a part of the course she participated in self-awareness groups, had a few individual counseling sessions, and wrote several papers dealing with the turning points in her own life. One of the requirements was to write an extensive autobiography that was based on an application of the principles of the counseling course to her own personal development. This course and her experiences with fellow students in it acted as a catalyst in getting her to take an honest look at her life. Ruth is not clear at this point who she is, apart from being a mother, wife, and student. She realizes that she does not have a good sense of what she wants for herself and that she typically lived up to what others in her life wanted for her. She has decided to seek individual therapy for the following reasons:

HISTORY OF PRESENTING PROBLEM (CONT'D)

*A physician whom she consulted could find no organic or medical basis for her physical symptoms and recommended personal therapy. In her words, her major symptoms are these: "I sometimes feel very panicky, especially at night when I am trying to sleep. Sometimes I'll wake up and find it difficult to breathe, my heart will be pounding, and I'll break out in a cold sweat. I toss and turn trying to relax, and instead I feel tense and worry a lot about many little things. It's hard for me to turn off these thoughts. Then during the day I'm so tired I can hardly function and I find that lately I cry very easily if even minor things go wrong."

*She is aware that she has lived a very structured and disciplined life, that she has functioned largely by taking care of the home and the needs of her four children and her husband, and that to some degree she is no longer content with this. Yet she reports that she doesn't know what "more than this" is. Although she would like to get more involved professionally, the thought of doing it does frighten her. She worries about her right to think and act selfishly, she fears not succeeding in the professional world, and she most of all worries about how becoming more professionally involved might threaten her family.

*Her children range in age from 16 to 19, and all of them are now finding more of their satisfactions outside of the family and the home and are spending increasing time with their friends. Ruth sees these changes and is concerned about "losing" them. She is having particular problems with her daughter Jennifer, and she is at a loss how to deal with Jennifer's rebellion. In general, Ruth feels very much unappreciated by her children.

*In thinking about her future, she is not really sure who or what she wants to become. She would like to develop a sense of herself apart from the expectations of others. She finds herself wondering what she "should" want and what she "should" be doing. Ruth does not find her relationship with her husband, John, at all satisfactory. He appears to be resisting her attempts to make changes and prefers that she remain as she was. But she is anxious over the prospects of challenging this relationship, fearing that if she does, she might end up alone.

*Lately, Ruth is experiencing more concern over aging and losing her "looks." All of these factors combined have provided the motivation for her to take the necessary steps to initiate individual therapy. Perhaps the greatest catalyst that triggered her to come for therapy is the increase of her physical symptoms and her anxiety.

PSYCHOSOCIAL HISTORY

Client was the oldest of four children. Her father is a fundamentalist minister, and her mother, a housewife. She describes her father as distant, authoritarian, and rigid; her relationship with him was one of unquestioning, fearful adherence to his rules and standards. She remembers her mother as being critical, and she thought that she could never do enough to please her. At other times her mother was supportive. The family demonstrated little affection. In many ways Ruth took on the role of caring for her younger brother and sisters, largely in the hope of winning the approval of the parents. When she attempted to have any kind of fun, she encountered her father's disapproval and outright scorn. To a large extent this pattern of taking care of others has extended throughout her life.

One critical incident took place when Ruth was 6 years old. She reported: "My father caught me 'playing doctor' with an 8-year-old boy. He lectured me and refused to speak to me for weeks. I felt extremely guilty and ashamed." It appears that Ruth carried feelings of guilt into her adolescence and that she repressed her own emerging sexuality.

In her social relationships Ruth had difficulty in making and keeping friends. She felt socially isolated from her peers because they viewed her as "weird." Although she wanted the approval of others, she was not willing to compromise her morals for fear of consequences.

She was not allowed to date until she completed high school; at the age of 19 she married the first person she had dated. She used her mother as a role model by becoming a homemaker.

beneficial experience for the client as a way of reviewing significant life experiences as well as a useful device for the therapist to gain insight into the client's self-perception.

Something I've become aware of recently is that I've pretty much lived for others so far. I've been the superwoman who gives and gives until there is little left to give. I give to my husband, John. I've been the "good wife" and the "good mother" that he expects me to be. I do realize that I need John, and I'm afraid he might leave me if I change too much. I've given my all to seeing that my kids grow up decently, and yet even though I'm trying my best, I often worry that I haven't done enough.

When I look at my life now, I must admit that I don't like what I see. I don't like who I am, and I certainly don't feel very proud of my body. I'm very overweight, and despite my good intentions to lose weight I just can't seem to keep off the pounds. I've always enjoyed eating and often eat too much. My family nagged me as a child, but the more they wanted me to stop, the more I seemed to eat, sometimes to the point of making myself sick. I make resolutions to start an exercise program and stick to a diet, but I've yet to find a way to follow through with my plans.

One of the things I do look forward to is becoming a teacher in an elementary school. I really think this would make my life more meaningful. Right now I worry a lot about what will become of me when my kids leave and there is just John and myself in that house. I know I should at least get out there and get that job as a substitute teacher in a private school that I've wanted (and have an offer for), yet I drag my feet on that one, too.

One big thing that troubles me a lot is the feeling of panic I get more and more of the time. I don't remember ever feeling that bad. I'll wake up at night with my heart beating very fast, in a cold sweat, and sometimes shaking. I feel a terrible sense of doom, but I don't know what over. I know that I worry about death—about my dying—a lot. Maybe I still fear going to hell. As a kid I was motivated by fear of fire and brimstone. Nine years ago I finally broke away from my strong fundamentalist church, because I could see that this was not me. Somehow taking that philosophy class in the community college years ago got me to thinking about the values I was taught. It was the gospel, and who was I to question? Well, when I was 30, I made the break from the fundamentalist religion that I had so closely lived by. I'm now attending a less dogmatic church, yet I still feel pangs of guilt that I am not living by the religion my parents brought me up with. They haven't formally disowned me, but in many ways I think they have. I know I'll never win their approval as long as I remain away from the religion that's so dear to them. But I find it more and more difficult to live by something I don't believe in. The big problem for me is that I so often feel lost and confused, wanting some kind of anchor in my life. I know what I don't believe, but I still have little to replace those values that I once lived by. I sometimes wonder if I really discarded those values, because I so often hear the voices of my parents inside my head!

As a part of my college program I took a course on introduction to counseling, and that opened my eyes to a lot of things. One of our guest speakers was a licensed clinical psychologist, who talked about the value of counseling for people even though they are not seriously disturbed. I began to consider the prospect of getting involved in my own therapy. Up until that time I had always thought you had to be a psycho before going to a psychotherapist. I see that I could work on a lot of things that I've neatly tucked away in my life. Yet even though I think I've almost made the decision to seek therapy, there is still this nagging fear within me, and I keep asking myself questions. What if I find out things about me that I don't like? What will I do if I discover there's nothing inside of me? What if I lose John while I'm getting myself together? I so much want those magical answers. All my life I've had clear answers to every question. Then nine years ago, when I became a questioner to some extent, I lost those neat answers. What if I open Pandora's box and too much comes out and I get overwhelmed even more so than I already am?

What I most want from therapy is that the therapist will tell me what I have to do and push me to do it, so that I can begin to live before it's too late. The trouble is that I think I could settle for my nice and comfortable life that I have now, even though a great part of it is driving me nuts. Sure, it's boring and stale, but I don't have to make any decisions either. Then again it's uncomfortable to be where I am. But new decisions are so scary for me to make. I'm scared I'll make the wrong decisions and that in doing so I'll ruin not only my life but John's life and the future of my kids. I feel I owe it to them to stay in this marriage. I guess I'm trapped and don't see a way out. And that would be the last straw if my father ever found out that I was seeing a psychotherapist! He'd tell me I was foolish—that all the answers to life are found in the Bible. Sometimes I wonder if I should turn my life over to God and let Him take over. I so much wish He *would* take over! I still don't know what my next step will be. I'm afraid and excited at the same time.

Recommended Supplementary Readings

Diagnostic and Statistical Manual of Mental Disorders (third edition, 1980) by the American Psychiatric Association (Washington, D.C.: Author) is the official system of classification of psychological disorders. It is the resource to consult for identifying patterns of emotional and behavioral problems. It provides a rationale and method for classifying particular psychological disorders, gives specific criteria for these classifications, and shows the differences that separate the various disorders.

DSM-III Case Book (1981) by R. L. Spitzer, A. E. Skodol, M. Gibbon, and J. Williams (Washington, D.C.: American Psychiatric Association) is a collection of case vignettes that grew out of the authors' experiences. The cases are designed as a learning companion to the DSM-III above. Most of the cases are brief descriptions of actual clients, and the discussions focus on ways of making an assessment and formulating a diagnosis.

"Counseling Theory: Understanding the Trend toward Eclecticism from a Developmental Perspective" (1985) by M. M. Brabeck and E. R. Welfel (*Journal of Counseling and Development*, volume 63, pp. 343–348) examines the current trend toward eclecticism from a developmental perspective. Recent surveys of practitioners' identification with eclecticism are discussed, as are suggestions for counseling professors and researchers.

"Models of Helping and Coping" (1982) by P. Brickman, V. C. Rabinowitz, J. Karuza, D. Coates, E. Cohn, and L. Kidder (*American Psychologist*, volume 37, pp. 368–384) offers a useful framework for clarifying the assumptions that guide one's therapeutic practice by drawing a distinction between attribution of responsibility for a problem and attribution of responsibility for a solution.

Great Cases in Psychotherapy (1979) edited by D. Wedding and R. J. Corsini (Itasca, Ill.: Peacock) consists of brief verbatim accounts of a variety of theoretical approaches to case histories. It stresses application of techniques advocated by different schools of therapy.

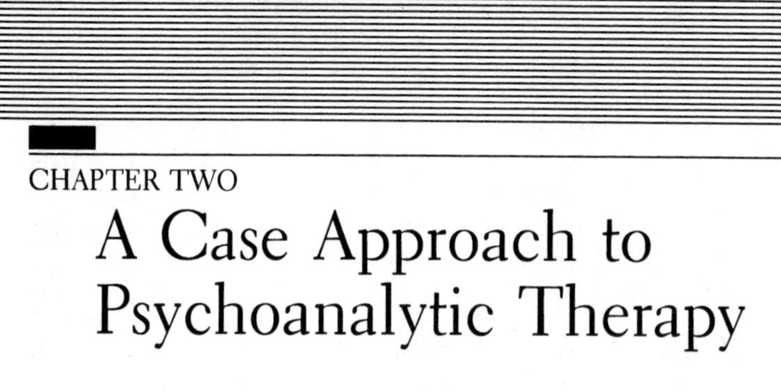

CHAPTER TWO

A Case Approach to Psychoanalytic Therapy

Introduction

In this chapter and the eight to follow I assume the identity of a therapist with the particular theoretical orientation being considered. As much as possible I attempt to stay within the spirit of each specific approach, but I again want to emphasize that you will be seeing my interpretation and my own style. For example, there are many differences in therapeutic style among practitioners who share the same theoretical orientation. There is not "one right way" of practicing psychoanalytic therapy or any of the other systems. I encourage you to do your best in assuming each of the separate theoretical perspectives as you follow the case of Ruth through the nine theory chapters and take up the other case example in each chapter. Doing this will help you decide which concepts and techniques you want to incorporate into your own therapeutic style.

In each of these nine chapters I am Ruth's therapist. I have read her intake form and her autobiography before meeting her for the first time. In each chapter I give an overview of the particular theory by describing the following: the basic assumptions underlying practice, my initial assessment of Ruth, the goals that will guide our work, and the therapeutic procedures and techniques that are likely to be employed in attaining our goals. The section on the therapeutic process shows samples of our work together. It is illustrated with dialogues between Ruth and myself, along with an ongoing process commentary that addresses my rationale for the interventions that I make and the general direction of her therapy.

A Psychoanalytic Therapist's Perspective on Ruth

Basic Assumptions

As I work with Ruth within a psychoanalytic framework, I am guided by both the *psychosexual perspective* of Sigmund Freud and the *psychosocial perspective* of Erik Erikson. My work with Ruth is also influenced to some extent by contemporary psychoanalytic trends, which are often classified in terms of self psychology and object-relations theory. I am moving beyond Freud to illustrate that contemporary psychoanalysis is an ever-evolving system rather than a closed and static model.

The *psychosexual* theory, as seen in traditional Freudian psychoanalysis, places emphasis on the internal conflicts of an individual during the first six years of life. It assumes that certain sexual and aggressive impulses, because they would produce extreme anxiety if they were to become conscious, are repressed during these formative years. Although these memories and experiences are buried in the unconscious, they exert a powerful influence on the individual's personality and behavior later in life.

The *psychosocial* theory, primarily developed by Erikson, emphasizes sociocultural influences on the development of personality. The assumption is that there is a continuity in human development. At each stage of life we face the challenge of establishing an equilibrium between ourselves and our social world. Each of the stages of the life cycle presents a crisis, or a turning point. We can either successfully resolve our conflicts or fail to resolve them. Although such a failure does not necessarily doom us to remain forever the victim of fixations, our lives are, to a large extent, the result of the choices we make at these stages.

The *newer psychoanalytic approaches* are represented by the writings of Margaret Mahler, Heinz Kohut, and Otto Kernberg, among others. Contemporary psychoanalytic practice emphasizes the origins and transformations of the self, the differentiation between the self and others, the integration of the self with others, and the influence of critical factors in early development on later development. Predictable developmental sequences are noted in which the early experiences of the self shift in relation to an expanding awareness of others. Once self/other patterns are established, they influence later interpersonal relationships. Human development can best be thought of as the evolution of the way individuals differentiate self from others. One's current behavior in the world is largely a repetition of the internal patterning during one of the earlier stages of development.

In viewing Ruth's case I make the assumption that her early development is of critical importance and that her current personality problems are rooted in repressed childhood conflicts. Borrowing from Kohut's thinking, I surmise that Ruth was psychologically wounded during childhood and that her defensive structure is an attempt to avoid being wounded again. I expect to find an interweaving of old hurts with new wounds. Thus, I pay attention to the consistency between her emotional wounding as a child and those situations that result in pain for her today. Much of our therapeutic work is aimed at repairing the original wounding.

The work of repairing early wounds takes time. Therefore, I expect to see Ruth at least a couple of times a week for a minimum of three years. One of the reasons that therapy will take so long is that it entails a reliving of early childhood memories and events and that, for it to be effective, the client must do some basic reorientation. I am interested in a characterological, or structural, change in Ruth, not in mere problem solving or in removal of symptoms. I see therapy as an uncovering process that delves into repressed experiences. I assume that for many years a person such as Ruth has been storing away conflicts, intense feelings, and other impulses. Even though she may not be conscious of how these repressed feelings influence her current behavior, they do determine the course of her life. It is important to note that I make many of these assumptions before meeting a client. The psychoanalytic perspective on the developmental process provides me with a conceptual framework that helps me make sense of an individual's current functioning. Although I do not force my client to fit this theoretical mold, I do make certain general assumptions about the normal sequence of human development.

Initial Assessment of Ruth

The following assessment is based on a few initial sessions with Ruth, her intake form, and her autobiography. Ruth's relationships with her parents are critically important from a therapeutic standpoint. She describes her father as "distant, authoritarian, and rigid." My hunch is that this view of her father colors how she perceives all men today, that her fear of displeasing her husband is connected to her fear of bringing her father displeasure, and that what she is now striving to get from her husband is related to what she wanted from her father. I expect that Ruth will view me and react to me in many of the same ways she did with her father. Through this transference relationship with me, she will be able to recognize connecting patterns between her childhood behavior and her current struggles. For example, she is fearful of displeasing her husband, John, for fear he might leave. If this were to happen, there would be a repetition of the pattern of her father's psychological abandonment of her after she had not lived up to his expectations. She does not stand up to John or ask for what she needs for fear that he will become disgruntled and abandon her. Ruth is defending herself against being wounded by John in some of the same ways that she was by her father.

From a *psychosexual perspective* I am interested in Ruth's early childhood experiences in which she learned about sexuality. Her father's response when he caught her in an act of sexual experimentation needs to be considered as we work with her present attitudes and feelings about sex. As a child and adolescent, Ruth felt guilty and ashamed over her sexual feelings. She internalized many of her father's strict views of sexuality. Because her father manifested a negative attitude toward Ruth's increased sexual awareness, she learned that her sexual feelings were evil, that her body and sexual pleasure was dirty, and that her curiosity about sexual matters was unacceptable. Her sexual feelings became anxiety provoking and were thus rigidly controlled. The denial of her sexuality that was established at this age has been carried over into her adult life and gives rise to severe conflicts, guilt, remorse, and self-condemnation. Her weight problem is probably connected to her denial of sexuality. She does not allow herself to experience sexual attraction to men, nor does she allow herself to enjoy her sexuality with her husband.

Ruth apparently gratifies her need for affection by overeating, which is a longstanding pattern. Just as she feels guilty over sexuality, Ruth feels guilty over her overeating. If she is not physically and sexually attractive to either herself or to others, she will not have to deal with feelings that produce anxiety.

Viewing Ruth from a *psychosocial perspective* will shed considerable light on the nature of her present psychological problems. As an infant she never really developed a sense of trust in the world. She learned that she could not count on others to provide her with a sense of being wanted and loved. Throughout her early childhood years she did not receive affection, a deprivation that now makes it difficult for her to feel that she is worthy of affection. The task of early childhood is developing a sense of *autonomy*, which is necessary if one is to gain a measure of self-control and an ability to cope with the world. In Ruth's case, she grew up fast, was never allowed to be a child, and was expected to take care of her younger brother and sisters. Although she seemed to become "mature" even as a child, in actuality she never developed a sense of autonomy.

Modern psychoanalytic thinking helps me understand Ruth's psychosocial dynamics. She will not feel truly independent until she feels properly attached and dependent. This notion implies that to be independent one must be able to depend on others. Ruth, however, never felt a genuine sense of attachment to her father, whom she perceived as distant, or to her mother, whom she viewed as somewhat rejecting. For Ruth to have developed genuine independence she would have needed others in her life whom she could count on for emotional support. But this support was absent from her background. During the school-age period Ruth felt inferior in social relationships, was confused about her sex-role identity, and was unwilling to face new challenges. During adolescence she did not experience an identity crisis, because she did not ask basic questions of life. Rather than questioning the values that had been taught to her, she compliantly accepted them. In part, Ruth has followed the design established by her parents when she was an adolescent. She was not challenged to make choices for herself or to struggle to find meaning in life. In her adulthood she managed to break away from her fundamentalist religion, yet she could not free herself of her guilt over this act. She is still striving for her father's approval, and she is still operating without a clearly defined set of values to replace the ones she discarded. A major theme of her life is her concern over how to fill the void that she fears will result when her children leave home.

Psychoanalytic theory provides a useful perspective for understanding the ways in which Ruth is trying to control the anxiety in her life. As one of her primary ego defenses, she readily accepted her parents' rigid morality because it served the function of controlling her impulses. Further, there is a fundamental split within Ruth between the "good girl" and the "bad girl." Either she keeps in control of herself and others by doing things for them, or she gets out of control when she enjoys herself, as she did when she was "playing doctor." She feels in control when she takes care of her children, and she does not know what she will do once they leave home. Coupled with this "empty-nest syndrome" is her ambivalence about leaving the security of the home by choosing a career. This change brings about anxiety because she is struggling with her ability to direct her own life as opposed to defining herself strictly as a servant of others. This anxiety will be a focal point of therapy.

Goals of Therapy

The goal of our analytically oriented work will be to gradually uncover the lid to the unconscious, so that Ruth can become aware of material that is not now accessible to her. In this way she will be able to use messages from the unconscious to direct her own life instead of being driven by her defensive controls. A further goal is the restructuring of Ruth's basic character by surfacing unconscious conflicts and working through them. Our process is aimed at the promotion of integration and ego development. The various parts of her self that she has denied will become connected, and there will be a movement from infantile dependence toward mature dependence. The ideal type of identity is an autonomous self, which is characterized by self-esteem and self-confidence.

Therapeutic Procedures

I expect that a major part of our work will entail dealing with resistance. In spite of the fact that Ruth comes voluntarily to therapy, there are any number of barriers that will make her progress slow at times. She has learned to protect herself against anxiety by building up defenses over the years, and she will not quickly surrender them. As we have seen, some of her primary defenses are repression and denial. I expect that she will have some ambivalence about becoming aware of her unconscious motivations and needs. Merely gaining insight into the nature of her unconscious conflicts does not mean that her therapy is over, for the difficult part will be the exploration and working-through of these conflicts.

I mentioned earlier that therapy would be a long process. One of the reasons is that much of our time will be devoted to exploring Ruth's reactions to me. I expect that I will become a significant figure in her life, for I assume that she will develop strong feelings toward me, both positive and negative. I expect that she will relate to me in some of the same ways that she related to her father. Working therapeutically with this transference involves two steps. One is to foster this development of transference; the second consists of working through patterns she established with significant others in her past as these feelings emerge toward me in the therapy relationship. This second step is the core of the therapy process. *Working-through* refers to repeating interpretations of her behavior and overcoming her resistance, thus allowing her to resolve her neurotic patterns. Although I do not use a "blank-screen" model, keeping myself mysterious and hidden, in this type of intensive therapy the client is bound to expect me to fulfill some of her unmet needs. She will probably experience again some of the same feelings she had during her childhood. How Ruth views me and reacts to me will constitute much of the therapy work, for this transference material is rich with meaning and can tell Ruth much about herself.

In addition to working with her resistances and with any transference that develops in our relationship, I will probably use a variety of other techniques to get at her unconscious dynamics. Dream analysis is an important procedure for uncovering unconscious material and giving Ruth insight into some areas of unresolved problems. She will be asked to recall her dreams, to report them in the sessions, and then to learn how to free-associate to key elements in them. Free association, a major procedure in our therapy, involves asking Ruth to clear her mind of thoughts and preoccupations and to say whatever pops into her head without censoring, regardless of how silly or trivial it may be. This procedure typically leads to some recollection of past experiences and, at times, to a release of bottled-up feelings. Another major technique at my disposal is interpretation, or pointing out and explaining to Ruth the meanings of behavior manifested by her dreams, her free-association material, her resistances, and the nature of our relationship. Timed properly, these interpretations (or teachings) can help Ruth assimilate new learning and uncover unconscious material more rapidly. This, in turn, will help her understand and deal with her life situation more effectively.

Therapeutic Process

The crux of my therapeutic work with Ruth consists of bringing her past into the present, which is done mainly through exploring the transference relationship. My aim is to do more than merely facilitate recall of past events and insight on her part; instead, I hope that she will see patterns and a continuity in her life from her childhood to the present. When she realizes how her past is still operating, character change is possible and new options open up for her.

Elements of the Process

Exploring Ruth's transference. After Ruth has been in therapy with me for some time, she grows more disenchanted with me because she does not see me as giving enough. She complains that she is the one doing all the giving and that she is beginning to resent how much I know about her and how little she knows about me. Here is a brief sample of a session in which we talk about these feelings.

RUTH: So, I want you to be more of a real person to me. It feels uncomfortable for you to know so much about me, when I know so little about you.

JERRY: Yes, it is surely the case that I know a lot more about your life than you know about mine and that you're more vulnerable than I am.

RUTH: Why can't you be more personal with me?

JERRY: How would you like me to be more personal? What would you like from me?

RUTH: Well, you seem so removed and distant from me. You're hard to reach. This is not easy for me to say . . . uhm . . . I suppose I want to know what you really think of me. You don't tell me, and I'm often left wondering what you're feeling. I work hard at getting your approval, but I'm not sure I have it. I get the feeling that what I'm doing isn't enough for you.

JERRY: Have you experienced anything like this before?

RUTH: Well, ah . . . you know that I felt this way around my father as long as I can remember. No matter what I did to get his approval, I was never really successful. And that's sometimes the way I feel toward you.

I am consciously not disclosing much about my reactions to Ruth at this point because she is finally bringing out feelings about me that she has avoided for so long. I encourage her to express more about the ways that she sees me as ungiving and unreachable and as not being what she wants. It is through this process of exploring some of her persistent reactions to me, I hope, that she will see more of the connection between her unfulfilled needs from the past and how she is viewing me in this present relationship. At this stage in her therapy she is experiencing some very basic feelings of wanting to be special and wanting proof of it. By working over a long period with her transference reactions, she will eventually gain insight into how she has given her father all the power to affirm her as a person and how she has not learned to give herself the approval she so much wants from him. I am not willing to reassure her, because I want to foster this expression of transference so that she has the tools to make these important discoveries.

Working with her mother. At another period in Ruth's therapy we spend many sessions exploring her reactions to her mother. We focus on how she felt toward her mother as a child and how she feels toward her mother now. For a long period during her childhood Ruth attempted to become to her father what her mother was, but she never managed to replace her mother in her father's eyes. She tried by becoming "mother" to her younger brother and sisters and by working as hard as she could for recognition. But this was to no avail, for she did not get the recognition that she wanted from either her father or her mother. Much later in her sessions we explore the parallels between Ruth's giving to her brother and sisters and the way that she has devoted much of her adult life to giving to her own children, only to feel a lack of appreciation and recognition for her efforts in being a good mother.

Process Commentary

Being guided by some of Kohut's thinking, I direct much of our therapy to the exploration of Ruth's old issues, her early wounding, and her fears of new wounds. The bruises to her self that she experiences in the here and now trigger memories of her old hurts. Especially in her relationship with me, Ruth is sensitive to rejection and any signs of my disapproval. Therefore, much of our therapeutic effort is aimed at dealing with the ways in which she is now striving for recognition as well as the ways in which she attempted to get recognition as a child. In short, Ruth has a damaged self, and she is susceptible to and fearful of further bruising. We therefore talk about her attachments, how she tried to win affection, and the many ways that she is trying to protect herself from suffering further emotional wounds to a fragile ego.

As Ruth's therapy progresses, she is able to let more material rise to consciousness. We focus on the conflicts between her id (the impulsive and "spoiled-brat" side of her personality, which craves indulgence in physical gratification immediately), and her superego (her conscience and all the morals and standards that she has incorporated into her self-system). It is obvious that Ruth has an extremely strong superego, one that was based on some unrealistically high standards of perfection and that punished with guilt as a motivator. A large part of her therapy consists of learning to relax the boundaries of her superego so that she will not be controlled by its demands for perfection.

Much of Ruth's work involves going back to early events in her life—recalling them and the feelings associated with them—in the hope that she can be free from the restrictions of her past. She comes to realize that her past is an important part of her and that some old wounds will take a long time to heal.

One of the major ways Ruth gains insight into her patterns is by learning to understand her dreams. We regularly focus on their meanings, and she free-associates with some symbols. She has a very difficult time giving up control and simply allowing herself to say freely whatever comes to mind in these sessions. She worries about "saying the appropriate thing," and of course this is material we examine in the sessions. Dream work is one of the major tools to tap her unconscious processes.

Ruth also discovers from the way she responds to me some key connections between how she related to significant people in her life. She looks to me in some of the same ways that she looked to her father for approval and for love. I encourage her regression to these past events, so that she can work through barriers that are preventing her from functioning as a mature adult.

Questions for Reflection

As you continue working with the nine therapeutic approaches described in this book, you will have many opportunities to apply the basic assumptions and key concepts of each theory to your own life. Some of the questions below will assist you in becoming more involved in a personal way. The rest of the questions are designed to give you some guidance in beginning to work with Ruth. They are intended to help you clarify your reactions to how I counseled Ruth from each therapeutic perspective. Select the questions for reflection that most interest you.

1. Reflecting on your own childhood, what do you consider to be some significant events that have an impact on your life today? (How did you get approval or disapproval? How much trust did you feel toward significant people in your life? What attitudes did you develop toward sex? How were your dependency needs met?)
2. Do you think that your relationships with your mother or father influence your life today, especially the ways you relate to significant women and men? What might you not have received from either parent that you are now seeking from other people?
3. What do you consider to be one of the most significant themes (from the analytic perspective) that you would focus on in your sessions with Ruth?
4. How might you respond to Ruth if she challenged you over your aloofness and your unwillingness to give of yourself personally? Might you become defensive if she compared you to her father and accused you of being just like him? If you were more revealing, how do you expect that your therapy would be any different with Ruth?
5. In what ways would you encourage Ruth to go back and relive her childhood? How important is delving into the client's early childhood as a factor leading to personality change?
6. What defenses do you see in Ruth? As her therapist, how do you imagine you would work to lessen these defenses?
7. Do you share the emphasis of this approach on the role given to her father's importance in her life? How might you go about exploring with her the ways in which conflicts with her father are related to some of her present conflicts?

Moe: A Passive/Aggressive Client Who Wants to Escape with Alcohol

Moe has been in therapy with me for one year. Besides describing his character and what he is doing in therapy, I will give a running commentary explaining why I am proceeding as I am and clarifying what is occurring between us.

Some Background Data

Moe is 35 years old. He originally became involved in analytically oriented therapy with me on the recommendation of his physician. It was clear to the physician that he had a major drinking problem, which was a manifestation of more deeply rooted personality problems. Initially, Moe resisted seeing himself as a "problem drinker," let alone a confirmed alcoholic. As an adjunct to his treatment in individual therapy with me he agreed to join Alcoholics Anonymous, which he now continues in by his choice. In AA he learned that his drinking controls him and that he is an alcoholic.

So far in therapy, we have done a lot of reviewing of Moe's early childhood years, which were rather traumatic. His mother died when he was 10, and his father sent him to a private boarding school in another state, for he was sure that he could not manage to bring up Moe by himself. Moe felt abandoned by both his parents—by his mother, who had died and left him, and his father, just at the time that he really needed love, companionship, and support.

Moe has had three marriages, each of which ended by his wife's leaving him. Typically, each woman left when she grew tired of his continual drinking binges and all that went with his alcoholism—getting fired from job after job, not being a father to his children, being abusive both verbally and physically to her, and being extremely dependent on her. Moe decided that he did not have what it took to keep a wife, and he grew increasingly hopeless about loving or being loved by a woman. He also grew increasingly bitter toward women—they *all* left him when he was most in need of them. One of his conflicts is his dependency on women and his hostility toward them.

Moe feels a great deal of anger toward a former boss who fired him from his executive position in a business firm. He has complained that, when "I was broke, financially and personally, my boss took my job away from me instead of giving me the support I needed." In Moe's eyes, important men always let him down. His father sent him away, and his boss sent him away; what few male friends he did have broke contact with him, mainly because they felt put off by his drinking.

Moe has many ambivalent feelings toward me, which we have been working on in our sessions. He feels a deep liking and respect for me, and he says he needs me. He also feels hostility, fears letting himself "become dependent" on me, and in many ways is constantly defying me and testing me to see if I will be like other men in his life. We are now working on his *resistance* and his feelings toward me.

Highlights of Moe's Therapy

My goals in working with Moe. Thinking within the analytic framework, I see psychotherapy as a process that involves major character changes on Moe's part. This reconstruction will be accomplished by assisting him to become aware of his unconscious needs and motives. Examples of some of his unconscious dynamics are his dependency on strong women to take care of him and his conflicts with his boss, whom he views as an authority figure. My focus will be on using therapeutic methods designed to open the doors to his unconscious processes. I work on the assumption that it is necessary to recall and relive early childhood memories and experiences. These experiences will be reconstructed, discussed, interpreted, and analyzed with the aim of significantly changing his personality. Although I do not want to direct the entire focus of therapy toward his drinking patterns, it will be imperative that we deal with his alcoholism. There will be a focus on the unconscious motivations and dynamics associated with his drinking, as well as with some of his other passive/aggressive and highly dependent character traits. I identify and diagnose Moe as a passive/aggressive client who is using alcohol as one of his major defenses and escape mechanisms.

To unlock Moe's unconscious, I focus on past experiences, such as the impact of his mother's death on him, his being sent away to a private boarding school, and other occasions when he felt a sense of abandonment and rejection. I pay special attention to linking these traumatic situations and feelings from the past with present situations. Working with some of his reactions toward me and his expectations of me, I help him to gradually acquire self-understanding. Some other analytic procedures that I use to meet therapy goals are dream analysis, free-association methods, analysis of resistance, and interpretation.

Moe begins to learn about his ego defenses. Moe is gradually developing insight into some of the typical defenses he uses to deal with anxiety. He is acquiring this understanding through talking about subjects that he typically avoids and through my interpretations. I am attempting to teach him the meaning of certain patterns of behavior by pointing out significant connections between dreams and his everyday behavior, by working with his resistances, and by exploring early events with him. For example, Moe will need to recognize that he typically numbs his feelings of sadness. He attempts by denial and avoidance to deaden himself to the hurt and abandonment he felt first as a child, when his mother died, and later as an adult, when his wives divorced him. He does this most strikingly by drinking. Moe is beginning to understand that *denial* is a way in which he has continued to deceive himself and thus ward off anxiety. His alcoholism is a fact that he has denied; he has kept himself from looking at his inability to handle alcohol by placing blame on others and looking to external events for his personal failures. If reality is too painful for him to accept, he typically ignores it.

Working with Moe's alcoholism. Moe is a chemically dependent person. It would be a mistake to treat only his symptoms while ignoring the chemical dependency itself. Theoretically, I view the dynamics of his alcoholism as a fixation at an infantile level (oral stage). He is still unconsciously striving to be loved and taken care in a way more appropriate to an infant. Part of my role with Moe will be to assist him in developing insight into how many of his personality problems are connected to his addiction to alcohol. As is true for most alcoholics, Moe feels socially isolated, unable to love others or receive love from them; he feels chronic guilt; he experiences depression and self-pity frequently; and he feels frightened in interpersonal relationships. Alcohol, a depressant drug, is probably a factor that promotes or deepens the depression that Moe experiences. Sexual dysfunctions are common among alcoholics, as are broken marriages. Eventually, Moe will have to be confronted in a caring and concerned manner with his alcoholism. At this point he is using excuses, rationalization, denial, and minimizations. If I am well-versed in the alcoholic's confused system of beliefs, all of these defenses can be effectively dealt with and eventually turned around and used as information leading to insight on Moe's part. Yet timing is critical. At this point he is not likely to "hear" interpretations pertaining to his alcoholism, so we begin with the exploration of issues that are less threatening for him to consider. Eventually, however, his problem of chemical dependency will need to be thoroughly dealt with in therapy. It is a good sign that Moe has agreed to attend AA meetings. I think it would be a helpful adjunct to his therapy with me if he continued attending these meetings. There is no reason why we cannot work on the problem of his chemical dependency and his underlying personality problems at the same time.

Procedures and Techniques Used with Moe

Free association. A basic tool for uncovering repressed material is free association, which consists of expressing whatever comes to mind, regardless of how painful, illogical, or irrelevant it may seem. At times I might begin a session with a free-association exercise that goes something as follows:

"Moe, I'd like you to close your eyes and try to clear your mind for a time. Let yourself say aloud whatever comes to your mind. Try not to make any sense out of what you're saying; just report any reactions, thoughts, and feelings you're experiencing. Simply flow with your words with as little censorship as possible."

The purpose of this free-association exercise is to encourage Moe to become more spontaneous and to uncover unconscious processes. During this time I pay attention to patterns in his associations, especially noting areas where he tends to block or censor. In one session, for example, it is evident that he is blocking and censoring any information pertaining to the times he became physically abusive to his wife in each of his marriages. This blocking is important to interpret and analyze. I am interested in identifying the patterns and themes that become apparent through Moe's therapy sessions. I simply listen carefully to what he is saying, how he is saying it, and what he is not saying. I may use this free-association technique with a particular word, especially when he makes a significant "slip." For example, in one session Moe inadvertently refers to "Mother" when he is talking about one of his former wives. Using this as a clue, I ask him to free-associate to the word *mother*. His associations are "never there . . . strong . . . doesn't care . . . all alone . . . [a long pause] lonely . . . dead and gone" [another pause, and he begins sobbing].

Following up on Moe's slip leads him to uncover some painful feelings toward his mother, which provide therapeutic material. This example shows that the free-association process may lead to a recall of past experiences that release intense feelings, which can then be explored in depth. In a later session we came back to explore the implications of Moe's slip in referring to his ex-wife as "Mother." This led to a series of discussions of his dependency on and resentment of women.

Working with Moe's dreams. I am extremely interested in Moe's dreams, for I see them as a rich avenue to tapping his unconscious wishes, fears, conflicts, needs, desires, and impulses. At times, he is reluctant to report his dreams, saying that he has "forgotten" them or that he has not been dreaming lately. Sometimes he does bring in a dream, and my task is to work with him to uncover disguised meanings by studying the symbols involved. Again, when it is appropriate, I attempt to teach him about himself and his current conflicts through interpreting the meanings of his dreams. The following excerpts represent the manner in which we work.

Moe reports a dream in which several large women are chasing him with clubs. He is frightened that they will catch him and beat him to a pulp. They get closer to him, he trips . . . Then he wakes up in a panic.

I ask Moe to free-associate with every element in the dream, even though every aspect is not necessarily symbolic. His associations to this dream are as follows:

"I'm afraid of those big clubs. They have thorns on them, and if I get hit, that could be it for me! Where can I run to and hide? I'm afraid I can't run fast enough, that I'll get caught and they'll hurt me. These women seem to hate me, and they want to do me in! I feel so helpless and scared. This is the way I felt so often when I was a child. I felt that I'd get hurt, and nobody would be around to protect me. I'm afraid I'll make a mistake, that I'll trip up, and that my mother will punish me by beating me. I tried to do my best, but I was always afraid I'd do the wrong thing and get hit. I remember wishing that my father would protect me, but he just looked the other way."

From these associations Moe arrives at the following interpretation of the meaning of his dream: "The women are my mother and other strong and oppressive women in my life who have the power and desire to hurt me. Nobody will protect me from the wrath of women!"

It should be emphasized that I do not rely on one dream to uncover meaningful connections between Moe's past and his present struggles. A dream is an additional resource for learning about his psychodynamics. Taken in conjunction with other material, it can provide clues to solving a puzzle.

Working with Moe's resistance. Resistance is Moe's way of avoiding opening the doors to unconscious material. Thus, a basic technique in analytic therapy consists of interpreting these avoidance patterns so that he can begin to work through these barriers. Moe understands that his resistances are something to be understood and worked with in therapy, for they are ways of learning about some painful reality in his past.

Some manifestations of Moe's resistance that I have observed include:

- not remembering many of his dreams
- "forgetting" to show up for some appointments
- being late to some sessions
- talking about superficial topics
- his failure to pay some of his bills on time
- his insistence at times that I tell him what to talk about in the session
- his typical style of looking outside of himself for reasons to justify any failures on his part
- attending a session drunk

I see avoidance behavior, in whatever form it may take, as representative of his defense against the anxiety that is aroused in him when he gets close to unconscious content. How do I deal with his resistances? First of all, they are not just something to be overcome. Both he and I need to recognize that his resistances are valuable indications of his defenses against anxiety, and they need to be understood and worked with. Generally, I call attention to the more readily observable resistances and work with these behaviors first. I take care not to criticize him, for this is likely to increase his resistance. Also, I do not make dogmatic pronouncements, telling him what a certain pattern of behavior means; instead, I ask him to think for himself about some of these patterns and what they may indicate.

Working with our relationship. As I mentioned earlier, Moe's reactions to me represent a rich resource for understanding conflicts that stem from relationships to significant people in his past. At times he treats me in many ways as a father figure—sometimes the father he feels he had and at other times the father he wishes he had had.

Moe went through a period of several months expecting me to "kick him out" of therapy. He felt that, because he was not a cooperative and ideal patient, I would abandon him by refusing to see him in therapy any longer. Of course, there is a connection between what he experienced with his father and what he feared he would experience with me. We worked in depth on these feelings that I would not be there when he needed me, sorting out what this meant to him. We also explored some of his expectations and needs of me. In a very hostile way, he continued asserting that I would not have the slightest interest in being with him if I were not being paid for the relationship. He felt resentment that he had to pay high fees to be listened to and cared about. We explored the reality of this situation, as well as some of his own narcissism relating to his expectation that he be cared about unconditionally on his terms. He continued thinking that I was not providing enough direction, and that merely letting him struggle would not get him anywhere. I agreed that I provided little structure, telling him that this is part of my therapy approach. Instead, I dealt with his reactions toward being in a situation in which I would not meet his demands and in which he had to decide what to bring up in his sessions.

We are devoting much of our time in current sessions to exploring Moe's dependency on me, which is primarily manifested by his wanting me to make important decisions for him. He looks to me for advice on how to proceed in life; when such advice is not forthcoming, he typically reacts with some kind of hostile remark. He also has loving feelings for me, which are frightening to him. He is learning that he denies these positive feelings at times, so that he can remain angry.

Most of Moe's resistances that emerge from the sessions are an unconscious attempt to set me up to dislike him and to ultimately reject him. This follows the pattern of his significant relationships in the past. Related to his resistive behavior is the importance of maintaining my own objectivity. I must not get caught up in my own feelings and counterdefensive reactions toward him. If I get entangled in countertransference, I miss opportunities to help him work through places where he is now stuck. By remaining objective and not overreacting personally to his behavior, I am able to foster his transference toward me so that we can analyze and interpret it. His reactions to me provide rich clues to the ways in which he was emotionally wounded as a child and how much of his current behavior is aimed at unconsciously defending him against being wounded again.

Paradoxically, the very thing that Moe wants to avoid—being rejected and abandoned—he is unconsciously repeating. The difficult and time-consuming part of our therapy consists of his gradually becoming aware of ways that he is replicating earlier interpersonal relationships. Once he gains insight into how he is bringing his past into present relationships in a self-defeating way, we will have to work through these barriers to his growth. In an early session, for example, Moe disclosed to me his appreciation for how much I had done for him and how much I meant to him. After expressing his affection and respect for me, he seemed very embarrassed and then made some indirect and sarcastic remarks. The next session he showed up 30 minutes late and drunk. The following week we dealt at length with his appearing for his appointment drunk. He expressed his fear that I had judged him and had decided that he was a worthless person with no hope of getting better. Instead, I confronted him with what he had done and then explored with him the meaning of his behavior. I did not judge him as a worthless person, and I did not abandon him, even though on some levels he was setting me up to do so, as he had set up other significant people to criticize and eventually leave him.

By staying with the focus of the unconscious meanings of Moe's behavior and by not reacting to him in negative ways that he is used to from past experiences, I am teaching him that there can be a new ending to certain life dramas. Thus, in this transference situation we have the basis for him to learn new lessons about interpersonal relationships. He acquires the ability to perceive people differently than he perceived his parents.

I see Moe as a very dependent person, one who is looking for me to "feed" him. In his childhood he was deprived of the love and guidance he so much needed. Now in this relationship with me he is hoping that I will meet some of his infantile needs by protecting him, reassuring him, telling him that he is a special patient, approving of him, recognizing any progress he makes in therapy, and in many ways replacing the father that he never had. Rather than merely meeting many of his dependency needs, I am more interested in his coming to understand how he is repeating in his relationship with me some of his ineffective attempts to secure approval and recognition as a child. If I cater to his wants, I merely support his passivity and his helplessness.

The core of much of our work in therapy consists of Moe's becoming aware of those feelings that he had toward men such as his father and his boss that he is now projecting onto (or attributing to) me. Since these transference feelings are so essential for him to both understand and to *work through* in his relationship with me, I want to foster a climate in which such feelings can be recognized, brought out into the open, discussed, and analyzed, so that he will eventually no longer need to make men such as myself into father figures and thus keep himself as a "little boy." My hope for Moe is that he can work through the transference relationship with me successfully, which means that he can give a *new ending* to our relationship—escaping the self-destructive ending he has had with other significant people in his life.

In order to create a therapeutic climate that will better enable Moe to both recognize the nature of his intense feelings toward me and to work through (resolve) these feelings, I do not engage in much self-disclosure. I keep many of my reactions from him, and in that way I keep myself an ambiguous figure. Because of this ambiguity, his manner of perceiving and responding to me will be largely a matter of his projections, which we work with in therapy.

If I am to be therapeutic for Moe, I must be aware of any of my own unresolved conflicts that can easily surface in my relationship with him. For example, I need to be aware of my reactions toward his dependency on me. If I have an unconscious need to keep him dependent on me, this can seriously impede therapeutic progress. If I am unaware of my feelings toward him when he responds to me in passive/aggressive ways, I can become ensnarled in my own countertransference feelings. If I have a need to be appreciated by him—and instead he is hostile and refuses to cooperate with me—then my own unconscious reactions toward him will prove counterproductive. Thus, it is essential that I be aware of my own needs, motivations, and unresolved personal issues from my past and of how these factors are likely to intrude in our work together.

It is clear that the task of personality restructuring in Moe's case will take several years of intensive work, for gaining insight into the origins of his present conflicts is not sufficient. It is also necessary that he integrate these insights into a fuller awareness of how he is bringing his unresolved conflicts into his relationships with people in his life today.

Follow-Up: You Continue as Moe's Therapist

When I ask you to imagine that I am referring a client to you for further therapy, my hope is that you will function as much as possible within the conceptual framework of the model under discussion in each chapter. Also, you will learn best if you think of other directions to move with the client, and if you use techniques other than the ones I have described. Assume that you can go beyond the point I left off with the particular client, which in most of these cases is just a beginning. Build on my work and what you know about the client, as well as *your reactions* to him or her, and modify the approach I have initiated in any way that you can think of.

In this case, I hope that you will let yourself *think psychoanalytically*, so that you can begin to get some sense of how you might approach Moe from an analytic perspective and draw on its techniques. Attempting to "get the feel" of the psychoanalytic approach by staying as much as possible within its spirit will help you determine what aspects of it you might incorporate into your own style of counseling.

Some questions for you to consider as you evaluate my work with Moe and decide on the direction you might proceed with him are:

1. What are some of your main reactions to the way in which I worked with Moe? What did you either like or not like? What would you modify? How? What might you focus on in your follow-up work with Moe?
2. What central reactions do you have toward Moe? Would you like to work with him as a client? Why or why not?
3. How might you deal with Moe's feelings toward you, especially if they were hostile? How do you imagine you would react if Moe were to treat you as his father? or his mother? or one of his ex-wives? or an all-wise authority figure?

4. How might you deal with the various manifestations of Moe's resistance? For instance, might you work with it therapeutically? Might your response be defensive? Might you push him and thus make him even more defensive?
5. What countertransference issues could come up for you in your relationship with Moe? Might you foster his dependency on you out of your needs? Might he remind you of certain traits in yourself that you would like to deny? Are you aware of any unresolved problems of your own that could interfere with a *therapeutic* relationship?
6. How would you proceed with Moe? Discuss some areas you would explore with him, as well as the techniques you might use.

Recommended Supplementary Readings

One Little Boy (1964) by D. Baruch (New York: Dell [Delta]) is a fascinating account of one boy's feelings and problems. Using play therapy, it reveals how his personal conflicts originated in family dynamics. The book gives the reader a sense of appreciation for the struggles most children experience during early childhood in relationship with their parents.

Childhood and Society (second edition, 1963) by E. Erikson (New York: Norton) uses a modified and extended version of psychoanalytic thought. The author describes a psychosocial theory of development, delineating eight stages and their critical tasks.

A Primer of Freudian Psychology (1954) by C. S. Hall (New York: New American Library) is a good place to begin if you are interested in expanding your knowledge of the Freudian approach. It presents a concise overview of the key concepts of psychoanalysis.

Listening Perspectives in Psychotherapy (1983) by L. E. Hedges (New York: Jason Aronson) is a useful resource for readers who have a serious interest in learning more about contemporary psychoanalytic trends. These are exemplified in the writings of Heinz Kohut, Otto Kernberg, and Margaret Mahler.

Psychoanalysis: The Impossible Profession (1982) by J. Malcolm (New York: Random House [Vintage]) is a popular book that captures some of the analytic process in an interesting and accurate way. Highly recommended as a nontechnical illustration of how the psychoanalytic process unfolds.

August (1983) by J. Rossner (New York: Warner Books) is a best-selling novel. It provides examples of client/therapist dialogue, helping bring to life many of the concepts and techniques of psychoanalysis.

Suggested Readings

Belkin, G. S. (1984). *Introduction to counseling* (2nd ed.). Dubuque, Iowa: William C. Brown (Chapter 7).

Corey, G. (1986). *Theory and practice of counseling and psychotherapy* (3rd ed.). Monterey, Calif.: Brooks/Cole (Chapter 2).

Corsini, R. (1984). *Current psychotherapies* (3rd ed.). Itasca, Ill.: Peacock (Chapter 2).

Gilliland, B., James, R., Roberts, G., & Bowman, J. (1984). *Theories and strategies in counseling and psychotherapy.* Englewood Cliffs, N.J.: Prentice-Hall (Chapter 2).

Hansen, J., Stevic, R., & Warner, R. (1986). *Counseling: Theory and process* (4th ed.). Boston: Allyn & Bacon (Chapter 2).

Patterson, C. H. (1986). *Theories of counseling and psychotherapy* (4th ed.). New York: Harper & Row (Chapter 9).

Prochaska, J. O. (1984). *Systems of psychotherapy: A transtheoretical analysis* (2nd ed.). Homewood, Ill.: Dorsey Press (Chapter 2).

Shilling, L. E. (1984). *Perspectives on counseling theories.* Englewood Cliffs, N.J.: Prentice-Hall (Chapter 2).

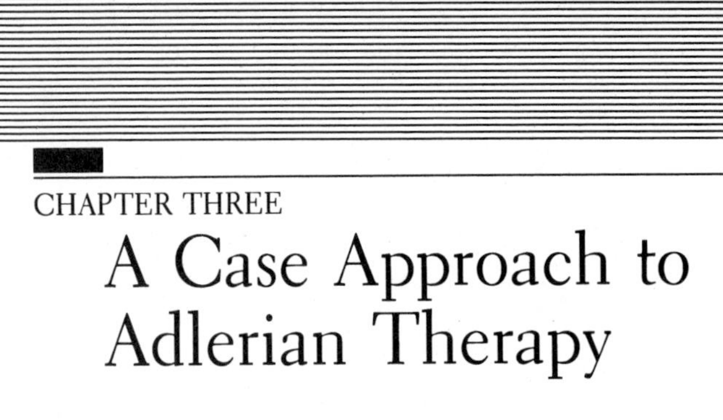

CHAPTER THREE

A Case Approach to Adlerian Therapy

An Adlerian Therapist's Perspective on Ruth

Basic Assumptions

As an Adlerian therapist I view my work with Ruth as teaching her better ways of meeting the challenges of *life tasks*. One assumption that will guide my interventions with her is that of self-determination, which means that, although she has been influenced by her past, she is not completely molded by it. This premise leaves little room for a client to take the role of a passive victim. I approach Ruth with the assumption that she has the capacity to influence and create events. What is crucial is not what she was born with but what she is making of her natural endowment. Because I operate from a phenomenological stance (dealing with the client's subjective perception of reality), I will want to find out from Ruth's perspective how she views the major events and turning points of her life. Our work will be guided by a sense of goal orientation, of looking for her purposes and meanings, and of looking to what she is striving toward in her future. I assume that she has created a unique style of life that helps to explain the patterns of her behavior. My attention will be on how she has developed her distinctive behaviors as they relate to the pursuit of her life goals.

Ruth's childhood experiences are of therapeutic interest to me, yet we will focus more on the social factors that impinged on her development rather than the psychosexual factors. True to the Adlerian spirit, I function as a therapist on the belief that it is not Ruth's childhood experiences in themselves that are crucial; rather, it is her *attitude* toward these events that is significant. Since these early influences may lead to the development of a *faulty style of life*, I will want to explore with Ruth what it was like at home as she was growing up. Our focus will be on understanding and assessing the structure of her family life (known as the family constellation) and her earliest recollections.

Initial Assessment of Ruth

Adlerian therapists typically use a life-style questionnaire to assess the client and help formulate the goals and directions for therapy. This questionnaire is designed to gather information about the client's childhood experiences, especially as they relate to family influences, birth order, relationships to each of the other family members, early memories, and other relevant material that will provide clues about the social forces influencing the client's personality formation. After this family background material is summarized and interpreted, it will provide a rich avenue for understanding Ruth and will highlight specific themes that we can pay special attention to during the course of therapy. What follows is Ruth's life-style assessment, which we complete during the intake session.

Family constellation and early memories. Ruth is first asked to list all the siblings from oldest to youngest, giving a brief description of each.

Ruth: responsible, hard working, organized, dedicated, capable, trustworthy, undemanding, self-critical, scared

Jill (4 years younger): bright, pretty, accomplished, conforming, well behaved

Amy (6 years younger): immature, admiring of me, demanding, seen by the family as a "trouble maker," hard working, independent

Steve (9 years younger): overprotected, liked by Mother, sensitive, argumentative with me, not too accomplished

Next, Ruth is asked to *rate the siblings on these traits*, from most to least: intelligent, achievement oriented, hard working, pleasing, assertive, charming, conforming, methodical, athletic, rebellious, spoiled, critical of others, feminine, easygoing, daring, responsible, idealistic, materialistic, fun loving, demanding, critical of self, withdrawn, sensitive.

Then comes a list of the following questions, along with Ruth's answers:

1. Q: Which sibling(s) was most different from you and how?
   A: Amy, who was immature, and Steve, who was protected by Mother.
2. Q: Which sibling(s) was most like you?
   A: Jill, who was a good girl and accomplished.
3. Q: Which played together?
   A: Nobody—play was frowned on in my house.
4. Q: Any unusual achievements?
   A: Jill won several honors at school.
5. Q: Any accidents or illnesses?
   A: None that I can remember.

Continuing on, Ruth is asked to complete the following sentences:

6. *As a child I:* was lonely, felt useful and needed, wanted approval from my folks, was a good girl, acted as the "mother" of my younger sisters and brother.
7. *For me, school was:* a challenge.
8. *My childhood fears were:* being alone, not feeling liked, doing something wrong, being yelled at by my father, seeing my mother disappointed.
9. *My childhood ambitions were:* to become a minister and have people look up at me.
10. *My role in my peer group was:* I don't remember feeling a part of social groups, and I sort of kept to myself and kept extremely busy.
11. *The significant events in my physical and sexual development were:* I remember being frightened about the changes in my body and very confused, and I felt guilty and ashamed about my body.
12. *In my social development:* I felt rather backward and didn't know what was expected.
13. *The most important values in my family were:* to be God-fearing, to live by the Bible, to do what was right, to obey, to be truthful, and to work up to your ability.
14. *What stands out the most for me about my family life is:* how scared I was of my father, and yet how much I wanted him to like me and think well of me.

Ruth is asked to report further on her family constellation, including information about parents. Below is a summary of this information about parental figures and relationships.

FATHER
Current age: 64
Occupation: minister

Kind of person: devoted to his work, stern, authority figure, respected, righteous, cool, detached

His ambitions for the children: that we grew up as God-fearing people who did what was right

Ruth's childhood view of father: distant, strict, ungiving

His favorite child: Jill—he liked her accomplishments

Relationship to children: he was rather aloof from all of us and insisted upon respect

Sibling most like father: Jill, because people respected her

MOTHER
Current age: 59
Occupation: housewife

Kind of person: hard-worker, rarely complained out loud, proper, dignified, self-sacrificing

Her ambitions for the children: that we never would bring shame to family and would work hard

Ruth's childhood view of mother: emotionally ungiving, serious, strict

Her favorite child: Steve—he did no wrong in her eyes

Relationship to children: she was devoted to seeing that we grew up right, but not personally involved

Sibling most like mother: myself in that we were both hard-workers

15. *My parents' relationship to each other was:* very formal and stiff. They did not argue; my mother stood behind whatever my father said or did; very little affection was demonstrated; and they rarely laughed.
16. *Siblings' relationship to parents:* Jill got along fairly well with my father; Amy and Steve were often in trouble with him, and I was never able to get his approval. Steve was close to Mother, and both Amy and I tried to please her without much success. Jill got along fairly well with her.
17. *Parents' relationship to the children:* Mother showed affection mainly to Steve. She appeared to be concerned about how we were growing up, but I rarely felt any kind of emotional closeness with her. At times she was supportive, however. Father seemed pretty distant from all us kids.
18. *Besides my parents, another parental figure for me was:* my grandmother, who seemed to understand me and take an interest in me.

I ask Ruth to describe her *earliest recollections,* which are recorded as follows:

Age 3: I remember my father yelling at me and then putting me in another room because I was crying. I don't remember why I was crying, but I know I was scared, and after he shouted, I was petrified.

Age 4½: I was in church and was talking with a boy. My mother gave me dirty looks, and my father, who was conducting the service, gave me a stern lecture when we got home.

Age 6: An 8-year-old neighbor boy and I had our clothes off and were "playing doctor" when my father caught us in my bedroom. He sent the boy home and then told me in a cold and solemn voice that what I had done was very wrong. He did not speak to me for weeks, and I remember feeling very dirty and guilty.

Age 7: I remember my second-grade teacher saying that I was not doing well in school and that I was going to get a bad report card. I tried so hard to do well, because I didn't want to bring home poor grades. This teacher didn't like me very much, and I couldn't understand what I had done wrong. I thought I was trying my best. I was scared.

Age 8: I was in a church play, and I worked for months at memorizing my lines. I thought I had them down perfectly. My parents came to the church play, and for a time I was doing fine, and I was hoping they would like my performance. Then, toward the end I forgot to come in when I was supposed to, and the director had to cue me. My mistake was apparent to my father, who later commented that I had spoiled a rather good performance by my lack of attention. I remember feeling sad and disappointed, because I had so hoped that they would be pleased. And I don't recall my mother's saying anything about the play.

Life-style summary. As is typical in Adlerian therapy, after collecting all of this information I make a summary of Ruth's family constellation and her early recollections. Then I interpret this summary in light of her "basic mistakes," the mistaken perceptions or faulty conclusions that she lives by, which she arrived at from a series of critical incidents in her early childhood. I summarize her major assets also, so that we can build on them in therapy. In the next session Ruth and I go over this life-style summary, and I help her understand some themes that appear to be running through her life.

1. *Summary of Ruth's family constellation.* Ruth was the oldest of four children, and she assumed the role of looking after her siblings. She describes the atmosphere of the family as serious, with little affection demonstrated to the children, and as one in which the father demanded unquestioning adherence to the rules and standards he set. There was a moralistic tone to most of the family discussions. When Ruth attempted to have fun, she was met with disapproval from her father. Guilt was a controlling factor in the family. A central theme for Ruth is that she did everything she could to win the favor of her parents but continued to feel that she had never done enough and that they expected more.

2. *Summary of early recollections.* A theme here is that Ruth had a fear of her father, whom she saw as aloof and difficult to please. Although she did everything to keep him from being upset, she eventually decided that she did not know how to prevent his disapproval.

3. *Summary of basic mistakes.* Ruth's pattern and profile show a number of mistaken and self-defeating perceptions, some of which are:

- If you can't please your own father, it is impossible to really please any man.
- I should be perfect, and if I ever manage to become perfect, my parents will finally love me the way I want them to.
- Don't be physically close or affectionate, because doing so might lead to trouble.
- Because the church has all the right answers, I don't have to think for myself.

- If I don't follow everything I was taught, I deserve to be punished, and I should feel guilty.
- I don't have a right to think of myself, for my proper place is to always put others first and to serve others.

4. *Summary of assets.* Personal assets are strengths that can be built on as a part of the therapy process. Some of the positive directions and strengths in Ruth's case are:

- She is beginning to question values that she uncritically accepted.
- She is coming to the realization that she has value as a person in her own right, not simply for the functions that she performs for others.
- She is beginning to have ideas of what she wants from life besides being a mother and a wife, and she seems committed to change.
- She is willing to tolerate some anxiety and uncertainty as she struggles to find her own way.
- She is fairly bright, is hard working, and had already taken some steps to change before she began therapy.

Goals of the Therapy

There are four major goals of Adlerian therapy, which correspond to the four phases of the therapeutic process. These goals are (1) to establish and maintain a good working relationship between equals; (2) to provide a therapeutic climate in which Ruth can come to understand her basic beliefs and feelings about herself and discover how she acquired these faulty beliefs; (3) to help her reach insight into her mistaken goals and self-defeating behaviors through a process of confrontation and interpretation; and (4) to assist her in developing alternative ways of thinking, behaving, and feeling by encouraging her to translate her insights into action.

Therapeutic Procedures

The four phases of Adlerian therapy that Ruth will experience are as follows. First, I emphasize establishing an empathic relationship with Ruth. It is important that our relationship be based on cooperation and mutual respect. Therapeutic cooperation requires that our goals be aligned, so Ruth and I develop a clear contract that specifies what she wants from therapy, that spells out our responsibilities in the therapeutic venture, and that guides the course of therapy.

Second is the phase of exploring Ruth's dynamics by conducting an assessment and analysis of her style of life and by seeing how her life-style affects her current functioning in all the tasks of life. (We have done this during the intake session via the life-style questionnaire that is described above.) We then spend several sessions summarizing, reviewing, integrating, and interpreting the material derived from the assessment.

This process leads to the third phase, insight. As an Adlerian I view insight as only a step toward change, which can best be defined as translating self-understanding into constructive action. Ruth can play a "Yes, but . . ." game if all she acquires are intellectual insights. Through well-timed interpretations, which I suggest as therapeutic hunches, Ruth can learn how she behaves as she does in the present and discover the purpose her behavior serves.

Phase four is reorientation. One of the aims of Ruth's therapy is to challenge her to take risks and make changes. Throughout the entire process, *encouragement* is of the utmost importance. My assumption is that with encouragement Ruth will begin to experience her own inner resources and the power to choose for herself and to direct her own life. By now she will ideally have challenged her self-limiting assumptions and will be ready to put plans into action. Even though she may regress to old patterns at times, I will ask her to "catch herself" in this process and then continue to experiment with and practice new behavior. Throughout her therapy I will use a variety of techniques aimed primarily at challenging her cognitions (beliefs and thinking processes). Adlerians contend that first comes thinking, then behaving, and then feeling. So, if we want to change behavior and feelings, the best way is to focus on Ruth's mistaken perceptions and faulty beliefs about life and herself. Drawing on a variety of techniques, some borrowed from other modalities, I will use confrontation, questioning, encouragement, assigning of homework, interpretation, giving of appropriate advice, and any other methods that can help her begin to change her vision of herself and her ability to behave in different ways.

Therapeutic Process

In many ways the process of Adlerian therapy can be understood by recalling some basic ideas of the psychoanalytic process. There is a tie between these two theories, especially on the issue of looking at how our earlier experiences are related to our present personality functioning.

Elements of the Process

Uncovering a mistaken belief. Ruth and I have been working together for some time, and she is beginning to see striking parallels between the role she assumed as an adolescent in her family by becoming the caretaker of her sisters and brother and her contemporary role as "supermother" to her own children. She has discovered that for all of her life she has been laboring under the assumption that, if she gave of herself unselfishly, she would be rewarded by being acknowledged and feeling a sense of personal fulfillment. As a child she wanted to be loved, accepted, and taken care of emotionally by her father, and she worked very hard at being the "good girl." For all her married life Ruth has outdone herself in being the perfect wife and the devoted mother to their children. In this way she hopes to relate to her husband so he will love and accept her. Yet she has never really felt appreciated or emotionally nurtured by him, and now she is realizing that she has built her life on a personal mythology—if people loved her, she would be worthwhile and would find happiness through her personal sacrifices.

Helping Ruth reach her goals. At this time in Ruth's therapy we are exploring some other options open to her. Lately we have been talking a lot about her goals and about her visions of herself in the years to come.

RUTH: I'm in college now, and I'm hoping to finish my degree and get a teaching credential. But I keep telling myself that I don't have a right to do this for myself. It seems so selfish. School is very demanding of my time and energies, and it means that I have that much less to give at home. If only I could throw myself more fully into my studies and at the same time feel good about that choice!

JERRY: And what stops you from doing what you say you want to do?

RUTH: I guess it's my guilt! I keep feeling I shouldn't be at school and should be at home. John keeps telling me how much he and the kids miss me. If only I could stop feeling that I should be the dedicated mother and wife! But then I wouldn't be sure of my place in the family, either, and everything would be up in the air.

JERRY: One way to free yourself is to imagine you could act as if you had the right to be a full-time student and could enjoy it—even for only a week. What would you need to ask of your family to help you do this? It might be beneficial to see what your kids and John could do if you didn't take it on yourself to do almost everything for them.

RUTH: What you're suggesting is awfully difficult. I'm realizing right now how rarely I ask my family to do anything for me and how often I assume that they either won't or can't do it. Just thinking about asking them to do more for me makes me feel very uncomfortable.

JERRY: So again I ask if you're willing to risk this uncomfortableness. For one week, are you willing to act as if you had a right to fully enjoy being a student?

I am hoping that, by forcing herself to act the way she says she would like to act, Ruth will discover some new possibilities. She may actually feel different by behaving differently and telling herself that she has a right to her own life. A week passes, and Ruth returns.

RUTH: Guess what? I did ask my family to do more things for themselves, and I delegated some of the housework. It went much better than I thought. I didn't feel nearly as guilty as I had expected to, and my family didn't fall apart as I had anticipated. Surprisingly, for the most part they were willing to help out.

JERRY: It must be satisfying for you to have followed through with your commitment. Now, what did you learn?

RUTH: That I can often do more than I think I can. But it's one thing doing this for only a week and another matter doing it for very long. Besides, there were several times that I started to feel guilty. Then my good feelings went away.

JERRY: Do you remember when we talked about catching yourself? At first you'll probably catch yourself falling into familiar traps too late, but as time goes on, you'll get better at catching yourself repeating these old patterns. [I want to encourage her not to give up merely because she didn't carry out her assignment perfectly. And I want her to give herself credit for what she did do and for her accomplishments.]

RUTH: If I hope to ever get my teaching credential, I'm going to have to get rid of my guilt. Don't you have any advice on how to do this?

JERRY: Sounds to me as if you're now in your old pattern, only this time it's your need to be the "perfect client." What would it be like if you could actually give yourself credit for what you did last week? Do you think you can brag to me about how well you carried out your assignment?

From here we proceed to talk in some detail about catching herself when she makes self-limiting statements. Then she is in a position to at least tell herself something different and also try different behavior. We also focus on specific plans for her to complete her education. We look at the barriers she is likely to encounter as she proceeds toward her goal—barriers from her parents, from her husband and children, from the environment, and, most importantly, from herself. Together we work on strategies that she can employ to successfully deal with these barriers. In short, we work out a short-range action program to meet her goals.

Process Commentary

My major aim in our sessions is to provide Ruth with both encouragement and challenge that will be instrumental in her considering alternative attitudes, beliefs, goals, and behaviors. Many times when I make suggestions, Ruth hesitates and then provides me with reasons why she cannot do what I am asking of her. For example, we discuss the prospects of her accepting a job as a substitute teacher. At first she seems excited and goes for a few interviews. Then she appears to give up on her plans, because she is sure that John would be very upset if she were gone more from the house.

At times I use a technique called "spitting in the client's soup." At these times I might reply "Do you really want to change your life, or do you want me to feel sorry for you?" I assure her that I do not feel sorry for her plight and let her know that to some extent she is maintaining her own helpless stance. More than once she becomes angry and accuses me of not really understanding her situation. But I persist in expecting her to actually do something different as a way of coming closer to the goals she has identified as important to her.

Once she has made some new decisions and modified her goals, I teach her ways to challenge her own thinking. At those times when Ruth is very critical of herself, I provide encouragement. Partly due to my faith in her and my encouragement, Ruth comes closer to experiencing her inner strength. She develops increased honesty about what she is doing, and she augments her power to choose for herself instead of merely following the values she uncritically accepted as a child.

A most important ingredient of the final stages of her therapy is commitment. Ruth is finally persuaded that, if she hopes to change, she will have to be willing to set specific tasks for herself and then take concrete action in dealing with her problems. Although she attempts to live up to what she believes is the role of the "ideal client," she eventually develops increased tolerance of learning by trial and error, and with this she becomes better at "catching herself" at repeating ineffective behavior.

Questions for Reflection

1. As you review the life-style-assessment form used to gather background information on Ruth, what associations do you have with your own early childhood experiences? If you were considering getting into therapy as a client, what do you imagine it would be like for you to complete the life-style questionnaire? Do you have any personal reactions to the information on Ruth?
2. As you think about your own family constellation, what most stands out for you? (As a child, how did you view your mother? father? How did they view and treat you? What was your parents' relationship to each other? What was their relationship to the other children? What was your position in your family? How did you get along with your siblings?) After reflecting on your early experiences in your family, attempt to come to some conclusions about the ways these experiences operate in your life today.
3. What are three of your earliest recollections? Can you speculate on how these memories might have an impact on the person you are now and how they could be related to your future strivings?
4. List what you consider to be the major "basic mistakes" in your life. Do you have any ideas about how you developed certain mistaken perceptions about yourself and about life? How do you think that your own "basic mistakes" influence the ways you think, act, and feel today?
5. Compare and contrast the Adlerian and the psychoanalytic ways of working with Ruth. What are some of the major differences? Do you see any ways that you could combine Adlerian and psychoanalytic concepts and techniques?
6. In Ruth's case, the counseling process began with a life-style assessment, which focused on her family constellation, her early recollections, and her basic mistakes. What are your ideas about conducting this type of assessment during the initial phases of therapy? From what you learned about Ruth through this questionnaire, what aspects of her life might you be most interested in focusing on? What are the themes running through her life that lend themselves especially well to Adlerian therapy?
7. One of the goals of Adlerian therapy is to increase the client's social interest. Can you think of ways that you could work with Ruth to help her attain these goals? (How might you help her develop new friendships or make her social involvements more meaningful?)

Julie: "It's My Father's Fault That I Can't Trust Men"

Some Background Data

Julie is interested in exploring her relationships with men. She says that she cannot trust me because I am a man, and that the reason for her inability to trust men is that her father was an alcoholic and was therefore untrustworthy. She recalls that he was never around when she needed him and that she would not have felt free to go to him with any of her problems because he was loud and gruff. She tells me of the guilt that she felt over her father's drinking because of her sense that in some way she was causing him to drink. Julie, who is now 35 and unmarried, is leery of men, convinced that they will somehow let her down if she gives them the chance. She has decided in advance that she will not be a fool again, that she will not let herself need or trust men.

Although Julie seems pretty clear about not wanting to risk trusting men, she realizes that this notion is self-defeating and that she would like to challenge her views. Though she wants to change the way she perceives and feels about men, somehow she seems to have an investment in her belief about their basic untrustworthiness. She is not very willing to look at her part in keeping this assumption about men alive. Rather, she would prefer to pin the blame on her father. It was he who taught her this lesson, and now it is difficult for her to change— or so she reports.

My Way of Working with Julie as an Adlerian Therapist

I would be inclined to begin my counseling of Julie with my own reactions to her not trusting me. I feel that she has lumped me into a category with "all men." With her present frame of mind there is no way that I can be anything but untrustworthy to her. I feel angry at being so categorized, and I hope to have the courage to let her know this. This in itself is an important place to begin with her. I fear that, if I ignore my own reactions to her stereotyping of me, I will not be able to counsel her very effectively.

Another reaction I have involves the degree to which she is failing to accept any of the responsibility for the way she feels and for the way she sees and treats men now. Granted, it was unfortunate that she had these experiences with her father, and I can accept that they have conditioned her toward men to a degree. Yet I see her as unwilling to look at all the power she continues to give to her father today. Part of our work will surely involve my confronting her on the way she clings to the notion that she cannot get close to men because her father was cruel and unavailable. I will probably ask her to consider what it might be like for her if she *were* to begin to accept her share of responsibility for her inability to trust men.

Even if it is true that her father was not trustworthy and treated her unkindly, my assessment is that it is a "basic mistake" for her to have generalized what she believes to be true of her father to all men. My hope is that our relationship, based on trust and cooperation, will be a catalyst for her in challenging her assumptions about men.

As a part of the assessment process I will be interested in exploring her early memories pertaining to her father, mother, brothers, and sisters. We will also explore what it was like for her as a child in her family. Some questions that I will pose, though not necessarily all at once, are:

- What do you think you get from staying angry at your father and insisting that he is the cause of your fear of men?
- What do you imagine it would be like for you if you were to act as if men were trustworthy? And what do you suppose really prevents you from doing that, because it is what you say you would like?
- If you could forgive your father, what do you imagine that would be like for you? for him? for other men?

- If you keep the same attitudes you have now until you die, how would that be for you?
- How would you like to be in five years?
- If you really want to change, what do you see that you can do to begin this process? What are you willing to do?

I have already indicated that I think that the relationship between Julie and me is the major vehicle to work with in the sessions. I pursue with her what, if anything, I have done to earn her trust or what warrants her continuing to treat me as she did her father. An honest exploration of the ways she thinks I have let her down might be appropriate. Also, I explore what she wants with me and why she continues coming for counseling. I expect her to explore whether she is getting what she wants from me and, if not, what is preventing her from getting what she wants. It is essential that I do much more than just listen to her; also vital is giving her my honest reactions to what I hear her saying and sharing with her the reactions that are generated in me when I am with her. It is necessary that I let her know that she is not *making* me have certain reactions, but that they are mine. This would be the most important therapeutic tool to work with.

Julie needs to take some action if she expects to change her views toward men. Thus, we work together to determine what she can do outside of the sessions. A number of possibilities occur to me.

First, she can write an uncensored letter to her father, explicitly airing all of her grievances. In her letter it is critical that she express her anger—that she tell him all the things she has been saying to me and other things that she has felt but kept to herself. I encourage her *not* to mail the letter, as this is only an exercise for her to symbolically work through some of the feelings toward her father. At the following session we can discuss what it was like for her to write this letter.

After she writes the letter, she and I can role-play many of the things that she told her father and what she would still like to say to him. I can be her father and respond in several ways. One way is to act as her father typically did; another idea is to respond in the way she wished her father would someday respond; another way is for her to talk to me as a representative of all men, especially those men whom she wants to get close to but will not. Of course, she has to coach me on playing the appropriate roles. Very useful to Julie is my telling her how I might feel if I were her father.

After role-playing various situations in our sessions, Julie can decide if she wants to actually initiate a meeting with her father. This may or may not be appropriate or necessary, although I will open the topic up for discussion with Julie if she does not mention it herself. If this is something she wants to do, I explore with her what she hopes to get from such a conversation. And I take steps to lessen the chances that she is setting herself up for failure (with more reasons and justifications for continuing to keep her distance from men). We also talk about the possibilities of her not being received by him the way she would like, along with how she might deal with such a situation. I impress on her the importance of giving her father a chance and of being careful to avoid attacking him and blaming him for all of her problems.

The letter writing and the role playing are avenues for Julie to vent her pent-up emotions; she could lose an opportunity for contact with him by merely wanting to castigate him and get revenge. Further, Julie can benefit by focusing on what *she* most wants to tell him about herself, rather than merely asking him a host of questions that would put him on the defensive.

A major part of my work with Julie is directed at confronting her with the ways she is refusing to take responsibility for the things in herself that she does not like and at encouraging her to decide on some course of action to begin the process of modifying those things.

A very important phase of therapy is the *reorientation* stage, which is an action-oriented process of putting one's insights to work. As an Adlerian therapist I am concerned that Julie do more than merely understand the dynamics of her behavior. My goal is that she eventually see new and more functional alternatives. This reorientation phase of her therapy consists of her considering alternative attitudes, beliefs, goals, and behaviors.

During this reorientation phase of counseling Julie is expected to make decisions and modify her goals. I encourage her to "catch herself" in the process of repeating old patterns. When she meets a man and then immediately assumes that he cannot be trusted, for example, it helps if she is able to observe what she is doing. She can then ask herself if she wants to persist in clinging to old assumptions or if she is willing to let go of them and form impressions without bias.

This phase of counseling is a time for setting tasks and making commitments. Thus, Julie will decide on the specific ways she would like to be different, and then it is essential that she develop some program that will help her achieve those changes she wants. Encouragement during the time that Julie is trying new behavior and working on new goals is most useful. This encouragement can take the form of positive reinforcement, of support, of recognizing the changes she makes, and of continuing to be psychologically available for her during our sessions.

Follow-Up: You Continue as Julie's Therapist

1. What are some of your impressions and reactions to the way I worked with Julie? What did you like or not like about the session? Knowing what you know about this session and Julie, what might you *most* want to follow up with if you could see her for at least a couple of months?
2. How much do you imagine that your approach with Julie would be affected by your life experiences and views? How much would you want to share of yourself with her in your sessions? What ways do you think you could use yourself as a person in your work with her?
3. How might you deal with her apparent unwillingness to accept personal responsibility and her blaming of her father for her inability to trust men now?
4. What are some additional Adlerian techniques you might use with Julie?
5. Outline some of the steps in Adlerian counseling that you would expect to take for a series of sessions with Julie, showing why you are adopting that particular course of action. Specifically, how would you (a) establish a good therapeutic relationship with her? (b) conduct an analysis and assessment of her individual dynamics,

including family constellation and early recollections? (c) help her gain insight into her dynamics? (d) assist her in the process of reorientation, or considering an alternative set of attitudes, beliefs, goals, and behaviors?

Recommended Supplementary Readings

Superiority and Social Interest: A Collection of Later Writings (third revised edition, 1979) by A. Adler (New York: Norton) is an excellent source for readers who want to review some of Adler's writings. The introduction, written by H. L. Ansbacher and R. R. Ansbacher, is a clear statement on the increasing recognition of Adler's position in the development of counseling. Part VI contains a comprehensive and interesting biographical essay of Alfred Adler. Part III deals with case interpretations and treatment.

The Encouragement Book: Becoming a Positive Person (1980) by D. Dinkmeyer and L. Losoncy (Englewood Cliffs, N.J.: Prentice-Hall [Spectrum]) presents skills and attitudes that can be translated into behaviors. It is a readable book that illustrates how the encouragement process can result in behavioral change.

Adlerian Counseling and Psychotherapy (1979) by D. Dinkmeyer, W. Pew, and D. Dinkmeyer, Jr. (Monterey, Calif.: Brooks/Cole) gives an excellent basic presentation of the theoretical foundations of Adlerian counseling. The specific focus is on stages of the counseling process, Adlerian techniques, applying Adlerian methods to a variety of populations, and working with individuals, groups, and families.

Individual Psychology: Theory and Practice (1982) by G. M. Manaster and R. Corsini (Itasca, Ill.: Peacock) is a highly readable overview of Adlerian psychology. There is a clear summary of basic Adlerian concepts, with emphasis on application of these principles to practice. An accurate, interesting, and clear book.

Suggested Readings

Belkin, G. S. (1984). *Introduction to counseling* (2nd ed.). Dubuque, Iowa: William C. Brown (Chapter 7).

Corey, G. (1986). *Theory and practice of counseling and psychotherapy* (3rd ed.). Monterey, Calif.: Brooks/Cole (Chapter 3).

Corsini, R. (1984). *Current psychotherapies* (3rd ed.). Itasca, Ill.: Peacock (Chapter 3).

Gilliland, B., James, R., Roberts, G., & Bowman, J. (1984). *Theories and strategies in counseling and psychotherapy*. Englewood Cliffs, N.J.: Prentice-Hall (Chapter 3).

Hansen, J., Stevic, R., & Warner, R. (1986). *Counseling: Theory and process* (4th ed.). Boston: Allyn & Bacon (Chapter 4).

Prochaska, J. O. (1984). *Systems of psychotherapy: A transtheoretical analysis* (2nd ed.). Homewood, Ill.: Dorsey Press (Chapter 6).

Shilling, L. E. (1984). *Perspectives on counseling theories*. Englewood Cliffs, N.J.: Prentice-Hall (Chapter 3).

CHAPTER FOUR

A Case Approach to Existential Therapy

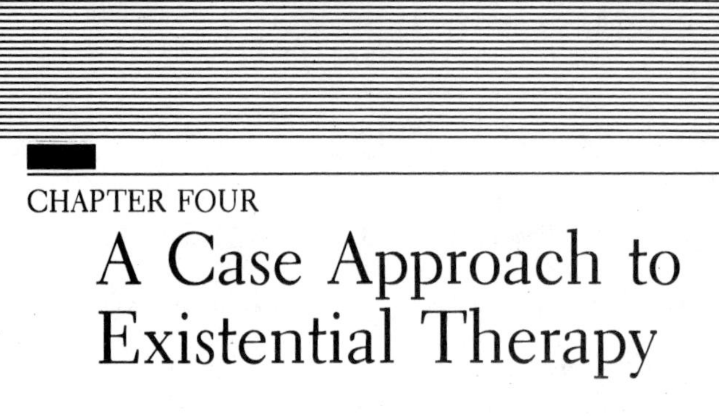

An Existential Therapist's Perspective on Ruth

Basic Assumptions

The existential approach to counseling is based on the assumption that the relationship the therapist establishes with the client is of the utmost importance in determining how successful therapy will be. Therapy is not something that I do *to* the person (in this case, Ruth); I am not the technical expert who acts on the passive client. I view therapy as a dialogue in the deepest and most genuine sense—an honest exchange between Ruth and myself. We will be partners traveling on a journey, and neither of us knows where it will end. At times we will not even have a clear idea of where we are heading. Ruth and I may both be changed by the encounter, and I expect that she will touch off powerful associations, feelings, memories, and reactions within me. My hope is to understand her world from a subjective viewpoint and at the same time to let her know what personal reactions I am having toward her in our relationship.

My approach emphasizes human factors such as self-awareness, freedom, responsibility, anxiety, meaning, the reality of death, and the challenges of shaping and creating one's own destiny. A fundamental part of this approach is respect for the client, which implies having faith in Ruth's capacity to recognize her part in creating her current life situation and in her potential to discover new ways of being. As Ruth's therapist my job is to assist her in understanding how she is dealing with the basic issues in her life, such as responsibility, choice, and meaning. My hope is that she will discover, through self-exploration in therapy and her willingness to take risks, that she can live without remaining committed to earlier assumptions about life that may no longer be valid or useful. Primarily through the therapeutic relationship that we create, she will find the resources to challenge some of the ways in which she is living a restricted existence, and she will be able to live more freely and responsibly.

Initial Assessment of Ruth

Ruth appears to be a good candidate for existential therapy. She is courageous enough to question the meaning of life and to challenge some of her comfortable, but dull, patterns. She is facing a number of developmental crises, such as wondering what meaning there is to life now that her children are preparing to leave home. As she begins to expand her vision of the choices open to her, her anxiety is increasing. The process has led to more questions, yet her answers are few. She is grappling with what she wants for herself, apart from her long-standing definition of herself as wife and mother. A major theme in her life is centered on the question "How fully am I living life?" One of her strengths is her willingness to ask such anxiety-producing questions. Another of her assets is that she has already made some choices and taken some significant steps. She did separate from her fundamentalist religion, which she no longer found personally meaningful, she has returned to college, she is motivated to change her life, and she has sought out therapy as a way to help her find the paths she wants to travel.

Goals of the Therapy

The purpose of existential therapy is not to "cure" people of disorders; rather, it is to help them become aware of what they are doing and to get them out of a "victim" stance. It is aimed at helping people like Ruth get out of their rigid roles and see more clearly the ways that they have been leading a narrow and restricted existence. The basic purpose of Ruth's therapy is to provide her with the insights necessary to discover, establish, and use the freedom that she possesses. In many ways she is blocking her own freedom, and she perceives herself as a victim. My function is to help her recognize her part in creating her life situation, including the distress she is experiencing. Until she recognizes and accepts her part in contributing to her dilemma, there is really no motivation to change. My central concern is to provide a climate in which Ruth can evaluate her past choices and freely choose for herself now. I assume that, as she sees the ways in which her existence is limited, she will be able to take steps toward her liberation. My hope is that she can create a more responsible and meaningful existence.

Therapeutic Procedures

As an existential therapist I do not rely on a well-developed set of techniques. Instead, I focus on certain themes that I consider to be part of the human condition, and I emphasize my ability to be fully present with my client by challenging her and by reacting to her. To give some idea of the questions I might pursue with Ruth, consider the following, any of which we might eventually explore in therapy sessions:

- "In what ways are you living as fully as you might? And how are you living a restricted existence?"
- "To what degree are you living by your own choices, as opposed to living a life outlined by others?"
- "What choices have you made so far, and how have these choices affected you now?"
- "What are some of the choices you are faced with now? How do you deal with the anxiety that is a part of making choices for yourself and accepting personal freedom?"
- "What are some of the changes that you most want to make, and what is preventing you from making them?"

My central concern is to provide a climate in which Ruth can evaluate her past choices and freely choose for herself now. I assume that, as she sees the ways in which her existence is limited, she will be able to take steps toward her liberation. My hope is that she can create her identity anew.

In essence, Ruth is about to engage in a process of opening doors to herself. The experience may be frightening, exciting, joyful, depressing, or all of these at times. As she wedges open the closed doors, she will also begin to loosen the deterministic shackles that have kept her psychologically bound. Gradually, as she becomes aware of what she has been and who she is now, she will be better able to decide what kind of future she wants to carve out for herself. Through her therapy she can explore alternatives for making her visions become real.

Therapeutic Process

At this point in her therapy Ruth is coming to grips more directly than she has before with the mid-life crisis that she is experiencing. She has been talking about values by which she lived in the past that now hold little meaning for her, about her feelings of emptiness, and about her fears of making "wrong" choices. Below are some excerpts from several of our sessions.

Elements of the Process

Examining Ruth's marital problems.

RUTH: So, at 39 I'm just now agonizing over who I am. Perhaps it's too late.

JERRY: Well, I don't know that there's a given time period when we should ask such questions. I feel excited for you and respect you for asking these questions now.

RUTH: What I know is that my life has been very structured up to this point, and now all this questioning is unsettling to me and is making me anxious. I wonder if I want to give up my predictable life and face the unknown. Sometimes I feel more powerful, and there are moments when I believe I can change some things about my life. But I wonder if it's worth the risk!

JERRY: I'm very touched by what you're saying and remember some of my own struggles in facing uncertainty. When you say that you're anxious, it would help me to understand you better if you could tell me some of the times or situations in which you feel this anxiety.

RUTH: Sometimes I feel anxious when I think about my relationship with John. I'm beginning to see many things I don't like, but I'm afraid to tell him about my dissatisfactions.

JERRY: Would you be willing to tell me some of the specific dissatisfactions you have with John?

Ruth then proceeds to talk about some of the difficulties she is experiencing with John. I also encourage her to share with me some of the impulses that frighten her. I am providing a safe atmosphere for her to express some new awarenesses without reacting judgmentally to her. I also give her some of my personal reactions to what she is telling me. Then I ask her if she talks very often with John the way she is talking with me. I am receptive to her and wonder out loud whether John could also be open to her if she spoke this way with him. We end the session with my encouraging her to approach John and say some of the things to him that she has discussed in this session.

Helping Ruth find new values. In a later session Ruth initiates her struggles with religion.

RUTH: I left my religion years ago, but I haven't found anything to replace it. I'm hoping that you can help me find some new values. You have so much more experience and you seem happy with who you are and what you believe in. On my own I'm afraid that I might make the wrong decisions, and then I'd really be messed up.

As we continue, it becomes clear that she is not trusting herself to find answers within, so she is hoping that I will give her those answers. For me, what therapy is all about is engaging in the struggle to find life's answers within oneself. Ruth feels lost in an unfriendly sea without any compass, and she very much wants me to point the proper direction so that she will feel more secure.

JERRY: If I were to give you answers, that would not be fair to you. It would be a way of saying that I don't see you as capable of finding your own way. Maybe a way for you to begin is to ask some questions. I know, for me, one way of getting answers is to raise questions.

RUTH: I know that the religion I was brought up in told me very clearly what was right and wrong. I was taught that once married, always married—and you make the best of the situation. Well, I'm not so willing to accept that now.

JERRY: How is that so?

RUTH: Sometimes I'm afraid that if I stay in therapy, I'll change so much that I'll have little in common with John, and I may eventually break up our marriage.

JERRY: You know, I'm aware that you have somewhat decided that your changes will cause the breakup of your marriage. Could it be that your changes could have a positive effect on your relationship?

RUTH: You're right, I haven't thought about it in that way. And I guess I've made the assumption that John won't like my changes. I more often worry that what I'm doing in therapy will eventually make me want to leave him, or he might want to leave me. Sometimes I have an impulse to walk away from my marriage, but I get scared thinking about who I would be without John in my life.

JERRY: Why not imagine that this did happen, and for a few minutes talk out loud about who you would be if John weren't a part of your life. Just let out whatever thoughts or images that come to your mind, and try not to worry about how they sound.

RUTH: All my life I've had others tell me who and what I should be, and John has picked up where my parents and church left off. I don't know what my life is about apart from being a wife and a mother. What would our kids think if John and I were to split up? How would it affect them? Would they hate me for what I'd done to the family? I know I'm tired of living the way I am, but I'm not sure what I want. And I'm scared to death of making any more changes for fear that it will lead to even more turmoil. John and the kids liked the "old me" just fine, and they seem upset by the things I've been saying lately.

JERRY: In all that you just said, you didn't allow yourself to really express how you might be different if they were not in your life. It's easier for you to tune in to how the people in your life might bc affected by your changes than for you to allow yourself to imagine how you'd be different. It does seem difficult for you to fantasize being different. Why not give it another try? Keep the focus on how you want to be different rather than how your family would react to your changes.

Dealing with Ruth's anxiety. Ruth has trouble changing. There is immediate anxiety whenever she thinks of being different. She is beginning to see that she has choices, that she does not have to wait around until John gives her permission to change, and that others do not have to make her choices for her. Yet she is terrified by this realization, and for a long time it appears that she is immobilized in her therapy. She will not act on the choices available to her. So, I go with her feelings of being stuck and explore her anxiety with her. Here is how she describes these feelings.

RUTH: I often wake up in the middle of the night with terrible feelings that the walls are closing in on me! I break out in cold sweats, I have trouble breathing, and I can feel my heart pounding. At times I worry that I'll die. I can't sleep, and I get up and pace around and feel horrible.

It should be remembered that, after Ruth mentioned her physical symptoms during the initial interview, I had her make an appointment with her physician for a complete physical. The results showed no organic basis for her symptoms.

JERRY: Ruth, as unpleasant as these feelings are, I hope you learn to pay attention to these signals. They're warning you that all is not well in your life and that you're ready for change.

I know that Ruth sees anxiety as a negative thing, something she would like to get rid of once and for all. I see her anxiety as the possibility of a new starting point for her. Rather than simply getting rid of these symptoms, I want to go deeply into their meaning. I see her anxiety as the result of her increased awareness of her freedom along with her growing sense of responsibility for deciding what kind of life she wants and then taking action to make these changes a reality.

Exploring the meaning of death. Eventually we get onto the topic of death and explore its meaning to Ruth.

RUTH: I've been thinking about what we talked about before—about what I want from life before I die. You know, for so many years I lived in dread of death because I thought I'd die a sinner and go to hell for eternity. I suppose that fear has kept me from looking at death. It has always seemed so morbid.

JERRY: It doesn't have to be morbid. As we talked about before, unless you can confront your own death, I don't think you'll be able to live life to its fullest. There are ways that you may be "dead" even though you're still physically alive.

RUTH: How do you mean that?

JERRY: Why don't you talk about aspects of your life where you do not feel really alive? How often do you feel a sense of excitement about living?

RUTH: It would be easier for me to tell you of the times I feel half dead! I'm dead to having fun. Sexually I'm dead.

JERRY: Can you think of some other ways you might be dead?

I am trying to get her to evaluate the quality of her life and to begin to experience her deadness. After some time she admits that she has allowed her spirit to die. Old values have died, and she has not planted new ones. She is gaining some dim awareness that there is more to living than breathing. It is important that she allow herself to recognize her deadness and feel it as a precondition for her rebirth. I operate under the assumption that, by really experiencing and expressing the ways in which she feels dead, she can begin to focus on how she wants to be alive, if at all. Only then is there hope that she can learn new ways to live.

JERRY: Ruth, I wonder if you would let yourself imagine that you're dying, and even fantasize your funeral. What might each of the significant people in your life say about you at your funeral?

I ask her to close her eyes and say aloud all the things that John, her parents, her brothers and sisters, and her children might say. Then I ask her to make up her own eulogy. I pose a number of questions about her life and ask her in fantasy to think about her answers. "What have you done with life so far? Whom have you touched? What have you left behind? What dreams never came to fruition? How did you make a difference by having lived? What regrets do you have? What do you wish you had done differently? What opportunities have you passed up? What choices have you not made? What unfinished projects are left behind? And what would you do differently if you could live all over again?" Although I do not ask her all of these questions at once, I do challenge her to reflect on what she might begin to do today to lessen the chances of having too many regrets.

Process Commentary

Ruth's experience in therapy accentuates the basic assumption that there are no absolute answers outside of herself. She learns that therapy is a process of opening up doors bit by bit and that, as she opens up these doors, she has more potential for choices. This happens largely because of the relationship between us. She becomes well aware that she cannot evade responsibility for choosing for herself. She learns that she is constantly creating herself by the choices she is making, as well as by the choices she is failing to make. As her therapist I support her attempts at experimenting with new behaviors in our sessions. Our open discussions, in which we talk about how we are experiencing each other, are a new behavior for her. These sessions provide a safe situation for her to extend new dimensions of her being. At the same time, I teach her how she might use what she is learning in her everyday life. She risks getting angry at me, being direct with me, and telling me how I affect her. We work on ways that she might continue this behavior with selected people in her environment.

Along with Ruth's willingness to risk behaving in different ways, both in the therapy sessions and in daily life, she comes to realize that, as her boundaries of personal freedom expand, so does her anxiety. One of my aims is to show her the connection between the choices she is making or failing to make and the anxiety she is experiencing. I do this by asking her to observe herself in various situations throughout the week. In what situations does she "turn the other cheek" when she feels discounted? When does she put her own needs last and choose to be the giver to others? In what specific instances does she fail to be assertive? Through this self-observation process, she gradually sees some specific ways that her choices are directly contributing to her anxiety.

My goal in working with Ruth is not to eliminate her anxiety; rather, it is to help her understand what it means. From my perspective, anxiety is a signal that all is not well, that a person is ready for some change in life; Ruth does learn that how she deals with her anxiety will have a lot to do with the type of new identity she creates. She sees that she can take Valium to dissipate the anxiety, or she can listen to the message that her anxiety is conveying. The goal of existential therapy is to enable individuals to act and to accept the awesome freedom and responsibility for action. With Ruth's increased sense of awareness of the factors that have limited her existence also comes an increased sense of her freedom to act.

Perhaps the critical aspect of Ruth's therapy is her recognition that she has a choice to make: She can continue to cling to the known and the familiar, even deciding to settle for what she has in life and quitting therapy. She can also accept the fact that in life there are no guarantees, that in spite of this uncertainty and the accompanying anxiety she will still have to *act* by making choices and then living by the consequences. She chooses to commit herself to therapy and find what she might.

My central task as Ruth's therapist is to directly confront her with the ways in which she is living a restricted existence and to help her see her part in having created her own restricted world and her deadness as a person. By holding a mirror up to her I help her engage in self-confrontation. She is able to see how she became the way she is, and she can also see alternative ways of enlarging the range of her living. Through the process of becoming aware of her past and of the stifling modes of her present existence, Ruth is able to begin to make new decisions and to accept responsibility for changing her future.

Questions for Reflection

1. What are some critical choices that you have made? Can you think of any turning points in your life? How have some of your choices affected the life you now experience?
2. What does freedom mean to you? Do you believe that you are the author of your life? that you are now largely the result of your choices? How do you suppose that your personal view of freedom would influence the way you worked with Ruth?
3. Can you recall any periods in your life when you experienced anxiety over the necessity of making choices? In looking at your own life, to what degree has your freedom led you to assume responsibility for your choices? In what ways have you experienced anxiety over the realization of your freedom and responsibility? In what ways are your answers to these questions relevant to the way you would approach Ruth?

4. What life experiences have you had that could help you identify with Ruth? Have you shared any of her struggles? Have you faced similar issues? How have you dealt with these personal struggles and issues? How are your answers to these questions related to your potential effectiveness as Ruth's therapist?
5. What were your general reactions to the way that I worked with Ruth? What did you like best? like least? What aspects of my counseling might you carry out in much the same manner? What different themes might you focus on? What different techniques might you use?
6. Compare this approach in working with Ruth with the previous approaches—psychoanalytic therapy and Adlerian therapy. What major differences do you see?
7. How might you work with Ruth's fears associated with opening doors in her life? Part of her wants to remain as she is, and the other part yearns for a fresh life. How would you work with this conflict?
8. Using this approach, how would you deal with her fears related to dying? Do you see any connection between her anxiety attacks and her view of death?

Walt: "What's There to Live for?"

Some Background Data

The question of meaning in life is especially critical to Walt, a retiree in his mid-60s who has lived with his son and daughter-in-law for the five years since his wife died. During this period he spent some time in a county hospital because of prolonged periods of depression, disorientation, and suicidal tendencies. As a part of his recovery he participates in a day-treatment program. As an outpatient he is involved in individual therapy a couple of times each week, and this therapy has continued for several months.

Walt has discussed a number of current life issues, including the following:

- He feels depressed most of the time and often wishes he could die so that he would not have to feel the loneliness, the emptiness, and the general feeling of being down and hopeless. He says that he does not have much to look forward to in his life; there is only a past that is filled with mistakes and regrets.
- Walt was very dependent emotionally on his wife, and when she died of cancer a big part of him died. He continues to feel lost and like a child in so many ways. He does not feel close to anyone, and he is convinced that his presence in his son's home is a burden to all.
- Before he was forced to retire, Walt taught English in a high school. When he was involved in this work, he felt good, because he had some measure of worth. He enjoyed working with young people, especially teaching them literature and encouraging them to think about the direction of their life. He was a fantastic teacher, well-liked by his students. After his wife died, Walt went into a long and deep depression; coupled with his age, this resulted in his dismissal and the beginning of his retirement years.

· For him, retirement is next to death. He feels "put out to pasture," simply passing time without getting in people's way. His major problem is the emptiness and lack of purpose for living. He is searching for something to take the place of his wife and his job, yet he sees little chance that he will find a substitute that will bring any meaning to his life.

My Way of Working with Walt as an Existential Therapist

My goal in working with Walt is to provide adequate support for him at a very difficult time in his life. What I see him as needing is an opportunity to talk about his regrets and what it feels like to be depressed; he needs to feel that he is being heard and cared for. At the same time, I must challenge him to begin to create his own meaning, even though most of his support systems are gone. To accomplish this goal I encourage Walt to talk, recounting things about his past that he regrets and wishes had been different. I urge him to talk about the loss he feels with his wife gone and his teaching career over. Early in his therapy, I believe, he needs to talk freely and to be listened to.

Walt's weaknesses and strengths. Where do I proceed with Walt? I do not ignore his depression, for this is a symptom that carries a message. By beginning with his full recognition and acceptance of his hopelessness, I may be able to help him change. I am especially interested in how Walt derived meaning through his work. I want to know the ways that work contributed to his feeling that he had something to offer people. So we talk of all the things that he got from teaching adolescents and what he learned about life from them. In many ways Walt, who did not have much of an adolescence, tried to make up for this gap in his youth through his work with young people. He found them floundering and lost, in search of who they were. He derived a great deal of personal meaning from seeing his students get excited about literature and in seeing them relate the struggles of the characters they were reading about to their own search for meaning in life.

Although Walt does need this opportunity to relive times from his past, I see a danger that we could stop here. And in this case our sessions would be little more than "talks" and remembrances of days gone by. I want more for Walt. This desire may be part of my own need to see him move in other directions. I may be fearful of getting lost in his depression with him. And if he does not find new hope and a will to continue to live, I could be threatened in many ways. For one thing, it might jar me into seeing that I could someday be faced with the same search for something to hope for. For another, if Walt does not move beyond his depression, then I will look at myself as a therapist and wonder if I have given him enough. Would he find a meaning for living if I were more of a person to him or more skilled in helping him at this juncture in his life?

Our therapeutic relationship. Let me proceed by saying more about how I see Walt and what is being generated within me as I work with him. Because the existential therapist assumes that therapy is an I/thou encounter and that what happens between the two people is central to determining outcomes, I will focus on this relationship. Questions that I will explore are: How do I see Walt at this time in his life? Where does he want to go? What does he want from me? How can I be instrumental in his life?

In some ways Walt is telling me that he is a *victim*—that his choices have mostly been taken from him, that there is little he can do about changing the situation he finds himself in, and that he is for the most part doomed to live out a sterile future. Although I think that it is necessary for me to perceive his world as he does, I find it hard to accept his conclusions. I want to provide a supportive atmosphere, so that he can relate to me what it is like for him to be in his world; yet at the same time I want to challenge his passive stance toward life. I surely would not tell Walt all the things I am about to mention in any single session. But over the course of our time together these are some of the points I would make:

- "You're not a helpless victim. If I see you as a victim and accept the stance you present, then I won't help you move beyond being stuck in this place. I want you to at least challenge the assumption that there is little you can do to change. It's this very assumption that's limiting your potential for change."
- "I see you leading a restricted existence. You've narrowed down the boundaries in which you can take action. I'll try to help you expand these boundaries and act in a greater range of ways."
- "You live in the past much of the time. In telling me all of your failures and dwelling on all of the missed opportunities, you *contribute* to your depression. You have wanted to talk about how your life *could* have been different. Now it may be time to look at what you can do to make *today* different, so that tomorrow you won't look back in regret over one more lost day. While I accept that your choices are somewhat limited, you do have possibilities for action that you're not recognizing."
- "I hope you can accept your past—even though it wasn't what you wanted—yet not be bound by it. Instead of looking back, I'd like to see you look ahead and begin walking, however slowly, where you want to go."
- "Think about your death. You've fantasized about suicide and thought that death would put an end to a miserable life. What are some of the things you want to end? What are some of the projects you haven't finished, ones you'd want to finish before you die? What do you want to be able to say at the time of your death about how you've lived? What can you do today to begin working on these projects that have some meaning to you?"

In terms of Walt's themes of not finding meaning in life and thinking about death, especially his suicidal fantasies, I think it is important to confront him with questions such as "What are you living for? What stops you from killing yourself?" I would not want to take lightly Walt's mention of suicide. In light of the fact that he experiences a good deal of depression, it is critical to make an assessment of how likely he is to attempt to take his life. To make such an assessment I want to find out how often he thinks about suicide and with what degree of detail. Is he preoccupied with suicidal impulses, or is such a fantasy rare? Has he a detailed plan? Has he cut off social contacts? Has he made any prior attempts on his life? Although I doubt that our therapy would be primarily focused on the suicide issue, it is essential to carefully consider how seriously he is considering suicide before we take up other themes in his life. This may be his cry for help or a signal that in some way he wants me to offer him hope for a better existence. I would arrange for a referral or hospitalization if Walt were acutely suicidal.

Let's briefly look at what I think Walt wants from me and some of the ways I can be instrumental as a person for him. As I indicated earlier, working with him challenges me to look at my own life. What would it be like to be in his place? How might I deal with life if I lost my wife and felt abandoned during my later years? What would become of me if I could not work? How might I handle feelings of meaninglessness in my life? I think that it can be useful for me to explore with Walt some of these questions in our sessions. I need to take the time to reflect on these questions, for the degree to which I can face and deal with them is the degree to which I will be a significant force in encouraging him to do the same thing in his life. How can I offer him any hope if I am not willing to struggle with my own potential for depression and hopelessness? If I avoid contemplating my eventual death and what I want to accomplish and experience before that time, then how can I challenge him to look to his death for some lessons in learning how to live? One of the most powerful means of understanding him lies within me and my willingness to explore what is being touched off in me as a result of our relationship.

I think that what Walt wants from me is the potential for an interchange of ideas and feelings. He does not want mere reassurance, nor does he want me to cooperate with him in perpetuating his view that there is nothing left to live for and little he can do to actively change his situation. Walt needs my honest responses, my support and caring, my gentle pushing, my insistence that he begin asking how he wants today to be different, and my exchanges with him as another human being. I do not know where we will end up, even where we are going. I am not aiming for major personality reconstruction in Walt's case, yet I am pushing for some significant steps that will lead to new action.

So much depends ultimately on Walt and what he is willing to choose and do for himself. I must not let myself be duped into thinking that I can create a will to live in his life, that I can do his changing for him, or that I will have an answer for him. Where he ends up will largely be determined by *his* willingness to begin to move himself by taking the initial steps. The best I can offer to him is the inspiration to begin taking those steps. I hope that, through our relationship, he will see that he can move further than he previously allowed himself to imagine.

Follow-Up: You Continue as Walt's Therapist

Thinking as an *existential* therapist, in what directions would you move with Walt?

1. What were some of your main reactions to my style of working with Walt? Did you get ideas of ways you might want to proceed differently or issues on which you would want to follow through with him?
2. How do you see Walt? What are your reactions to him? Would you be willing to accept him as a client? Why or why not?
3. As Walt's therapist, what would you see as your main function? Would you want

mainly to support him? confront him? guide him into specific activities? teach him skills? be his friend?

4. In what ways does Walt's depression (and feeling of utter hopelessness—that there is nothing left to live for) affect you personally? How are you likely to respond to him as a result? Might you tend to give him answers? or cheer him up? or agree that his life *is* hopeless? or reassure him that he *can* find a new meaning in life?
5. I spent time in his sessions allowing him to talk about his past mistakes, regrets, and losses, as well as his memories of what gave his life meaning. For an older person such as Walt, what potential value do you see in the reminiscing? Or do you think that you might steer him away from such discussion about his past by encouraging him to talk about his life *now* or the future he hopes for?
6. The existential approach is based on the therapist's seeing the world through the perspective of the client. In Walt's view he is a victim with little chance of changing his destiny. He feels that he is doomed to a meaningless existence, and he has resigned himself to simply marking time. What implications do you see of accepting and responding to him from his vantage point? Can you think of ways that you are likely to reinforce his very perceptions that change is unlikely? How might you help him open up to other possibilities for a different future?
7. How might you respond to Walt's talking about his suicidal fantasies? What would you feel (and probably do) if he told you that he was going to kill himself because he saw no real hope for his future? How do you think that your views and values related to suicide would affect the way in which you would work with him?
8. In what ways do you think that you could be a positive force in Walt's life? What life experiences or personal characteristics of yours might be instrumental in establishing a *therapeutic* relationship with him? In what ways might your own needs, problems, values, and lack of life experiences actually get in the way of forming a relationship that would be of benefit to him?

Recommended Supplementary Readings

Psychotherapy and Process: The Fundamentals of an Existential-Humanistic Approach (1978) by J. F. T. Bugental (Reading, Mass.: Addison-Wesley) is a clear and descriptive picture of the therapeutic journey. The author captures the essence of the existential approach to individual therapy.

Man's Search for Meaning (1975) by V. Frankl (New York: Pocket Books) describes the author's experiences in a concentration camp. Frankl shows how it is possible to find meaning in life through suffering. His thesis is that we all have a need to discover meaning.

Freedom and Destiny (1981) by R. May (New York: Norton) focuses on the paradoxes of freedom and destiny and develops implications of these concepts for the practice of psychotherapy. Key issues given attention include choice, freedom and anxiety, death and life's meaning, the renewal of life, and despair and joy.

Existential Psychotherapy (1980) by I. D. Yalom (New York: Basic Books) is a comprehensive treatment of four basic human concerns—death, freedom, isolation, and meaninglessness—with implications for therapeutic practice. In this exceptionally fine work Yalom provides numerous clinical cases to illustrate existential themes in therapy.

Suggested Readings

Belkin, G. S. (1984). *Introduction to counseling* (2nd ed.). Dubuque, Iowa: William C. Brown (Chapter 8).

Corey, G. (1986). *Theory and practice of counseling and psychotherapy* (3rd ed.). Monterey, Calif.: Brooks/Cole (Chapter 4).

Corsini, R. (1984). *Current psychotherapies* (3rd ed.). Itasca, Ill.: Peacock (Chapter 10).

Patterson, C. H. (1986). *Theories of counseling and psychotherapy* (4th ed.). New York: Harper & Row (Chapter 15).

Prochaska, J. O. (1984). *Systems of psychotherapy: A transtheoretical analysis* (2nd ed.). Homewood, Ill.: Dorsey Press (Chapter 3).

CHAPTER FIVE

A Case Approach to Person-Centered Therapy

A Person-Centered Therapist's Perspective on Ruth

Basic Assumptions

My view of counseling is that it should be directed at more than merely solving problems and giving information. It is best aimed at assisting clients to tap their inner resources, so that they can better deal with their problems, both current and future. In the case of Ruth, I think that I can best accomplish this goal by creating a climate that is threat free, one in which she will feel fully accepted by me. I work on the assumption that my clients have the capacity to lead the way in our sessions and that they can profit without my active and directive intervention. Therefore, I do not pin a diagnostic label on clients, for I think that such categories are limiting. I rarely make interpretations, because I believe that clients will be able to learn about themselves without such judgments from me. I will not direct Ruth to go into her past or point her in any other direction. Basically, the sessions will be focused on her, and she will be the one to decide the direction we take. Likewise, I will avoid any analysis of so-called transference. If she is having reactions to me, there is no reason to assume that she is reacting to me as she did to her mother; she may be reacting to me personally.

I do not operate on the assumption that Ruth will move forward in therapy only if she is directed, pushed, rewarded, punished, or in some other way controlled. I have a deep faith in her capacity to identify her problems and to find the resources within herself to solve them, providing that I can create a climate of safety, respect, and trust. Thus, my approach rests on the assumption that three attributes on my part are necessary and sufficient to release her growth force:

1. *Genuineness:* I am real, without a false front, during the therapy sessions. In other words, I am congruent—my outer expression matches my internal experience.
2. *Unconditional positive regard and acceptance:* My caring for Ruth is not contaminated by evaluation or judgment of her feelings, thoughts, and behaviors.
3. *Accurate empathic understanding:* I can understand sensitively and accurately her present experiencing and can convey this understanding to her.

If I genuinely experience these attitudes toward Ruth and successfully communicate them to her, she will decrease her defensive ways and move toward becoming her true self, the person that she is capable of becoming. Therapy is not so much a matter of my doing something to Ruth; rather, it is establishing a relationship that she can use to engage in self-exploration and ultimately find her own way.

Initial Assessment of Ruth

In talking to Ruth it becomes apparent that she is disappointed with where she is in life and that she is not being herself around her friends or family. Her therapy is based on this concern.

As I review Ruth's autobiography I see her as asking "How can I discover my real self? How can I become the person I would like to become? How can I shed my phony roles and become myself?" My aim is to understand how she sees herself and her world, to accept her as she is, and to create an atmosphere in which she can freely, without judgment and evaluation, express whatever she is feeling. If she can experience this freedom to be whatever she is in this moment, then she will begin to drop the masks and roles that she now lives by.

Ruth exists largely in response to the demands of others. She seems to have no self of her own, and the source of her values lies outside of herself. She has spent much of her life attempting to think, feel, and behave in the way that others believe that she *ought* to think, feel, and behave. As a result, she is not in contact with what she really values and wants for herself. In order for her to discover her sense of self, she needs a place where she can look nondefensively at the way she is now. The starting point for her change will be her recognition and acceptance of the way in which she now thinks, feels, and behaves.

Goals of the Therapy

My basic goal is to create a therapeutic climate that will help Ruth discover the kind of person she is, apart from being what others have expected her to be. When her facades come down as a result of the therapeutic process, four of her characteristics should be enhanced: (1) an openness to experience, (2) a greater degree of trust in herself, (3) an internal source of evaluation, and (4) a willingness to live more spontaneously. These characteristics constitute the basic goals of person-centered therapy.

Therapeutic Procedures

When clients begin therapy, there is usually a discrepancy between the way they see themselves and the way they would like to be. Initially, they tend to look to me to provide direction and magical answers. They often have rigid beliefs and attitudes, an internal blockage, a sense of being out of touch with their feelings, a basic sense of distrust in themselves, and a tendency to externalize problems. As therapy progresses, I find, clients are generally able to express fears, anxiety, guilt, shame, anger, and other feelings that they have deemed too negative to incorporate into their self-structure. Eventually they are able to distort less, express more feelings that were previously out of awareness, and move in a direction of being more open to all of their experience. They can be in contact, moment by moment, with what they are feeling, with less need to distort or deny this experience.

Therapeutic Process

Elements of the Process

During the early stages of her therapy Ruth does not share her feelings but talks instead about externals. To a large degree she perceives her problems as external to herself. Somehow if her father would change, if her husband's attitude would change, and if her children would present fewer problems, she would be all right.

Getting in touch with Ruth's feelings. Further, Ruth is not very aware of the nature of her feelings, for she blocks off any that she deems inappropriate. She does not permit herself to freely accept the flow of whatever she might be feeling. Notice how she puts it:

RUTH: It's hard for me to feel. Sometimes I'm not sure what it is that I feel.
JERRY: From moment to moment you're not aware of what feelings are flowing inside of you.
RUTH: Yeah, it's difficult enough for me to know what I'm feeling, let alone express it to someone else.
JERRY: So it's also hard for you to let others know how they affect you.
RUTH: Well, I've had lots of practice in sealing off feelings. They're scary.
JERRY: It's scary not knowing what you're feeling, and it's also scary if you know.
RUTH: Sort of . . . When I was a child, I was punished when I was angry. When I cried, I was sent to my room and told to stop crying. Sometimes I remember being happy and playful, only to be told to settle down.
JERRY: So you learned early that your feelings got you in trouble.
RUTH: Just about the time I start to feel something, I go blank or get confused. It's just that I've always thought that I had no right to feel angry, sexual, joyful, sad—or whatever. I just did my work and went on without complaining.
JERRY: You still believe it's better to keep what you feel inside and not express feelings.
RUTH: Right! And I do that especially with my husband and my children.
JERRY: It sounds as if you don't let them know what's going on with you.
RUTH: Well, I'm not so sure they're really that interested in my feelings.
JERRY: Like they really don't care about how you feel. [At that point Ruth begins to cry.] Right now you're feeling something. [Ruth continues crying, and there is a period of silence.]
RUTH: I'm feeling so sad and so hopeless.
JERRY: Right now you're able to feel, and you can tell me about it.

In this interchange it is important for Ruth to recognize that she can feel and that she is able to express feelings to others. My acceptance of Ruth encourages her to come in contact with her emotions. This is a first step for her. The more difficult task is for her to begin to recognize and share her emotions with the significant people in her life.

Exploring Ruth's marital problems. In another session Ruth brings up her marital difficulties and explores how she does not trust her own decisions and how she is looking outside of herself for the answers to her problems.

RUTH: I wonder what I should do about my marriage. I'd like to have some time to myself, but what might happen to our family if I made major changes and nobody liked those changes?
JERRY: Thinking about what would happen if you expressed your feelings stops you.
RUTH: Yes, I guess I do stop myself because I don't want to hurt my family.
JERRY: If you ask for what you want, others are liable to get hurt, and there's no room in your life to think both about what's good for others and what's good for yourself.
RUTH: Yes, I didn't realize that I was saying it has to be either me or them. I do wonder if they will be angry if I start doing some things for me.

Process Commentary

We proceed with how Ruth's fear of others' anger keeps her from asking what she really wants in her life. She then begins to seek answers from me. Not trusting that she knows what is best for herself, she thinks I have the experience and wisdom to provide her with at least some answers. She continues to press for answers to what she should do about her marriage. It is as though she is treating me as her authority who has the power to fix things in her life. She grows very impatient with my unwillingness to give her answers. She is convinced that she needs my validation and approval if she is to move ahead.

We explore Ruth's feelings toward me for not giving her more validation and not providing reassurance that she will make correct decisions. I express my irritation at her during a session when she continues to press me for answers. She tells me that I do not really care about her and that, if I did care, I would give her more direction and do more for her than I am doing. She tells me that all I ever do is listen, that she wants and expects more, and that I am not doing my job properly. I let her know that I do not like her telling me what I am feeling about her. I also tell her that I do care about her struggle but that I refuse to give her answers because of my conviction that she is able to find answers within herself. I hope she will learn that I can be annoyed with her at times yet not reject her.

Ruth continues to risk sharing more of her feelings with me, and with my encouragement she begins to share more of her feelings with her family. Gradually she becomes more willing to begin thinking about her own approval. She demands less of herself by way of being a fixed product, such as the "perfect person," and allows herself to open up to new experiences, including challenging some of her beliefs and perceptions. Slowly she is showing signs of accepting that the answers to her life situation are not to be found in some outside authority but inside of herself.

Although it is not easy for me to refuse to provide answers and direction for Ruth, I believe that to do so would imply a lack of faith in her capacity to find her own way. Therefore, I do not rely on techniques, nor do I fall into the trap of being the guru. We focus on Ruth's feelings about not trusting herself, and she explores in depth the ways that she is discounting her ability to take a stand in many situations. At times I become angry with her when I feel set up by her. I think it is important for her to learn that I can express my anger toward her and at the same time not feel disapproving of her. Ruth learns that she can evoke feelings in others and that she can express her own feelings.

I do value support, acceptance, and personal warmth; yet at the same time I try to challenge Ruth to look at what she is saying and doing. If I am to be an influence in her life, I have to be more than a mirror that simply reflects back what she is projecting. Thus, I attempt to give of myself in our sessions. By relating to Ruth personally, I allow her to feel an increased freedom to express whatever she is thinking and feeling. Ruth can actually use our relationship as the basis for her growth.

Basically, Ruth can use our relationship to learn to be more accepting of herself, with both her strengths and limitations. She has the opportunity to express her fears and feelings of guilt without being judged. This encourages her to explore the ways in which she feels judged by her parents, the feelings that she has denied or distorted, and her lack of confidence in being able to find her own answers.

Questions for Reflection

1. To what degree have you been willing to struggle with finding your own answers to life? Are there ways in which you have avoided this responsibility by looking to others to provide you with answers? How would your personal experiences with searching within yourself for answers affect how you would work with Ruth?
2. Knowing what you do of Ruth, how would it be for you to develop a therapeutic relationship with her? Is there anything that might get in your way? If so, how do you think you would deal with this obstacle? To what degree do you think you could understand her subjective world?
3. What were some of your general reactions to the way that I approached and worked with Ruth? What did you particularly like? What did you like least? What aspects of her therapy would you have duplicated? What would you have done differently?
4. With both this approach and the previous one (existential therapy) the client/therapist relationship is central, and the focus is on clients' choosing their way in life. Do you agree that Ruth has this potential for directing her life and making wise choices? Would you be inclined to let her select the topics for exploration, or might you suggest topics? Would you be more directive than I was?
5. Do you think that understanding and caring are enough to lead to personality change? This particular approach assumes that, if the therapist is genuine, accepts the client fully and unconditionally, and respects, cares for, and deeply understands the client (and communicates these attitudes), this is sufficient for constructive change to occur. To what degree do you agree with this assumption? Do you think anything else is necessary? If so, what?
6. Staying within this model, show how you would continue to work with Ruth and what general direction you would expect your sessions to take.

Don, Who Is Sure He Has to Prove Himself

Some Background Data

Don, an Air Force officer, comes to see me on the basis of a referral from a military doctor. He consulted with the physician because of continuing heart pains. Even though he is only in his mid-30s, he has had two mild heart attacks. These resulted in his being hospitalized and required that he take a sustained period off from work. He is about 30 pounds overweight, has very high blood pressure, suffers at times from angina, and develops severe headaches that are of a chronic nature under stressful conditions. His physician insisted that, if he was interested in continuing to live, he would have to learn how to relax and meet stress in more constructive ways. Because his physician was convinced that Don's psychological characteristics and the perpetual stress he was under called for psychological as well as medical treatment, he was referred to me.

Our First Session

At our first meeting Don fills me in on his medical problems. In doing so, he also talks of his feelings about being sent to see a psychologist, including what he hopes to get from our contract. To give a flavor of his view of himself, as well as the manner in which I might work with him from the person-centered perspective, I will present the following dialogue. I want to emphasize that this will be my own style of working with person-centered concepts; I do not want to give the impression that the following is necessarily characteristic of all those who identify themselves as person-centered counselors.

DON: Well, Doctor, it's really hard for me to admit that I have to see a man like you. I mean, no offense or anything, but I never dreamed I'd be sent to a psychologist.

JERRY: I'd like to hear how it feels for you to be here now. Could you tell me in what ways seeing me is hard for you to accept?

DON: Sure. I thought I'd never die, until I had my first heart attack, and then I realized that I might kick over long before my time. It's hard enough for me to admit that my body can't take it. Now to be told that I have psychological problems that I also have to learn to deal with—that's too much.

JERRY: It seems easier to do something about your physical problems than to do something about your feelings.

DON: The physician I've been seeing says there's not much more he can do for me, besides giving me the medication. I know my job is a stressful one. I'm under constant pressure from the upper brass to produce and keep my outfit in order. I'm responsible for a lot of other men in my unit, and that's what's hard to handle. I can handle my own responsibilities, but being expected to make sure that the other men under me follow through almost does me in. I worry constantly about whether or not they'll pull their end. If they don't, it's my ass that gets kicked, not theirs.

JERRY: As you talk, I hear how unsupported you feel, as well as how difficult it is for you to carry the weight for the rest of your men. You have all this burden on your shoulders.

DON: It's part of my job. I'm the top man in my unit, and I've gotta make damn sure that nobody under me messes up, because our unit is a vital unit in a chain. If we're a weak link, the rest of the chain will be useless. And it's my job to make sure that we're effective at all times and that there aren't any slipups! If I don't keep a close watch on the entire operation, everything is liable to go to pot. And I can't live with myself knowing that I haven't done all that was expected of me—and then some.

JERRY: As I look at you, I see the weariness in your face. You look *very* tired and extremely tense. Sitting with you here I can feel your tension. I'm feeling tired just listening to you. It seems that you don't see any way out of assuming all this responsibility.

DON: Not really. That's why I'm coming to see you. I hope you can teach me some relaxation methods and some better ways of living with this stress that's a part of my job.

JERRY: I'm wondering if the stress is only with your job. I'd like to hear about areas of your life besides your work. How are things for you apart from work?

DON: I carry my work home with me. I have so much to do that I have to bring hours of paperwork home every night. In the military, filling out papers is what counts. I can't get behind in that damn paperwork whatever I do. And there's no way I can do all that I have to do on the job and still get my paperwork done properly and in on time. Besides, even when I'm at home, I always get calls from my subordinates asking me my opinion on this or that matter that needs immediate attention.

JERRY: So you're on constant call. I feel the sense of how overwhelming all this is to you. No matter how hard you try to keep up, there are always other decisions to be made, more papers waiting for you to complete, and more responsibility than you can handle. There's no place you can go to escape those who depend on you.

DON: You hit on a good point. I do feel exhausted and very tight. That's just the way I am—and that's the way I've been for years. But I don't know how to change that. I look at the other officers who have positions of command, and they seem to be able to deal with the stress far better than I can. It doesn't get to them. Most of the guys are much older, and they don't have heart problems. I keep asking myself what's wrong with me that I can't take this stress more in stride. I *should* be able to get the job done without my body giving out on me. This is a hard one for me to take!

JERRY: It's hard for you to accept that your body has its limits and that you can push yourself only so far.

DON: Yeah, like why can't I be like the rest of the guys and handle things? Not only do I have trouble handling stress on the job, but I have a hell of a time dealing with stress at home.

JERRY: It's just the same at home?

DON: Yeah, I feel that I've got to be the one in charge there, too. I've got to plan for laying aside money to send my kids through college. I've got to be the one who keeps peace in the family. I've got to make sure that Millie, my wife, feels important and special. I've got to be the counselor for my kids and be able to give them answers when they come to me with problems. I've got to ride herd on my teenage boys to do their chores properly, and I've got to keep nagging at my daughters to keep the house in order. Sure, I'm the one who's the head of the house, and it's up to me to see that our family functions smoothly. When there's a fight in the house between the kids, I can't stand the arguing. I feel it's my job to get them to resolve their differences or else all hell will break loose. So I can't relax at home either.

JERRY: I'm struck with all the responsibility you take on yourself. You've got to do everything or it won't get done right. There's no one you can trust to take responsibility.

DON: Well, it's true! When I do trust others in the family to do something, inevitably things go sour. Then I've got to get involved and clean up the mess that others made. I don't like being in that position either. I'd like to change it, but I know it's easier said than done. But I tell you, I hate having to be the strong one *all the time!*

JERRY: Even though you'd like to change the way you are, you're at a loss to know where to begin. You hate being this superstrong person all the time, but you *have* to be this way. How would it be for you if you weren't so strong *some* of the time?

DON: I don't think you can understand. In my head I say to myself that a man is strong and doesn't buckle under with burdens. I'm the kind of guy who can't show feelings of weakness. I'm supposed to be able to meet these challenges of life. I can't afford to be weak and let down. I've gotta hang in there and make it.

JERRY: You have to hang in there at all costs?

DON: At all costs. Even if it kills me. I'm the kind of guy who can't stop running. What I set out to do, I've determined that I'll succeed in. I can't let my body get the best of me.

JERRY: Your body is speaking a loud message, and yet you're not willing to listen to what it's telling you. I sense how hard it is for you to accept that you can't manage everything in life by yourself. And I see you as willing to hang onto the notion that somehow you'll find a way to be superhuman.

DON: You're hearing me! What I'd hope you could tell me is how I *can* be that superman.

Some Observations on Our Session

During this session I'm interested in seeing the world through Don's eyes. I want to understand what it's like for him to feel driven to prove himself, to be consistently strong, to meet all his obligations (and then some), to take on the responsibilities of everyone, and to keep moving ahead even if it kills him. At the same time, I want him to know I have some understanding of how his life is. But I want to do more than merely reflect what I hear him saying. I want to get him to begin to look at the obvious signs his body is sending him. I hope that he can pay attention to his own body and allow himself to tune into his own tiredness and his own pain of always having to be strong.

I do not think that he will change merely from my telling him that he *should* be different—that he *should* allow himself to be weak, *should* delegate responsibilities, or *should* slow down and take it easy. He has heard this from his physician, and he *knows* (intellectually) that this is what he should do; yet he *feels* (emotionally) that he has to stay together at all costs. My assumption is that Don will be better enabled to change if I encourage him to share openly with me what it feels like for him to live the way he does. Without directly trying to insist that he be different from the way he is, I want to encourage him to talk more about his striving for being on the top, to express his frustrations over his body's failure to stand up under the pressure, and to express his dire need to be strong and capable. At the same time, I am hoping that he will eventually consider whether he really does need to assume the responsibility for everyone else. I hope that he will begin to question how hard he is on himself and that he may eventually challenge himself on the necessity of maintaining such standards. He may decide to give up some of his burdens and to stop putting himself in the position of being completely responsible for the functioning of his family.

In getting Don to take this look at himself, I want to share what is being evoked in me as I sit with him. I feel tense and very tired as I try to be with him. If I can be myself with him, I think he is more likely to be himself with me. He may be willing to show whatever he might be attempting to cover up with his strength and drivenness. I do not need to give him answers, even though on some levels he would like answers to "the way" to cope with stress. If I can stay with him and encourage him to express whatever he is feeling, I believe, this itself will provide the needed direction for us to move in future sessions. He is giving plenty of clues to pursue, if I will listen and follow these clues. I do not need to rely on techniques to get him to open up or techniques to resolve his problems. The best I can offer to him is the relationship that we can develop, regardless of how brief it may be. If I am able to accept him in a nonjudgmental way, I see a good chance that he will begin to listen to himself (including his body) and that he will grow toward self-acceptance, which can be the beginning of real change for him.

Follow-Up: You Continue as Don's Therapist

1. How do you see Don? What do you see as the major themes of his life that need to be focused on and explored more fully? How do you personally respond to him?
2. Assume that I were to refer Don to you for continued therapy (in the person-centered style). How do you imagine that it would be for you to work with him? How might a person such as Don relate to you?
3. Assuming that you will be seeing Don for at least six more sessions, what are some specific issues that you most want to explore? How might you go about doing this with him?
4. This approach was characterized by my listening and responding to him rather than by my active and directive intervention with therapeutic procedures and techniques. Do you think you would feel comfortable in staying in such a role as mine in your work with Don? Why or why not? Are there other techniques that you might want to introduce?
5. Don is driving himself relentlessly, and his body is telling him that he will probably kill himself if he does not change. Can you think of anything you might do or say to him to increase the probability that he will pay attention to the messages his body is sending him?

Recommended Supplementary Readings

Dibs: In Search of Self (1976) by V. Axline (New York: Ballantine) gives a touching account of a boy's journey from isolation toward self-awareness and self-expression. It emphasizes the crucial effects of parent/child relationships on the development of a child's personality. It also describes how play therapy can be a tool for developing an autonomous individual.

Client-Centered Counseling: A Renewal (1982) by A. V. Boy and G. J. Pine (Boston: Allyn & Bacon) is a readable source that presents a refinement of the person-centered perspective. There are some excellent chapters on the role of values in counseling, the role of the counselor, the client/therapist relationship, and the process by which a client changes.

On Becoming a Person (1961) by C. Rogers (Boston: Houghton Mifflin) compiles many of Rogers' significant essays on education, therapy, communication, family life, and the healthy personality. Case examples illustrate the process of person-centered therapy in action.

A Way of Being (1981) by C. Rogers (Boston: Houghton Mifflin) contains a series of updated writings on Rogers' personal experiences and perspectives, as well as chapters on the foundations and applications of a person-centered approach.

Suggested Readings

Belkin, G. S. (1984). *Introduction to counseling* (2nd ed.). Dubuque, Iowa: William C. Brown (Chapter 8).

Corey, G. (1986). *Theory and practice of counseling and psychotherapy* (3rd ed.). Monterey, Calif.: Brooks/Cole (Chapter 5).

Corsini, R. (1984). *Current psychotherapies* (3rd ed.). Itasca, Ill.: Peacock (Chapter 5).

Gilliland, B., James, R., Roberts, G., & Bowman, J. (1984). *Theories and strategies in counseling and psychotherapy*. Englewood Cliffs, N.J.: Prentice-Hall (Chapter 4).

Patterson, C. H. (1986). *Theories of counseling and psychotherapy* (4th ed.). New York: Harper & Row (Chapter 14).

Prochaska, J. O. (1984). *Systems of psychotherapy: A transtheoretical analysis* (2nd ed.). Homewood, Ill.: Dorsey Press (Chapter 4).

Shilling, L. E. (1984). *Perspectives on counseling theories*. Englewood Cliffs, N.J.: Prentice-Hall (Chapter 9).

CHAPTER SIX

A Case Approach to Gestalt Therapy

A Gestalt Therapist's Perspective on Ruth

Basic Assumptions

Approaching Ruth as a Gestalt therapist, I assume that she can deal effectively with her life problems, especially if she becomes fully aware of what is happening in and around her. My central task as her therapist is to help her fully experience her being in the here and now by first realizing how she is preventing herself from feeling and experiencing in the present. My approach is basically noninterpretive; instead, I will ask her to provide her own interpretations of her experiences. I expect her to participate in experiments, which consist of trying new ways of relating and responding.

I will encourage Ruth to experience directly in the present her "unfinished business" from the past. (Unfinished business involves unexpressed feelings such as resentment, rage, hatred, pain, anxiety, grief, guilt, abandonment, and so on. Because these feelings are not fully expressed in awareness, they linger in the background and are carried into present life in ways that interfere with effective contact with oneself and others.) A basic premise of Gestalt therapy is that by experiencing conflicts directly, instead of merely talking about them, clients will expand their own level of awareness and integrate the fragmented and unknown parts of their personality.

Initial Assessment of Ruth

Viewing Ruth from a Gestalt perspective, I see her as having the capacity to assume personal responsibility and to live fully as an integrated person. Because of certain problems in her development, she devised various ways of avoiding problems, and she has therefore reached impasses in her quest for personal growth.

There are a number of ways in which Ruth is presently stuck. She has never learned that it is acceptable to have and to express feelings. True, she does feel a good deal of guilt, though she rarely expresses the resentment that she must feel. Any person who is as devoted to others as she is must feel some resentment at not having received the appreciation that she believes is due her. She does not allow herself to get angry at her father, who has punished her by withholding his affection and approval. She does not experience much anger toward John, despite the fact that here again she does not feel recognized. The same is true for both of her sons and both of her daughters. Ruth has made a lifetime career out of giving and doing for her family. She maintains that she gets little in return, yet she rarely expresses how this arrangement affects her. I think that keeping all of these feelings locked inside of her is getting in her way of feeling free. Therefore, I believe that she needs to embrace feelings that she is now excluding. A lot of her energy is going into blocking her experience of threatening feelings, sensations, and thoughts. Our therapy will encourage her to express her moment-by-moment experience so that her energy is freed up for creative pursuits instead of being spent on growth-inhibiting defenses.

Goals of the Therapy

My goal is to challenge Ruth to move from environmental support to self-support and to assist her in gaining awareness of her present experience. With awareness Ruth will be able to recognize denied aspects of herself and thus proceed toward the reintegration of all her dimensions. Therapy will provide the necessary intervention and challenge to help her gain awareness of what she is doing, thinking, and feeling now. As she comes to recognize and experience blocks to maturity, she can then begin experimenting with different ways of being.

Therapeutic Procedures

As a Gestalt therapist, I work to foster clients' ability to stand on their own two feet. Thus, in my work with Ruth I will not do her seeing, nor will I listen for her, because she has eyes and ears. Although philosophically I accept the existential view of the human condition, I draw heavily on experiential techniques that are aimed at intensifying here-and-now experiencing. These techniques are designed to help clients focus on what is going on within their body and to accentuate whatever they might be feeling. In this sense I will be directive and active in my sessions with Ruth. I will take my cues from her, but I will also pay attention to what she is saying both verbally and nonverbally. From the cues I pick up, I will invent action-oriented techniques that will enable her to heighten whatever she is experiencing.

I have a bias against having clients simply *talk* about conflicts or situations in their life. In Ruth's case, she could go on forever talking about issues and abstractly analyzing matters to death. Clients find that they do not get rid of feelings within them, but they can learn how to live with these feelings—love/hate, wanting to be tough/tender—even though such feelings may seem contradictory at times. In my sessions with Ruth we will work with some of these polarities that she generally does not express. For example, she tends to be critical and judgmental, so we may focus on the dimension of self-acceptance, which does not get recognized or expressed. In this way she will find sides of herself that can be developed and integrated.

Along this line, I will be asking Ruth to carry out some experiments. These may entail giving expression to unexpressed body movements or gestures, or they may involve talking in a different tone of voice. I may ask her to experiment with rehearsing out loud those thoughts that are racing through her, ones that she usually keeps to herself. My style is to invite clients to try new behavior and see what these experiments can teach them. I assume that, if clients learn how to pay attention to whatever it is that they are experiencing at any moment, this awareness itself can lead to change.

Therapeutic Process

At one of our early sessions Ruth feels the necessity of bringing me up to date by describing her history. I direct her to continue to talk but to act as if what she is saying is happening right now. She is somewhat resistant to getting into the present tense and keeps falling back into talking in the past tense. I let her know that, when she speaks in the present tense, I experience her as more animated and easier to listen to. I give Ruth a general rationale for the things I will be asking her to try. She initially has some difficulty in working with fantasy and bringing significant people in her life symbolically into the room with me, so we explore her fears of looking foolish and doing dumb things. Because she cannot see much value in carrying out the experiments I am suggesting, I spend more time preparing her for participating in Gestalt therapy. I ask her to risk trying experiments in the safety of the therapeutic setting and afterwards deciding for herself whether the new behavior works for her. I want her to trust her own direct experience, rather than relying on my judgment of the value of these techniques.

Elements of the Process

Ruth works with her daughter, Jennifer. Ruth brings up the topic of how guilty she feels about disappointing her daughter Jennifer, who is 18 and who lives at home.

JERRY: Ruth, rather than telling me about how guilty you feel over not having been the mother you think you should have been to Jennifer, would you simply list all the ways that you feel this guilt?

RUTH: Oh, that's not hard—there are so many ways! I feel guilty because I haven't been understanding enough, because I've been too easy on her and haven't set limits, because I haven't touched her enough, because I've been away at college when she needed me during her difficult years. And in some ways I feel responsible for her getting kicked out of school, for her drug problem—I could go on!

JERRY: So go on. Say more. Make the list as long as you can. [I am encouraging her to say aloud and unrehearsed many of the things that I assume she tells herself endlessly in her head. She continues to speak of her guilt.]

RUTH [letting out a deep sigh]: There! That's it!

JERRY: And what is that sigh about?

RUTH: Just relief, I suppose. I feel a little better, but I still have a sense that I've done wrong by Jennifer.

I am aware that Ruth is not going to rid herself forever of her guilt. If she does not let her guilt control her, however, she could make room for other feelings. Based on my hunch that behind guilt is usually resentment, I propose another experiment.

JERRY: Ruth, if you're willing to go further, I'd like you to repeat your list of guilts, only this time say "I resent you for . . ." instead of "I feel guilty over . . ."

RUTH: But I don't feel resentment—it's the guilt!

JERRY: I know, but would you be willing to go ahead with the experiment and see what happens?

RUTH [after some hesitation and discussion of the value of doing this]: I resent you for expecting me to always be understanding of you. I resent you for demanding so much of my time. I resent you for all the trouble you got yourself into and the nights of sleep I lost over this. I resent you for making me feel guilty. I resent you for not understanding me. I resent you for expecting affection but not giving me any.

My rationale for asking Ruth to convert her list of guilts into a list of resentments is that doing so may help her direct her anger to the sources where it belongs, rather than inward. She has so much guilt because she directs her anger toward herself, and this keeps her distant from some people who are significant to her. Ruth becomes more and more energetic with her expression of resentments.

JERRY: Ruth, let me sit in for Jennifer for a bit. Continue talking to me and tell me the ways in which you resent me.

RUTH [Speaking to her daughter directly, she immediately becomes more emotional and expressive.]: It's hard for me to talk to you. You and I haven't really talked in such a long time. [Tears well up in her eyes.] I give and give, and all you do is take and take. There's no end to it!

JERRY: Tell Jennifer what you want from her.

RUTH [There is a long pause, and then, with a burst of energy, Ruth shouts at Jennifer.]: I want to be more like you! I'm envious of you. I wish I could be as daring and as alive as you . . . Wow, I'm surprised at what just came out of me.

JERRY: Keep talking to Jennifer and tell her more how you're feeling right now.

With Ruth's heightened emotionality she is able to say some things to Jennifer that she has never said but has wished she could. She leaves this session with some new insights: her feelings of guilt are more often feelings of resentment; her anger toward Jennifer is based on envy and jealousy; and the things that she dislikes about Jennifer are some of the things that she would like for herself.

Exploring the polarities within Ruth. In later sessions we continue working with some of the splits within Ruth's personality. My aim is not to get rid of her feelings but to let her experience them and learn to integrate all the factions of her personality. She will not get rid of one side of her personality that she does not like by attempting to deny it, but she can learn to recognize the side that controls her by expressing it.

RUTH: For so many years I had to be the perfect minister's daughter. I lost myself in always being the proper "good girl." I'd like to be more spontaneous and playful and not worry constantly about what other people would think. Sometimes when I'm being silly, I hear this voice in my head that tells me to be proper. It's like there are two of me—one that's all proper and prim and the other that wants to be footloose and free.

JERRY: Which side do you feel most right now—the proper side or the uninhibited side?

RUTH: Well, the proper and conservative side is surely the stronger in me.

JERRY: Here are a couple of chairs. I'd like you to sit in this chair here and talk for the proper side of you, which is sitting in this other chair.

RUTH: I wish you would grow up! You should act like an adult and stop being a silly kid. If I listened to you, I'd really be in trouble now. You're so impulsive and demanding.

JERRY: OK, how about changing and sitting in the chair over here and speaking from your daring side? What does she have to say to the proper side over there?

RUTH: It's about time you let your hair down and had some fun. You're so cautious! Sure, you're safe, but you're also a very, very dull person. I know you'd like to be me more often.

JERRY: Change chairs again, talking back to the daring side.

RUTH: Well I'd rather be safe than sorry! [Ruth's face flushes.]
JERRY: And what do you want to say back to your proper side?
RUTH: That's just your trouble. Always be safe! And where is this getting you? You'll die being safe and secure.

This exchange of chairs goes on for some time. Becoming her daring side is much more uncomfortable for Ruth. After a while she lets herself get into the daring side and chides that old prude sitting across from her. She accuses her of letting life slip by, points out how she is just like her mother, and tells her how her being so proper stops her from having any fun. This experiment shows Ruth the difference between thinking about conflicts and actually letting herself experience those conflicts. She sees more clearly that she is being pulled in many directions, that she is a complex person, and that she will not get rid of feelings by pretending that they are not inside of her. Gradually, she experiences more freedom in accepting the different parts within her, with less need to cut out certain parts of her.

A *dialogue with Ruth's father.* In another session Ruth brings up how it was for her as a child, especially in relation to a cold and ungiving father. I direct her not merely to report what happened but also to bring her father into the room now and talk to him as she did as a child. She goes back to a past event and relives it—the time at 6 years old when she was reprimanded by her father in the bedroom. She begins by saying how scared she was then and how she did not know what to say to him after he had caught her in sexual play. So I encourage her to stay with her scared feelings and to tell her father all the things that she was feeling then but did not say. Then I say to Ruth:

JERRY: Tell your father how you wish he had been with you. [She proceeds to talk to her father. At a later point I hand her a pillow.] Let yourself be the father you wished you had, and talk to little Ruth. The pillow is you, and you are your father. Talk to little Ruth.
RUTH: [This brings up intense feelings in Ruth, and for a long time she says nothing. She sits silently, holding "Ruth" and caressing her lovingly. Eventually, some words follow.]: Ruth, I have always loved you, and you have always been special to me. It has just been hard for me to show what I feel. I wanted to let you know how much you mattered to me, but I didn't know how.

Process Commentary

During the time that Ruth is doing her work, I pay attention to what she is communicating nonverbally. When she asks why I "make so much fuss over the nonverbals," I let her know that I assume that she communicates at least as much nonverbally as through her words. As she is engaged in carrying on dialogues with different parts of herself, with her daughter, and with her father, she feels a variety of physical symptoms in her body. For example, she describes her heart, saying it feels as if it wants to break; the knots in her stomach; the tension in her neck and shoulders; the tightness in her head; her clenched fists; the tears in her eyes; and the smile across her lips. At appropriate moments I call her attention to her body and teach her how to pay attention to what she is experiencing in her body. At different times I ask her to try the experiment of "becoming" her breaking heart (or any other bodily sensation) and giving that part of her body "voice."

When she allows herself to speak for her tears, her clenched fists, or her shaking hands, Ruth is typically surprised by what her body can teach her. She gradually develops more respect for the messages of her body. In the same manner, we work with a number of her dreams. When she feels free enough to become each part of a dream and then act out her dreams, she begins to understand the message contained in them.

Ruth exhibits some resistance to letting herself get involved in these Gestalt experiments, but after challenging herself and partially overcoming her feelings of looking foolish, she is generally amazed at what comes out of these procedures. Without my interpretations she begins to discover for herself how some of her past experiences are related to her present feelings of being stuck in so many ways.

A theme that emerges over and over in Ruth's work is how alive material becomes when she brings an experience into the present. She does not merely intellectualize about her problems, nor does she engage in much talking about events. The emphasis is on trying out action-oriented techniques and experiments to intensify whatever she is experiencing. In most cases, when she does bring a past event into the present by actually allowing herself to reexperience that event, it provides her with valuable insights. Ruth does not need interpretations from me as her therapist, because by paying attention on a moment-to-moment basis to whatever she is experiencing she is able to see the meaning for herself.

Ruth's awareness is by itself a powerful catalyst for her change. Before she can hope to be different in any respect, she first has to be aware of how she is. The focus of much of her work is on *what* she is experiencing at any given moment, as well as *how*. Thus, when she mentions being anxious, she focuses on *how* this anxiety is manifested in a knot in her stomach or a headache. I focus her on here-and-now experiencing and away from thinking about *why*. Asking *why* would remove Ruth from her feelings. Another key focus is on dealing with *unfinished business*. This case shows that unfinished business from the past does seek completion. It persists in her present until she faces and deals with feelings that she has not previously expressed.

Questions for Reflection

1. Gestalt techniques are useful in working with the splits and polarities within a person. As you can see, Ruth has problems because she is not able to reconcile or integrate polarities: good versus bad, child versus adult, dependent versus independent, giving to others versus asking and receiving, feelings versus rational ideas, and the need for security versus the need to leave secure ways and create new ways of being. Are there any of Ruth's polarities that you are aware of struggling with in your life now?
2. Knowing what you do of Gestalt therapy, what kind of client do you imagine you'd be in this type of therapy? How free would you be to try experiments? to engage in

fantasy dialogues? to allow yourself to intensify whatever you were feeling? to stay focused in the here and now? Do you see any connection between the type of client you'd be and the type of therapist you'd be within a Gestalt therapy framework?

3. Can you think of some ways to blend the cognitive focus of Adlerian therapy with the emotional focus of Gestalt therapy in working with Ruth? Provide a few examples of how you could work with her feelings and cognitions by combining techniques and concepts from the two approaches.
4. How does the Gestalt approach work with Ruth's past in a way different from that of the psychoanalytic approach? Which style of dealing with the past do you prefer? Why?
5. What main differences do you see between the way I worked with Ruth as a Gestalt therapist and the way I worked with her as a person-centered therapist? Which approach do you prefer? Why?
6. If you were counseling Ruth, what other Gestalt techniques might you have applied? In what directions do you think you might have gone with her?
7. What did you particularly like and not like about the way I worked with Ruth? What are some other possibilities you see for working with her?
8. What are the specific areas of unfinished business that are most evident to you as you read about Ruth? Does any of her unfinished business ignite any of *your own* unfinished business from the past? Are there any unresolved areas in your own life or any feelings that might interfere with your ability to work effectively with her? If so, what are they? How might you deal with these feelings if they came up for you as you were counseling her?

Christina: A Student Works with Her Feelings toward Her Supervisor and Her Father

To demonstrate the flavor of my personal style of working with a client, I dramatize a session in which Christina begins by saying she wants to work on her feelings toward me. I will use a dialogue to show how I draw on Gestalt concepts and employ Gestalt techniques. At the same time I will give a running commentary on the process and my rationale for using the techniques I am using.

Some Background Data

Christina was a student in my counseling practicum class. She says that she was constantly uncomfortable in the class, that the course and I threatened her, and that she would like to deal with some of the feelings she sat on during that entire semester. She has taken the initiative to ask for an individual counseling session to work on these feelings and on her relationship with me.

The following imaginary dialogue is a sample of a typical way I would work *if* I were to stay within a Gestalt framework.

A Dialogue with Christina

JERRY: What would you like to get from this session, Christina?

CHRISTINA: I just get so down on myself for the way I let other people make me feel unimportant. I really became aware of this in your class. So I want to work on the feelings I had toward you then.

JERRY: Feelings you *had?* If you still have any of those feelings now, I'd like to hear more about them.

CHRISTINA: Oh, I suppose I still have those feelings, or at least it wouldn't be too difficult to get them back again. I just don't like the way you make me feel, Jerry.

JERRY: I still don't know what *those feelings* are, but I do know you're making me responsible for them. I *make* you feel? I don't like being put in that position.

CHRISTINA: Well, you *do* make me feel inadequate when I'm around you. I'm afraid to approach you, because you seem so busy, and I think you'll just brush me off. I don't want to give you the chance *not* to listen to me. I'm afraid you'll have too many other things to do and that you wouldn't want to spend the time with me to hear my feelings. So that's why I stayed away from you that semester I had your class.

Without getting defensive, I want to let Christina know that *I* would like to be allowed to decide whether I have the time or the willingness to listen to her. I do not like being written off in advance or being told *who* I am and *how* I am without being given the chance to speak for myself. I let her know this directly, because I think my honest reactions toward what she is saying will be a vital component to building the kind of relationship between us that is needed to effectively deal with her feelings. Further, I call her on her unwillingness to accept responsibility for her own feelings, as expressed in her statements of "You make me feel . . ."

JERRY: So Christina, if you're willing, I'd like you to try an experiment. Would you just rattle off all the ways that you can think of that you feel around me, and after listing each of them I'd like you to add "*And you make me feel that way!*" OK?

CHRISTINA: Sure, now I get my chance. This could be fun! Are you ready for this? When I'm around you, I feel so small and so inadequate—and you make me feel this way! When I'm around you, I feel judged. I feel that whatever I do isn't what you expect, and that whatever I do it won't be enough to please you—and you *make* me feel that way! [She seems more excited and is getting into the exercise with her voice and her postures and gestures.] I have to read all those damn books you've written. And then I feel I'll never be able to write papers that are clear enough for you and I'll feel stupid and inferior. And it's *your* fault that I feel this way—you *make* me feel this way! You're always rushing around doing so many things that I can't catch you long enough to get you to listen to me. Then I feel unimportant, and you *make* me feel this way.

I want Christina to say out loud many of the things that I imagine she has said silently to herself. As she lists all the ways she feels around me, as well as restating over and over that I make her feel those ways, I listen and encourage her to continue. I want her to become aware of her resentments and *experience her feelings*, not just to talk abstractly about them. I see this awareness as essential before any change can occur. While she is doing this, I pay attention to the *way* she is delivering her message, because her body provides excellent leads to follow up on. I listen for changes in the tone and pitch of her voice. I notice any discrepancies between her words and facial expressions. I pay attention to her pointed finger or to her clenched fist. I notice her tapping of her foot. I also notice her blushing, her moist eyes, and any changes in her posture. All of these provide rich possibilities for exploring in this session, and there are any number of possibilities that I can follow through on. All the while I will be frequently checking in with her on what she is feeling right now. This will determine the direction we take next.

JERRY: What are you experiencing now?
CHRISTINA: I'm afraid you're judging me.
JERRY: What do you imagine I'm saying about you?
CHRISTINA: You're thinking I'm really immature and stupid. I'm feeling small again. And I'm also feeling vulnerable . . . weak . . . helpless . . . but mostly like you're up there and I'm down here looking up at you. And I don't like feeling little and making you that important.
JERRY: What would your "littleness" say to me now?
CHRISTINA: I'm feeling hopeless. Like I'll never be able to touch you or really reach you? [A long pause follows.]
JERRY: What are you experiencing now?
CHRISTINA: I'm thinking about my father.
JERRY: What about your father? Let me be him, and you talk to me.
CHRISTINA: I'll never be able to touch you or really reach you. I feel so dumb with you. [Another long pause]
JERRY: And what else do you want to say to your father right now?
CHRISTINA: I'd love to really be able to talk to you.
JERRY: You're talking to him right now. He's listening. Tell him more.
CHRISTINA: I've always been scared of you. I'd so much like to spend time with you and tell you about my pains and joys. I like that you're listening to me now. It feels so good.
JERRY: It feels good . . . What is it?
CHRISTINA [smilingly]: I feel good. [Another pause]
JERRY: What do you want to do next?
CHRISTINA: I'd like to give you a hug, Dad. [She gives Dad a hug, sits down.]
JERRY: You look different now than you looked earlier.
CHRISTINA: I feel more at peace with myself.
JERRY: Anything else you'd like to say?
CHRISTINA: To my Dad or to you?
JERRY: To either or both of us?
CHRISTINA: You know, Jerry, right now you don't seem as much *up there* as you did. I think I could actually talk to you now and feel straight across with you—in fact, I'm feeling that way now. It feels good to me not to give you all that power, and the

more I talk the less scared I feel. Like right now I'm feeling a real strength. I think you can see me for what I am, and I *am* worth something! I *am* important! And looking at you now, I feel that you're with me, and that you're *not* judging me and putting me down. I'm feeling good saying all this.

JERRY: Sitting across from you and looking at your face now and hearing you, I'm feeling good too. I don't like being put in unreachable places and then told how distant I am. I feel good sensing a quiet power in you and I really like being treated like a human being by you.

I continue by telling her some of the observations I had of her work and sharing what I was feeling at different points in our dialogue. I also tell her how I experience her very differently when she is soft, yet direct and powerful, instead of whining and giving me critical glances. I again offer her support and recognize the difficulty of her work.

Commentary on the Session

I think Gestalt techniques are powerful ways to help bring feelings out and also into focus. There is a vitality to Christina's work as she lets herself assume the identities of various objects. She can begin to reclaim disowned sides of herself and to integrate parts within herself. She is doing far more than reporting in an abstract fashion details from the past. She is bringing this unfinished business from her past into the present and dealing with whatever feelings arise in her.

Although I value Gestalt techniques as a way to take Christina further into whatever she is experiencing, I want to stress that these techniques cannot be used as a substitute for an honest exchange and dialogue between us. I can use myself and my own feelings to enhance the work of the session. Even though I will be departing from "pure" Gestalt, I want to integrate some cognitive work by asking Christina to put into words the meaning of what she has experienced and encourage her to talk about any associations between her work in our session and other aspects of her life. She may continue to talk about her awareness of how she puts *all* authority figures up high and what this is like for her. In my view, blending this cognitive work with her affective work seems to result in longer-lasting learning.

Follow-Up: You Continue as Christina's Therapist

Assume that Christina and I decide that it is best that she continue her counseling with another therapist, one with a Gestalt orientation. I refer Christina to you.

1. Overall, what are your general impressions of Christina? Does she evoke any reactions in you? Knowing what you know of yourself and of Christina, how do you imagine that she would respond to you?
2. How comfortable would you be using Gestalt techniques similar to the ones I demonstrated in my work with Christina? Are there any techniques I used that you would *not* use? Why? Are there other Gestalt techniques you would like to try in your sessions with her?

3. I put a lot of emphasis on helping Christina pay attention to whatever she was feeling or experiencing at the moment. Why do you think I did this? What value, if any, do you see in this?
4. Does my work with Christina bring to the foreground any unfinished business in yourself that you recognize? How might any of your own conflicts affect your work with her?
5. Where would you go from here with her? How?

Recommended Supplementary Readings

Gestalt Therapy Now (1970) by J. Fagan and I. Shepherd (New York: Harper and Row) has some excellent readings dealing with the theory, techniques, and applications of Gestalt therapy.

Gestalt Approaches in Counseling (1975) by W. Passons (New York: Holt, Rinehart, & Winston) is a very useful resource for learning how Gestalt techniques can come alive in individual counseling sessions. The chapters contain many clear examples of dealing with fantasy, bringing the past or the future into the present, working with both verbal and nonverbal messages, and using techniques appropriately.

Gestalt Therapy Verbatim (1969) by F. Perls (Moab, Utah: Real People Press) is a useful book to get a flavor of Gestalt concepts and a first-hand account of the style in which Fritz Perls worked. Many examples of clients working with Perls provide a sense of how Gestalt techniques bring the past into the here and now.

You're in Charge: A Guide to Becoming Your Own Therapist (1979) by J. Rainwater (Los Angeles: Guild of Tutors Press) is an excellent self-help book based on principles and techniques of Gestalt therapy. The author suggests exercises to increase self-awareness. She has useful ideas for keeping a journal, the uses of autobiography, working with dreams, the constructive use of fantasy, and the art of living in the here and now.

Creative Process in Gestalt Therapy (1978) by J. Zinker (New York: Brunner/Mazel) is an exceptionally good book that captures the essence of Gestalt therapy as a combination of phenomenology and behavior modification. The author provides many excerpts from therapeutic sessions to show how the therapist functions much as an artist. The book shows how Gestalt therapy can be practiced in a creative and eclectic style.

Suggested Readings

Belkin, G. S. (1984). *Introduction to counseling* (2nd ed.). Dubuque, Iowa: William C. Brown (Chapter 8).

Corey, G. (1986). *Theory and practice of counseling and psychotherapy* (3rd ed.). Monterey, Calif.: Brooks/Cole (Chapter 6).

Corsini, R. (1984). *Current psychotherapies* (3rd ed.). Itasca, Ill.: Peacock (Chapter 8).

Gilliland, B., James, R., Roberts, G., & Bowman, J. (1984). *Theories and strategies in counseling and psychotherapy*. Englewood Cliffs, N.J.: Prentice-Hall (Chapter 5).

Hansen, J., Stevic, R., & Warner, R. (1986). *Counseling: Theory and process* (4th ed.). Boston: Allyn & Bacon (Chapter 7).

Patterson, C. H. (1986). *Theories of counseling and psychotherapy* (4th ed.). New York: Harper & Row (Chapter 13).

Prochaska, J. O. (1984). *Systems of psychotherapy: A transtheoretical analysis* (2nd ed.). Homewood, Ill.: Dorsey Press (Chapter 5).

Shilling, L. E. (1984). *Perspectives on counseling theories*. Englewood Cliffs, N.J.: Prentice-Hall (Chapter 8).

CHAPTER SEVEN

A Case Approach to Transactional Analysis

A TA Therapist's Perspective on Ruth

Basic Assumptions

Transactional analysis emphasizes the cognitive, rational, and behavioral aspects of personality and is oriented toward increasing awareness so that the client will be able to make new decisions. TA is rooted in an antideterministic philosophy and asserts that we are capable of transcending our conditioning and early programming. It acknowledges that we were influenced by the expectations and demands of significant others, especially because our early decisions were made at a time in life we were highly dependent on others. But these decisions can be reviewed and challenged, and, if they are no longer appropriate, new ones can be made.

As I review Ruth's case, it becomes readily apparent that she accepted many parental injunctions that still have control over her life. (Injunctions are messages that tell children what they have to do and be in order to get recognition.) As a child Ruth accepted a host of injunctions and made some significant early decisions based on them.

Initial Assessment of Ruth

Perhaps the clearest way to describe my initial assessment of Ruth is to present in shortened and modified form her responses to the TA *personal life-script questionnaire.* Early in the course of TA therapy, beginning with the intake interview, I start asking for information that forms the basis of the life script of a client. (A life script is a personal life plan, which individuals create by a series of early decisions regarding themselves, others, and their place in the world.) I ask Ruth the following questions as the basis for this general assessment, and I expect that from a summary of this information we can develop a therapeutic contract that will give structure and direction to the course of therapy.

1. *How do you see yourself now?* as a person who has made a lifetime career out of thinking of and serving others
2. *Three things that I'd most like to change about myself are:* being able to feel that I was worth getting affection; being able to have fun; and being able to think of myself and do what I want without feeling guilty.
3. *What has prevented me from changing these things is:* my sense of duty and obligation to other people in my life and my fear of the consequences if I don't carry out my duties.
4. *To what degree are you living up to the expectations of others?* I have done what others expect of me for so long that I don't have a clear idea of what I want for myself or what is right for me.
5. *How do you see your mother?* as a self-sacrificing martyr who had no life of her own
6. *How are you like your mother?* We are both serious, and we both have lived to serve others.
7. *How are you unlike your mother?* I am not satisfied with my present state, and I am motivated to change.

8. *When my mother compliments me, she says:* You're a good person.
9. *When my mother criticizes me, she says:* Don't be so selfish, and you're not trying hard enough.
10. *Her main advice to me is:* to follow the Bible and not make a fuss.
11. *What could you do to make her happy?* do everything that was expected—but even then, she was not happy with me!
12. *What could you do to disappoint her?* Bring shame to the family. We all had an image to live up to, and, if we didn't, she showed her displeasure by her sad face.
13. *How did you see your father?* as a stern, authoritarian, hard-working man who was quick to criticize
14. *How are you like your father?* We both are very concerned about what people think.
15. *How are you unlike your father?* I want to have fun, and he thinks having fun is a sin.
16. *When my father compliments me, he says:* His compliments are so rare that I don't remember what he says.
17. *When my father criticizes me, he says:* You could have done much better if you had tried harder.
18. *His main advice to me was:* Always do what is right, and you'll find true happiness.
19. *I could disappoint him by:* giving up my religion.
20. *Some of the main* do's *that I have learned and accepted are:* Do follow the Bible. Respect the Lord. Do for others, and ask nothing in return. Do suffer in silence, and offer it up as atonement for your sins. Live in a moral and decent manner. Be proper. There is virtue in not complaining about the crosses that you must carry in this life.
21. *Some of the main* don'ts *that were programmed into me were:* Don't be close. Don't be a child. Don't be frivolous. Don't be sexy. Don't get angry. Don't think for yourself.
22. *One important early decision I made as a child was:* I'll strive for perfection so that someday I'll be loved and accepted.
23. *One early decision that I feel I have changed is:* Well, I am still struggling with the one about thinking I have a right to get an education, which is something I've really wanted.
24. *What is one new decision that you would like to make?* that I could treat myself as well as I treat others
25. *What I most like about myself is:* my determination. I just won't give up.
26. *What I least like about myself is:* how scared of life I am.
27. *What did your mother tell you (either directly or indirectly) about:*
    a. *you?* that I had to earn my place in life
    b. *life?* that it was given by God
    c. *death?* that it comes like a thief in the night and I should always be prepared
    d. *love?* that it has to be earned
    e. *sex?* that it is a necessary means of procreation
    f. *marriage?* that it is the expected path and a sacred union
    g. *men?* that I shouldn't get too close or too friendly

h. *women?* that they are meant to have children and to serve
i. *your birth?* that I was extremely difficult and caused her much pain

28. *What did your father tell you (either directly or indirectly) about:*
    a. *you?* that I did not count in his life
    b. *life?* that it was to be lived in accordance with the word of the Lord
    c. *death?* that it ushers the way to either heaven or hell
    d. *love?* that it doesn't involve sex
    e. *sex?* that it is the source of many a person's downfall
    f. *marriage?* that it is a serious matter, never to be broken
    g. *men?* that they are the head of the house
    h. *women?* that they reach their zenith by bearing children
    i. *your birth?* I have no idea!
29. *How did you see yourself as a child?* as compliant, quiet, obedient, hard-working, striving to please, scared, lonely, lost
30. *How did you see yourself as an adolescent?* as scared, without friends, responsible, mature, hard-working, studious, eager to please
31. *How did you see yourself five years ago?* as the supermother, superwife, and as one who simply did what was expected of her
32. *How would you like to see yourself five years from now?* as a professional woman with satisfactions both in the home and outside of it
33. *What are you doing to make that ideal become real?* I am beginning therapy, which is difficult for me to do.
34. *If you were to write your own epitaph, what would it say?* Here lies Ruth, who thought about everyone, yet she forgot about herself.
35. *What words do you fear might appear on your tombstone?* I fear that there will be no tombstone—that I will be forgotten.
36. *What do you wish your mother had done differently?* I wish she had shown me affection and let me know that she appreciated all my efforts in taking care of my sisters and brother.
37. *What do you wish your father had done differently?* I wish he had been more gentle with me, hugged me, and told me that he approved of me.
38. *What do you most want out of life?* to feel really alive—to be able to have fun and still to accomplish
39. *If you could have three wishes, what would they be?* that John would appreciate the changes I am making and support me in them; that I could become a teacher; and that I could dump the guilt I so often feel
40. *What was a critical turning point in your life?* a few years ago, when I decided to enroll in college

After Ruth has answered this questionnaire, we look for patterns. Many of her injunctions fit together. It becomes clear that Ruth accepted most of the parental messages uncritically. A major injunction was for her not to think, question, or to have a life of her own. By way of summary, *the major message she received from her father* was: live in a moral and decent manner; emotions will lead you astray, so keep on the right path and pray for guidance to always be strong. *From her mother, the main message* was: suffer in silence; never let people know how difficult things are for you; there is virtue in not complaining about the crosses you must carry in this life. United, her parents would say: be proper; whatever you do, don't shame us.

In terms of stroking, or signs of recognition, Ruth got mainly "conditional strokes." She had to earn recognition. Yet even when she lived up to the expectations set by her parents, she did not typically feel appreciated or recognized by them.

A review of Ruth's responses will point the way to areas that she can consider changing. First, she will have to decide which specific changes she wants to make, and then together we will establish a therapeutic contract.

Goals of the Therapy

Specific goals are defined by Ruth and stated in her contract. After reviewing the life-script questionnaire, she asserts that she does not want to act out the rest of her life by her parents' design and end her life according to their plan. One of the points of her contract is to talk directly to her husband and to tell him specific ways that she wants their marriage to be different. She agrees that she is willing to risk displeasing him by stating how she would like to change their family life.

Therapeutic Procedures

Transactional analysis attempts to take the mystery out of the therapeutic process, for the client and therapist work together on goals that are mutually agreed on. Ruth's contract is not a rigid and legal document; it is a procedure that puts the responsibility on her to state what she is willing to initiate in the sessions. Her contract can be modified as she goes along, and in this sense it is an open one. It will prevent me from digging into her past like an archeologist looking for interesting artifacts.

I like to teach my clients about the fundamentals of transactional analysis so that we have a simple common vocabulary. In this way clients are half of the therapeutic partnership, as opposed to my being the "expert" and keeping what I know about them to myself. I will ask Ruth to read a few books that describe how TA actually works and this reading will help her apply these concepts to herself. We will be working with the *ego states* of Parent, Adult, and Child, which she will learn to recognize in herself, so that she can choose which one to function in at any given time. We will look at any *games* that she plays. These are "crooked" transactions between her and others that prevent intimacy from occurring and result in bad feelings. We will explore in depth the ways that she has programmed herself and how she behaves now as a result of some of her early decisions. I hope that she can see that some of her decisions may have been needed for her survival at one time as a child but that she may be clinging to decisions that are both archaic and nonfunctional. Working with her life script will be a large part of what we do in the sessions.

Transactional analysis integrates the cognitive and the affective (feeling) dimensions. It is fair to say that I emphasize the cognitive aspects of therapy, yet I realize that changing entails actually experiencing feelings. In my view, however, experiencing feelings alone is not enough to bring about a substantive change in behavior.

Therapeutic Process

Elements of the Process

When I first mention to Ruth that our work will be defined by a therapeutic contract, she seems resistant. She thinks it sounds so formal and legalistic, and she wonders why it is necessary.

JERRY: A contract sets the focus for TA therapy. As the client you decide what specific beliefs, emotions, and behaviors you plan to change in order to reach your stated goals.

RUTH: But I'm not quite sure what I want to change. After we went through that life-script questionnaire, I was counting on *you* to point out to me what I should work on. There's so much to change, and frankly I'm at a loss where to begin.

JERRY: Part of our work here will be for you to take increasing responsibility for your own actions.

Helping Ruth define her goals. At this point Ruth and I discuss this issue in some detail. The essence of what I let her know is that TA is based on the expectation that clients focus on their goals and make a commitment. It emphasizes the division of responsibility and provides a point of departure for working.

RUTH [after some exploration]: I just want to be me. I want to be happy. I'm tired of taking care of everyone else, and I want to take care of me.

JERRY: That's a start, but your statements are too global. Can we narrow them down? What would make you happy? What do you mean by taking care of yourself? How will you do this? And what ways are you not being you?

I work with Ruth until she eventually comes up with clear statements of what she wants from therapy, what steps she will take to get what she wants, and how she will determine when her contract is fulfilled. After much discussion and a series of negotiations, she is able to come up with a list of changes she is willing to make.

RUTH: For one, I'm willing to approach my husband and tell him what I feel about our relationship. I know you say that I can't change him and that I can only change myself, so I'll tell him what I intend to do differently. And later, I would like to deal directly with my four children. They all take advantage of me, and I intend to change that. I can begin by telling them what I'm willing to do and what I'm no longer willing to do.

Although the above list is more specific than her original goals, there is still a need for greater specificity. Thus, I proceed by asking her exactly what she does want to change about each area she has mentioned, including what she intends to do differently. One part of her contract involves asking her husband to attend at least one of the sessions so that she can tell him the specific things she most wants to change in their relationship.

Role-playing Ruth's marriage. In another session Ruth and I do some role playing in which I stand in for John. Ruth tells me, as John, how frightened she is of making demands on me, for fear that I might leave. Out of that session Ruth begins to be aware of how intimidated she has allowed herself to become. I point out to her that she has made John her Critical Parent. She continues to set John up to punish her by giving him the power to make her feel scared and guilty. As a homework assignment I ask her to write a letter to John, saying all the things she really wants him to hear, but not to mail it. The writing is geared to getting her to focus on her relationship with him and what she wants to be different. (In an earlier session I gave her a similar assignment of writing a detailed letter to her father, which she agreed not to send him but to bring in for a session with me.) I make the observation to Ruth that in many ways she is looking to John for the same things she wanted from her father as a child and adolescent. Further, she assumed the role of doing whatever she thought would please each of them, yet she typically ended up feeling that, no matter how hard she tried, she would never succeed in pleasing them. From here I try to show Ruth that she will have to change her own attitudes if she expects change in her relationships, rather than waiting until her father or her husband might change. This is a new discovery for Ruth, and it represents a different direction for her.

Holding a joint session with John. Later I remind Ruth of her contract, and I suggest that she ask John to attend a therapy session with her so that we can deal directly with some of the issues that surface. Initially, Ruth gives a list of reasons why she is sure that John will never come in. After some discussion with me she does agree to ask John directly and clearly to attend at least one session (which we will also role-play first). To her surprise, he agrees to join her. What follows are a few excerpts from this initial conjoint session.

RUTH: I brought John here today even though I don't think he really wanted to be here. [Notice that she speaks for him.]

JERRY: John, I'd like to hear from you about what it's like to attend this session.

JOHN: When Ruth asked me, I agreed because I thought I might be of some help to her. I know I don't need therapy for myself, but I couldn't see any harm in giving it one shot.

RUTH: Now that he's here, I don't know what to say.

JERRY: You could begin by telling him why you wanted him here.

RUTH: It's that our marriage just can't go on this way much longer. Things are no longer satisfactory to me. I know that for many years I never complained—just did what was expected and thought that everything was fine—but the truth is that things are not fine by me.

JOHN [turning to me]: I don't know what she means. Our marriage has always seemed OK by me. I don't see the problem. If there's a problem, *she's* got it [said in a manner like a critical parent].

JERRY: How about telling Ruth this? [I want Ruth and John to talk *to* each other directly, rather than talking *about* each other. My guess is that at home they are very indirect. By having them speak to each other in this session, I get a better sense of how they interact.]

RUTH: See, *that's* the problem. Everything is fine by John—I'm the one who's crazy! Why is he so contented while I'm so discontented?

JERRY: Tell John. You're looking at me. He needs to hear from you, not me.

RUTH: Why, John, am I the only one who is complaining about our marriage? Can't you see anything wrong with the way we're living? Do you really mean that everything is just fine by you? Why is everything on me?

JERRY: Wait a minute, Ruth, I hear lots of questions. Rather than asking all these questions of John, tell him what you really want him to hear.

RUTH [again turning to me and addressing me]: But I don't think he ever hears me! That's the trouble—I just don't think he cares or that he listens to me when I talk about our life together.

JERRY: Ruth, I can understand why he might not hear you. You're not telling him what you want, and you're not giving him a chance. You know, Ruth, part of the problem I'm seeing is that you aren't telling him about you. If this is the way it is at home, I can see why you feel you're not listened to. Are you willing to hang in there with him and tell him directly what you say you'd like him to hear?

RUTH [with raised voice and a great deal of emotion]: John, I'm tired of being the perfect wife and the perfect mother, always doing what's expected of me. I've done that for as long as I can remember, and I want a change. I feel that I'm the only one holding up our family. Everything depends on me, and all of you depend on me to keep things going. But I can't turn to any of you for emotional support. I'm the nurturer, but no one nurtures me. And there are times that I need to know that I matter to you, and that you recognize me.

JOHN: Well, sure—and I appreciate your hard work. I know you do a lot in the home, and I'm proud of you.

JERRY: How does it feel to hear John say that to you?

RUTH: But you never say that—you just don't tell me that you appreciate me. I need to hear that from you. I need to feel your emotional support.

JERRY: Ruth, you still didn't tell John how you were affected by what he said to you. [I am calling to Ruth's attention that in this brief interaction, for one short moment, her husband responded to her in a way that she says she would like him to. She does not acknowledge it, and instead continues with her litany of complaints. I am letting her know that John may be more likely to change if he gets some positive stroking.] How could you stroke John right now?

RUTH: I like it when you tell me that you're proud of me. It means a lot to me.

JOHN: I'm just not used to talking that way. Why make a lot of useless words? You know how I feel about you.

JERRY: John! That's just the problem. You don't tell Ruth how you feel about her and what she means to you, and she is not very good in asking that from you. Both of you are very stingy with each other in giving strokes.

RUTH: Yeah, I agree. It hurts me that you think I want to hear useless words. I'm missing affection from you. It's so hard for me to talk about my life with you—about you and me—about our family—oh! [Ruth's eyes grow moist, she lets out a sigh, and then she grows quiet.]

JERRY: So, don't stop now, Ruth. Keep talking to John. Tell him what your tears and that heavy sigh are about. [My hunch is that Ruth often feels defeated and stops there, seeing herself as misunderstood. I am encouraging her to stay with herself and continue to address John. Even though he is looking very uncomfortable at this point, he seems receptive.]

JOHN: Sometimes I find it hard to talk to you because I feel criticized by you. It's as if you were a victim of my insensitivity. But how can I be sensitive when you don't tell me what you want?

JERRY: Sounds like a reasonable request. Will you tell him?

RUTH: You may not know how important going to college really is for me. I so much want to finish and get my credential. But I can't do that and be responsible for the complete running of our house. I need for the kids to pitch in and do their share, instead of always expecting me to do everything. I need some time to myself—time just to sit and think for a few minutes—when I'm at home. And I would like to be able to sit down with you, John, after dinner and just talk for a bit. I miss talking to you. The times we do talk, the topic is household maintenance.

JERRY: What are you hearing, John, and how does this sound to you?

JOHN: Well, hell, we have to talk about chores. I just don't understand what she wants me to say. [John continues for a time with a very critical voice, and in many ways belittling Ruth. Yet eventually he does admit that the children don't help as much as they could and that he might be willing to do a bit more around the house.]

RUTH: Well, I'd really like your help at home. And what about spending time with me? Do you want to talk with me?

JOHN: Yes, I do, but too often I just want to relax after busting my butt at work all day. I want it to be positive at home after a long day.

JERRY: It sounds like both of you would like to talk to each other. Would you be willing to set aside some time during the next week when you can have some uninterrupted conversation?

Together we develop a realistic contract that specifies when, where, and how long they will spend uninterrupted time with each other. John agrees to come in for another joint session. In the meantime, I ask Ruth to monitor what she actually does at home for two weeks and to keep these notes in her journal. I suggest that she write down a specific list of the changes she wants at home, along with what she could do to make these changes happen.

Process Commentary

As a part of Ruth's therapy I ask her to keep a daily journal so that she can record specifics of how she is meeting her contract. Toward the end of her therapy, which lasts eight months, I request any summary statements that she can make so that I can get a glimpse of her view of her basic progress. We devote the last two therapy sessions to reviewing the progress she has made, as well as making specific plans for what she can do now that she is ending therapy. She agrees to call within two months to give a follow-up report on how she is carrying out her plans. Following are the summary statements that she excerpts from her journal.

> I've completed eight months of TA therapy with Jerry and as a result I've changed some of the decisions I made *for life* as a child. Much of the latter stages of my therapy focused on redecision work. One of the most significant redecisions I've made is to stop trying to be the perfect person, my father's "good girl"—all in the hope that he'll one day give me his love. My therapy taught me that I can't directly change him into a loving person. I see how for so many years I hung onto my unhappiness in order to get Father to change; now I see that I'm responsible for myself and for finding love in my own life, and I'm not waiting around forever for him to learn to give me this love. Another important lesson for me was that I now believe that there isn't necessarily something basically wrong or evil about me that makes me unlovable. My father's inability to show love is *his problem*, not a fault of mine.
>
> I've worked on many parental messages that I accepted, and I've changed some of the decisions I made in response to those messages. At one time I accepted the injunction *Don't think*. So I decided not to think for myself. Who was I to make a decision? I now realize that I can think for myself and come up with pretty good decisions! *Don't be sexy*—that one still gives me trouble, but I'm making progress. I'm able to say to the parents inside me that you had your standards, but I don't want them for me. I've learned that there are many new decisions I *can* make—that I don't have to be bound by some of the inappropriate ones I made when I felt helpless as a child. And I'm learning how to ask for more for myself, and feel good about asking and getting!

Ruth and I spend several sessions working with her part in creating and maintaining the difficulties she is experiencing in her marriage. Rather than focusing on John and what he can do to change, Ruth is challenged to focus on what she can do to change her own attitudes and behaviors, which will inevitably lead to changes in her relationship with John. Eventually, Ruth sees how she has made John into a Critical Parent and the ways that she has become an Adapted Child around him. She begins to see how difficult it is for her to make requests of him or ask him for what she needs emotionally. Although she initially resists the idea of telling John directly what she wants with him and from him, she eventually sees some value in learning to ask for the strokes she wants. One of the games that she has been playing is deciding in advance that he (and others) will not take care of her emotionally, and with this expectancy she has blocked off possibilities of feeling emotionally nourished by others. There are many times when Ruth becomes aware of ways that she is slipping into old patterns, many of which were developed as a child, yet she becomes increasingly aware of when she is about to fall into these traps and is able to behave in more effective ways.

I do a fair amount of teaching with Ruth, because TA is a didactic therapy. Although her therapy does involve reliving earlier events that are associated with intense emotions, I am interested in helping her to cognitively understand the nature of certain decisions that she made as a child. The majority of our sessions consist of reviewing and critically examining these early decisions, with the aim of determining the degree to which they are still functional. When I am working with early scenes that Ruth recalls from her childhood, what I have in mind is to provide her with an opportunity to recreate these situations with as much emotional intensity as she felt at that time. Yet our work does not stop with this role playing and reliving of past events; instead, I continually challenge her to think about what she decided about herself and her place in life at these moments. Before her therapy she was not aware of the parental messages she had incorporated. By the end of her therapy she has given considerable thought to both the implied and expressed messages she accepted from her parents. She has also developed a clearer perspective on the ways she has been perpetuating many of these injunctions and how she has still been trying to live up to the standards of her father. I consistently ask that she raise the question "Will I wait forever for my father's approval, or will I begin to work for my own approval?"

Questions for Reflection

1. What general reactions do you have to the way I worked with Ruth? What are some things you like about the approach? What do you like the least? How might you approach Ruth differently within the TA model?
2. What injunctions of Ruth's do you recognize in yourself, if any? Have you made any early decisions that resemble hers? If so, what are they? What have you done to challenge your early decisions? To what degree do you think that your potential effectiveness with Ruth would directly depend on how well you know your own injunctions?
3. What do you think about the idea of beginning therapy with a clear contract, one that spells out what the client wants from the process and states the functions and responsibilities of the therapist? What differences do you think there are between working with a contract and not using one? Which is your preference? Why?
4. What techniques might you introduce to help Ruth work on some of the injunctions and early decisions that she mentioned?
5. What major differences do you see between the TA approach to working with Ruth and the psychoanalytic approach? the Adlerian approach? the person-centered approach? What does TA have in common with the existential approach? What possibilities do you see for a merger of TA concepts with Gestalt techniques? In working with Ruth, can you think of ways that you might combine TA with Gestalt?
6. In reviewing the TA life-script questionnaire, how would you answer some of the questions yourself? If you were a TA client, what would it be like for you to begin therapy with an extensive survey such as this questionnaire? What kind of contract would you make, based on these life-script data?
7. What are some of the main themes in Ruth's life that you would pursue in her therapy sessions? What kinds of information from the questionnaire could you tap and use in therapy?
8. Compare the TA life-script questionnaire in this chapter with the life-style assessment questionnaire in the Adlerian chapter. What similarities and differences do you notice?
9. Do you see any similarities between Ruth's injunctions and early decisions (TA) and her "basic mistakes" (Adlerian)? Can you think of ways to combine an Adlerian and a TA perspective as you explore the major themes in Ruth's life?

Betty: Almost a Doctor

Some Background Data

Betty is a counselor in a community clinic who has also completed all her course work for a doctoral program in counseling psychology. To get her Ph.D. she needs to complete her dissertation, most of which is already done. Of course, she will have an oral examination in which her doctoral committee asks her questions about her dissertation. She has been putting off the final phases of this project for well over a year in spite of promptings from her chairman. She comes to me because she knows that transactional analysis is my orientation, and this approach is her favorite one. She even chose one facet of TA to study as the basis for her dissertation. Assuming a TA orientation, I will demonstrate the way I might proceed in working with Betty in a single session.

The Contract as a Starting Place

As a TA therapist I stress a therapeutic contract setting the focus for counseling. Betty will have to decide specifically what she wants in terms of beliefs, feelings, and behavior. She will need to clearly say what she plans to change about herself in order to reach whatever goals she sets for herself.

Betty is vague in stating what she wants. She tells me that she is confused about her wants. Then, with more pushing from me, she finally says that she wants to get rid of "parent tapes," that she wants to change her "life script," and that she wants to feel like an OK person instead of the not-OK person she feels like now. She would also like to deal with her Resistant Child and, while she is at it, she would like to "let my Child out to play more often."

At this point I let Betty know that I see her misusing TA concepts and vocabulary as a way of keeping herself vague. Although it may seem like an advantage that she has knowledge of how TA works, this very psychological sophistication might well get in the way of her taking an honest look at herself. She could easily deceive herself into thinking that she is further down the road to self-actualization than she actually is.

One way that I can assist Betty in using concrete and personal language is by asking her specific questions that call on her to use descriptive language instead of psychobabble. I could ask her, for example, "What do you hear your parents telling you now? When you say you want to change your life script, what would you most want to change? Who in your life now do you not feel OK about? What aspects of your life don't you like? In what ways would you like to be more of a child?" Such questions show respect for Betty, yet at the same time she is learning how to speak plain English.

We stay with the issue of defining what Betty wants and what she is willing to do to get it. After working together to narrow down her goals, we finally come up with a clear statement: she wants to take whatever steps are necessary to complete the writing of her dissertation and to apply for her oral and written doctoral examinations. She agrees to do this within a particular time frame, and together we outline specific steps she will take to accomplish her objectives. As important as it is, however, completing her doctoral dissertation is not the answer to her problems. She realizes that this situation fits into a pattern of hers—she rarely finishes projects. She very enthusiastically initiates diverse projects, and then, just as she is at the point of successfully completing them, she typically finds some way to put off whatever is needed for completion. As a part of her contract Betty wants to explore the meaning and the implications of this behavior pattern.

We Work with Betty's Life Script

As a basic part of working on the latter part of her contract—dealing with her choice to explore the meanings of her failure to complete projects—we review the components of her life script. In this script, or plan, many life events have made an impression on her, she has accepted and learned definite roles, and she now rehearses and acts out these roles according to the script. Her psychological life script outlines where she will go in life and what she will do when she gets there. A TA concept is that there is a compelling quality that drives people to live out their life plan. The components of Betty's life script that would be of interest include parental messages that she has incorporated, the early decisions that she made in response to such messages, the patterns of stroking she received, the games she plays to maintain her decisions, and the *rackets* (a collection of old and familiar feelings such as depression, guilt, and anger) she uses to justify her decisions. Working with her life script, as can be seen, is somewhat complex, but it does involve paying attention to a number of interrelated factors.

Injunctions and early decisions. In TA work we pay attention to parental injunctions telling children what they have to do or be in order to get stroked (to gain recognition). Betty has probably heard many verbal and direct messages, as well as some subtle ones that were inferred from her parents' actions.

Betty heard a lot of *Don't make it* or *Don't succeed* messages as a child. We find this out in our session by reviewing some events that she remembers from her adolescent and childhood years. She was actually stroked for *not* succeeding, and, on those occasions when she did succeed, she was *negatively* stroked (which in essence says "I don't like you"). Together we go through memories of past events, and Betty reports that in many situations her parents ignored her when she did make it. In one situation that she recalled, her folks responded with a polite "That's very nice, dear" when she was chosen as the valedictorian at her high school graduation. Betty's perception is that she was not supposed to go on to college and succeed academically or professionally. Her parents actively encouraged and supported her older brothers' educational and professional endeavors. One became a physician and the other a lawyer. Betty reports a series of events:

"Both of my parents, and especially my mother, would tell me that it was a waste of my time to think of going on to college. They thought it was fine that I had graduated from high school, but they asked what I was trying to prove when I kept up my interest in college. To their way of thinking, I should learn all the domestic talents, and I should get my sights set on some desirable and successful man. Marriage was seen as the ultimate in my parents' plan for me. Any hint on my part that I wanted to get not only a bachelor's degree but also a Ph.D. in counseling psychology was unthinkable. They didn't want to hear about any of my academic accomplishments. When I tried to tell them about professional opportunities that I'd accepted as a counselor, they abruptly changed the subject—often by talking about the successes of my brothers in the law firm or the hospital."

A major injunction of Betty's was *Don't make it!* Based on this strong parental message, we discovered, Betty had made an early decision: "While I'll go ahead and do what I want, I won't complete important ventures in life." This decision follows Betty to this day. Even though she is mostly finished with a doctoral program, which far exceeds the programming in her life by her parents, she finds some way *not* to ultimately succeed. There is an added dimension here—this way she never has to admit failure. She can always use as an excuse that she is not yet finished with something and that, *if* she did finish, *then* she would be successful.

Fear of success. We devote some time to looking at Betty's anxiety over going beyond what her parents had actually done for themselves in their lives and beyond *their expectations* of her. We talk about the many ways in which she sabotaged herself so that she would somehow typically fail to succeed in endeavors that had meaning to her. This involved looking critically at her *games.* (In TA a game is a series of transactions that ends in at least one of the players feeling badly. It develops for the purpose of supporting an original decision—in this case, "I won't finish anything, and that way I won't have to enjoy success." And it is a basic part of one's life script, necessary to survive in the world.)

For example, one of the games of Betty's that we analyze is her encouraging people to push her to complete a project, at which time she resists all the more, telling herself that she is not going to do something *because* they want this of her. Another game consists of Betty's convincing herself that those people who did not push her obviously did not care enough about her to give her a nudge. Therefore, she did nothing, and she blamed them for what happened because of their lack of caring. We explore some of the typical games she played as a child and as an adolescent, and we see the parallel between those and the ones she plays now. For example, she sees some connections between her past and the present in the situation of her chairman's pushing her to complete her doctoral project and her increasing defiance against complying with reasonable requirements or deadlines.

We Move toward Action

Understanding the patterns that fit into her life script is one matter. Yet if Betty hopes to change, she will have to take *action* and do something about changing, not merely talk about the prospects of change. Thus, because TA is an action-oriented therapy, Betty and I think of ways that she can practice some behavior that will challenge the early decisions she made. We begin to plan for ways that she can, for a change, actually complete a very meaningful project—in the situation at hand, her Ph.D. We go through each of the steps and practice in our session what she has typically done to procrastinate and what she can do differently this time. We predict problems with her typist in finishing the typing of her dissertation, and we look at ways that Betty might take steps not to let this stop her in completing the task. We look at her fear of the board of examiners and predict the worst of outcomes, yet we still look at what Betty can do to complete this venture. Betty is convinced this once to finish the job, at least to comply with the contract she made.

A Closing Commentary

If we had more sessions, I would work with Betty on the *redecision* process. This would mean that she go back in both an emotional and an intellectual way to an early scene in which she made her decision not to complete matters. From that psychological frame of reference she would make a different decision—this time one that is more functional. In Betty's case this could be "I am going to make it professionally and academically. Even if it's not what you want or what you have in mind for me for life, this is what I want and what I'll get." At least our work will move Betty closer to being able to make such a redecision.

Follow-Up: You Continue as Betty's Therapist

Assume that Betty continues counseling with the goal of working toward making a *new decision*. On my referral she comes to see you. Show how you would work with her from a TA perspective.

1. Do any of Betty's injunctions and early decisions touch off any associations with your life? To what degree have you faced, or do you now face, similar issues? How do you think this will either facilitate or interfere with your work with her?
2. Can you see different directions from those I began in which you would like to take Betty? What are some of the most pressing themes in her life that you think need focus? What TA techniques might you draw on in helping her in this exploration?
3. What advantages and disadvantages do you see to beginning therapy with a contract? What might you do if Betty consistently offered excuses or reasons for her failure to live up to her contract? If she failed to complete her dissertation by the time she had said she would, what might you say and do?
4. What are some of your main reactions to the way I worked with Betty? What are some things that you either liked or did not like in this session? What might you do differently?
5. To what degree might you focus on Betty's past in your work with her? If you did choose to explore her past, what are some of the possible techniques you might use?
6. TA is an action-oriented therapy. What kind of action in the real world would you most like to see Betty take? Why?
7. TA tends to stress the cognitive aspects of therapy. What advantages, if any, do you see to integrating affective dimensions into the cognitive work Betty is doing? How might you blend these two dimensions of human experience?

Recommended Supplementary Readings

What Do You Say After You Say Hello? (1975) by E. Berne (New York: Bantam) demonstrates how we learn certain scripts that determine our present behavior and how we can change them.

Changing Lives through Redecision Therapy (1979) by M. Goulding and R. Goulding (New York: Brunner/Mazel) is an excellent presentation of the major concepts of TA. This text deals in depth with concepts such as injunctions, early decisions, and redecisions. Many examples of therapy sessions show how TA concepts can be integrated with techniques from many other therapeutic approaches.

The Power Is in the Patient (1978) by R. Goulding and M. Goulding (San Francisco: TA Press) is a collection of essays on personal growth from a TA perspective. Articles deal with the therapeutic impasse, basic concepts of TA, methods of helping clients make new decisions, and various techniques in action.

Born to Win: Transactional Analysis with Gestalt Experiments (1971) by M. James and D. Jongeward (Reading, Mass.: Addison-Wesley) is a readable guide to combining TA concepts with Gestalt exercises for the goal of personal growth. Topics include scripts, games, early decisions, injunctions, and autonomy.

All My Children (1970) by J. Schiff (New York: Evans) is an interesting account of how the severely disturbed can be "reparented" by TA methods.

Suggested Readings

Belkin, G. S. (1984). *Introduction to counseling* (2nd ed.). Dubuque, Iowa: William C. Brown (Chapter 9).

Corey, G. (1986). *Theory and practice of counseling and psychotherapy* (3rd ed.). Monterey, Calif.: Brooks/Cole (Chapter 7).

Corsini, R. (1984). *Current psychotherapies* (3rd ed.). Itasca, Ill.: Peacock (Chapter 11).

Gilliland, B., James, R., Roberts, G., & Bowman, J. (1984). *Theories and strategies in counseling and psychotherapy*. Englewood Cliffs, N.J.: Prentice-Hall (Chapter 6).

Hansen, J., Stevic, R., & Warner, R. (1986). *Counseling: Theory and process* (4th ed.). Boston: Allyn & Bacon (Chapter 5).

Patterson, C. H. (1986). *Theories of counseling and psychotherapy* (4th ed.). New York: Harper & Row (Chapter 12).

Prochaska, J. O. (1984). *Systems of psychotherapy: A transtheoretical analysis* (2nd ed.). Homewood, Ill.: Dorsey Press (Chapter 8).

Shilling, L. E. (1984). *Perspectives on counseling theories*. Englewood Cliffs, N.J.: Prentice-Hall (Chapter 4).

CHAPTER EIGHT

A Case Approach to Behavior Therapy

A Behavior Therapist's Perspective on Ruth

Basic Assumptions

A basic assumption of the behavioral approach is that therapy is best conducted along systematic and scientific lines. Although behavior therapy represents a variety of principles and therapeutic procedures, its common denominator is a commitment to objectivity and evaluation. Due to the above-mentioned diversity, it is difficult to enumerate a set of agreed-on assumptions and characteristics that apply to the entire field. Some general characteristics, however, are part of all the behavioral approaches:

1. As a behavioral practitioner, I value a good client/therapist relationship. Although I see the quality of this relationship as having a bearing on therapeutic outcomes, I do not place emphasis on these relationship variables.
2. I begin therapy with an assessment of the client, as a way of determining present problems, personal liabilities, and major strengths.
3. The assessment focuses on current influences on behavior, as opposed to past influences. I am primarily concerned with how the client is functioning and the stimuli that are maintaining present behavior.
4. Treatment goals are established in specific and concrete terms.
5. After the client and I identify the goals for therapy, we work out a treatment plan, which includes a set of procedures or techniques designed to attain these goals.
6. Assessment and evaluation are a part of the entire therapeutic process. Procedures are continually evaluated, so that, if they are not working, new techniques can be tried. In this way we have an objective measure of how well therapy is proceeding.

Initial Assessment of Ruth

As a behavior therapist I typically use some type of questionnaire as a basis for making an initial assessment of the client. In Ruth's case, I select Arnold Lazarus' *multimodal life-history questionnaire*. Its purpose is to obtain a comprehensive picture of Ruth's background for use in designing and carrying out any therapeutic program. This assessment begins with the intake session and continues during the next session if necessary. The following are some areas of information tapped by this questionnaire:

1. general information
2. the nature and description of the presenting problems
3. a personal and social history, including information about family, childhood and adolescent years, past problems, and current ambitions
4. an analysis of the current problem

This fourth section is designed to identify specific problems in some detail so that therapy can be tailored to the needs of the client. Each area of human behavior is followed by a list that the client can underline if applicable. This analysis is done in the following areas: behavior, feelings, physical sensations, images, thoughts, interpersonal relationships, and biological factors. For each of these areas, specific questions are asked so that a comprehensive assessment of the client's current functioning is possible.

Gathering these data on Ruth takes two sessions. By way of summary, Ruth and I come up with the following problem areas that she wants to focus on: (1) She feels tense to the point of panic much of the time and wants to learn ways to relax. (2) From the standpoint of her interpersonal relationships, she does not have the skills to ask for what she wants from others, she has trouble in stating her viewpoints clearly, and she often accepts projects that she does not want to get involved in. (3) She says she has a weight problem that she has battled for years, with very little success. She would like to take weight off and keep it off.

Goals of the Therapy

After making the assessment of Ruth's strengths and weaknesses, I clarify with her the behaviors that she wants to increase or decrease in frequency. She will now set specific goals in her three problem areas. Before treatment, we establish *baseline data* for those behaviors that she wants to change. The baseline period is a point of reference against which her changes can be compared during and after treatment. In this way we will be able to determine therapeutic progress. There is continual assessment throughout therapy to determine the degree to which these goals are being effectively met. Thus, before we begin therapy I expect Ruth to monitor those behaviors that she wants to modify. Before establishing goals pertaining to weight control, for example, it is important for her to note when and what she eats and the conditions surrounding her eating habits. In addition, I ask her what behaviors she has previously used in order to lose weight.

The general goal of behavior therapy is to create new conditions for learning. I view Ruth's problems as related to faulty learning. The assumption underlying our therapy is that learning experiences can ameliorate problem behaviors. Much of our therapy will involve correcting faulty cognitions, acquiring social and interpersonal skills, and learning techniques of self-management so that Ruth can become her own therapist. Based on my initial assessment of her and on another session in which she and I discuss the matter of setting concrete and objective goals, we establish the following goals to guide the therapeutic process:

1. to learn stress-management techniques
2. to learn assertion-training principles and skills
3. to develop a behavioral self-management program to control her weight

Therapeutic Procedures

Behavior therapy is a pragmatic approach. I use what works, and I am concerned that the treatment procedures be effective. I have skills in using therapy procedures, and I will draw on various cognitive and behavioral techniques to help Ruth reach her stated goals. If my clients do not make progress, I must assume much of the responsibility, because it is my task to select appropriate treatment procedures and use them well. As a behavior therapist I am continually evaluating the results of the therapy process to determine what approaches are working. Ruth's feedback in this area is important. I will expect her to become active to accomplish her goals; this will include work outside the sessions.

In my view, therapy is not purely a technical matter or an impersonal process. Quite the contrary—I value the importance of the two of us establishing rapport so that we can work effectively. But a trusting and caring relationship, while essential, is not sufficient to produce a change in behaviors. For behavioral change to occur, we will need to work systematically on eliminating undesirable behaviors and on learning new and effective ones. As I mentioned, Ruth will be active in the sessions and outside of them. I will ask her to keep records of her daily behaviors, monitor those behaviors, and put her newly acquired skills into action in the everyday world.

I expect that our therapy will be relatively brief, for my main function is to teach Ruth skills that she can use in solving her problems and living more effectively. My hope is that she will learn how to become her own therapist. My ultimate goal is to teach her self-management techniques, so that she will not have to be dependent on me to solve her problems.

Therapeutic Process

Elements of the Process

The therapeutic process consists of gathering baseline data on the specific goals that Ruth has selected. In her case, much of the therapy will consist of learning how to cope with stress, how to be assertive in situations calling for this behavior, and how to develop a self-directed weight-control program.

Learning stress-management techniques. Ruth indicates that one of her priorities is to cope with tensions more effectively. I ask her to list all the specific areas that she finds stressful, and I discuss with her how her own expectations and her self-talk are contributing to her stress. We then developed a program to reduce unnecessary stress and to cope more effectively with the inevitable stresses of daily life.

RUTH: You asked me what I find stressful. Wow! There are so many things. I just feel as if I'm always rushing and never accomplishing what I should. I feel pressured so much of the time.

JERRY: List some specific situations that bring on stress. Then maybe we can come up with some strategies for alleviating it.

RUTH: Trying to keep up with my schoolwork and with the many demands at home at the same time. Dealing with Jennifer's anger toward me and her defiance. Trying to live up to John's expectations and at the same time doing what I want to do. Getting involved in way too many community activities and projects and then not having time to complete them. Dealing with how frazzled I feel in wearing so many hats. Feeling pressured to complete my education. Worrying that I won't be able to find a good teaching job once I get my credential . . . How's that for starters?

JERRY: That's quite a list. I can see why you feel overwhelmed. We can't address all of them at once. I'd like to hear more about what being in these stressful situations is like for you. Tell me about one of these situations, and describe what you feel in your body, what you're thinking at the time, and what you actually do in these times of stress. [I want to get a concrete sense of how she experiences her stress, what factors bring it about, and how she attempts to cope with her stresses.]

RUTH: Well, I often feel that I wear so many hats—I just have so many roles to perform, and there's never enough time to do all that's needed. I often lie awake at night and ruminate about all the things I should be doing. It's awfully hard for me to go to sleep, and then I wake up in the morning after hours of tossing and turning feeling dog tired. Then it's even harder for me to face the day.

JERRY: And as you're lying in bed, what are some of the things you tell yourself?

I pursue this line of questioning because I am interested in finding out what she tells herself that is contributing to, if not causing, her high levels of stress. I also want to find out what she actually does at these times, so that we can talk about alternative behaviors. After some time on these topics, I eventually suggest teaching her some relaxation exercises.

JERRY: Earlier you mentioned you have panic attacks, especially at night. I'd like to teach you some simple ways to use the relaxation response just before you go into a full-scale panic. You'll need to identify the cues that appear before a panic attack. I'd then like to teach you some simple and effective relaxation methods. Instead of wasting time lying there trying to sleep, you could be practicing a few exercises. It's important that you practice these self-relaxation exercises every day, for 20 minutes.

RUTH: Oh my! That's 20 minutes of one more thing I have to cram into my already busy schedule. It may add to my stress.

JERRY: Well, that depends on how you approach it.

We talk at some length, because I am afraid that she will make this a chore, rather than something that she can do for herself that she will enjoy. She finally sees that it does not have to be a task that she does perfectly, but a means of making life easier for her. I then teach her how to concentrate on her breathing and teach her some visualization techniques in which she imagines a very pleasant and peaceful scene. Then, following the guidelines described in Herbert Benson's book *The Relaxation Response*, I provide her with these instructions: "Find a quiet and calm environment with as few distractions as possible. Sit comfortably in a chair and adopt a passive attitude. Rather than worry about performing the technique, simply let go of all thoughts. Repeating a mantra, such as the word *om*, is helpful. With your eyes closed, deeply relax all your muscles, beginning with your feet and progressing up to your face. Relax and breathe." A week later, Ruth tells me how difficult it was to let go and relax.

RUTH: Well, I didn't do well at all. I did practice every day, and it wasn't as bad as I thought. But it's hard for me to find a quiet place to relax. I was called to the phone several times, and then my kids wanted me to do their wash another time, and on and on. Even when I wasn't disturbed, I found my mind wandering, and it was hard to just get into the sensations of feeling tension and relaxation in my body.

JERRY: I hope you won't be too hard on yourself. This is a skill, and like any skill it will take some time to learn. But it is essential that you block off that 20 minutes in a quiet place without disturbances.

Ruth and I discuss how difficult it is for her to ask to have this time for herself. I reinforce the point that this is an opportunity to practice specifically asking others for what she wants and seeing to it that she gets it. This addresses another of her goals—to work on being assertive in asking for what she wants.

As our sessions go on, Ruth sticks by her relaxation practice fairly well, and it is working for her. It does reduce stress considerably but does not eliminate it. One day Ruth comments that she would love to have a professional massage. I suggest a homework assignment. Knowing how difficult it is for Ruth to treat herself to any luxuries, I recommend that she spend one day in a spa and get a massage. Although she finally does so, and loves it, she experiences reluctance. At first she thinks it is silly, then she complains about one more thing to do, then she feels guilty about spending money on herself in this way—and finally, after going through this list, she agrees to do something she wants, that will be for herself. Of course, the following week we get therapeutic mileage out of her experience. We explore all the things she tells herself that are self-defeating, and I suggest some new sentences that she can practice in place of these old and ineffectual ones.

Learning how to say no. Ruth tells me that she has been a giver all of her life. She gives to everyone but finds it difficult to ask anything for herself. We have been working on the latter issue, with some success. Ruth informs me that she does not know how to say no to people when they ask her to get involved in a project, especially if they tell her that they need her. Ruth wants to talk about her father, especially the ways that she thinks he has caused her lack of assertiveness. I let her know that I am not really interested in going over past experiences in childhood or in searching for reasons for her present unassertiveness. Instead, I ask her to recall a recent time when she found it difficult to say no and to describe that scene.

RUTH: Last week my son Adam came to me late at night and expected me to type his term paper. I didn't feel like it at all, because I had had a long and hard day, and besides, it was almost midnight. He begged me, saying that it was due the next day and that it would only take me an hour or so. I got irked with him for giving it to me so late, and at first I told him I wasn't going to do it. Then Adam got huffy and pouty, and I finally gave in. Then I didn't sleep much that night because I was mad at myself for giving in so quickly. But what could I do?

JERRY: You could have done many things. Can you come up with some alternatives?

I want Ruth to search for alternative behaviors to saying yes when she is clear that she wants to say no. She does come up with other strategies, and we talk about the possible consequences of each approach. Then I suggest some behavioral role playing. First, I play the role of Adam, and she tries several approaches other than giving in and typing the paper. Her performance is a bit weak, so I suggest that she play

Adam's role, and I demonstrate at least another alternative. I want to demonstrate, by direct modeling, some behaviors that she does not use, and I hope that she will practice them.

As the weeks progress, there are many opportunities for Ruth to practice a few of the assertive skills that she is learning. Then she runs into a stumbling block. A community group wants her to be its president. Although she enjoys her membership in the group, she is clear that she does not have time to carry out the responsibilities involved in being the president. In her session she says she is stuck because she doesn't know how to turn the group down; because no one else is really available. We again work on this problem by role-playing techniques. I play the role of the people pressuring her to accept the presidency, and I use every trick I know to tap her guilt. I tell her how efficient she is, how we are counting on her for this, how we know that she won't let us down, and so on. We stop at critical points and talk about Ruth's hesitation in her voice, her guilty look on her face, and her habit of giving reasons to justify her position. I also talk with her about what her body posture is communicating. Then we systematically work on each element of her presentation. Paying attention to her choice of words, her quality of voice, and her style of delivery, we study how she might persuasively say no without feeling guilty later. As a homework assignment I ask her to read the paperback *Your Perfect Right*, by Alberti and Emmons. There are useful ideas and exercises in this book that Ruth can think about and practice in between our sessions.

The next week we talk about what she has learned in the book, and we do some cognitive work. I especially talk with her about what she tells herself in these situations that gets her into trouble. In addition to these cognitive techniques, I continued to teach Ruth assertive behaviors by using role playing, behavioral rehearsals, coaching, and practice.

Working on Ruth's weight problem. Ruth brings up her struggle with her diet thusly:

RUTH: Ever since I can remember, I've had a weight problem. When I get depressed, I eat even more, which gets me even more depressed, and then I get down on myself. I really would like to do something about taking off the pounds and then keeping them off.

JERRY: You sound pretty determined about making this change. As you know, we usually attack problems such as this in a systematic way.

RUTH: Well, I *am* determined, but I'm always this way at first, and then when things don't work out I get discouraged and drop the program. I'm afraid I'll repeat history.

JERRY: Your thinking sounds fatalistic, as if you're setting yourself up for failure. [I discuss with her negative expectations and self-fulfilling prophecies. We then explore new statements that she can make, in the hope that she can program herself for success instead of for defeat.]

RUTH: I need some help in working out a program, and then I need you to push me to stick with it.

JERRY: Well, I'm willing to work with you on developing a self-management program to control weight, and I'll negotiate a contract with you. But I'm not comfortable in assuming the role of pushing you.

I tell her why my pushing might end up defeating her purposes, and then I explain the nature of the program. First of all, I ask her to get baseline data by recording her eating habits for a one-week period. At the same time, we agree on realistic goals. At first Ruth declares that she will lose 20 pounds in a month. I recommend that she consult with her physician before embarking on a weight-control program. I also express my fears of her setting unrealistic goals and then getting discouraged and giving up the entire program. After getting a physical examination and discussing the matter with her doctor, she finally agrees to lose five pounds (or more) in a month's period.

We then discuss what eating behaviors Ruth will need to change. This is where her self-monitoring phase is of real value, for we look at when she eats, what she eats, how she eats, and events leading up to her wanting to eat. She decides on specific behaviors that she wants to increase or decrease. Coupled with her monitoring of food intake and cutting certain high-calorie foods out of her diet, she also agrees to resume riding her bicycle daily. At first she will ride for 15 minutes each day, then work up to 25 minutes, and then discuss with me whether she will ride 45 minutes daily. She is learning not to set herself up to fail. Now she is agreeing to smaller subgoals and then increasing them after enjoying success. All during this period she keeps charts and graphs of her eating patterns and continues to weigh herself daily. In this way she has feedback on how well she is meeting her goals.

Ruth sticks to her plan. By the end of the month she has lost eight pounds, which is three pounds more than the minimum she contracted for. She is proud of herself for following through with the program, and she comments that she liked the reinforcement and support she got from me along the way. She is looking trimmer and feeling better. As a reward, she treats herself to another visit to the spa, which is still difficult for her, because she is not used to spending money on herself in such a fashion!

Process Commentary

As a part of teaching Ruth a method of self-monitoring and as a way of keeping track of her progress toward meeting her goals, I suggest that she keep a journal in which she records how she acts in certain situations (as well as how she feels and what she is thinking as she faces problematic situations). In the final phase of her therapy she summarizes some of the major things she has learned and describes some of her reflections on her work. Below are these reflections.

> I just finished three months of behavior therapy, and I thought I'd write down a few notes on what that was like for me. I see that I have a lot more control over my behavior than I thought I could. Reading those books on assertion training, relaxation methods, and plans for weight loss were extremely helpful. It also helped greatly to be listened to by Jerry and to be taken seriously. I often felt that I was exaggerating my problems and that I should be grateful for the good life I have. Working with Jerry these few months has shown me that I have it within my power to actually change those behaviors I want to change. I don't know about changing the person I am, but I'm surely doing something about some of the things that really bugged me about myself. I've lost those eight pounds, and I'm losing more. I'm staying in the weight-loss program, and this is the first program that I've ever stuck to. I feel good about that. I'm continuing my relaxation exercises each day, and I'm also taking a course in

> meditation. I'm pleased to report that I'm much less uptight over finishing everything on time; I don't have as many anxiety attacks in the middle of the night as I used to. And when I do, I've learned to use deep-breathing exercises. I learned that I make matters worse by breathing in a shallow way, and now I actually hyperventilate. There are still many problem areas in my life that I don't feel are taken care of. Like I still wonder what I want to do with my life besides what I've done. But I'm meeting some practical problems better than I ever have.

In this approach Ruth is clearly the person who decides what she wants to work on and what she wants to change. She makes progress toward her self-defined goals because she is willing to become actively involved in challenging her assumptions and in carrying out behavioral exercises, both in the sessions and in her daily life. My function is to present methods she can use that will help her make the changes she desires. She makes progress in dealing with stress and learning to relax because she is disciplined enough to practice the relaxation exercises I have taught her. She learns how to ask for what she wants and to refuse those requests that she does not want to meet, not only by making resolutions but also by regularly keeping a record of the social situations in which she was not as assertive as she would have liked to be. She takes risks in practicing in everyday situations those assertive skills that she has acquired in our therapy sessions. Her willingness to carry out homework assignments is also instrumental in increasing her assertive behavior, which in turn helps her in the area of weight control—*she* decides that losing weight is a priority. Rather than speculating about the causes of her overeating or creating excuses for her weight problem, she accepts the problem and follows through with a regular action program designed for self-change. Although I help Ruth learn *how* to change, she is the one who actually chooses to apply these skills, thus making change possible.

Questions for Reflection

1. What are some of the features that you liked best about my approach? What did you like least? How might you have proceeded differently, still working within this model, in terms of what you know about Ruth?
2. This model assumes that the therapist's technical skills are essential to behavior change. What are your reactions to this assumption in light of the assumption of some other approaches that the therapeutic relationship itself is a sufficient condition for change?
3. What is your reaction to my attempt to get Ruth out of therapy as fast as possible so that she can apply self-management skills on her own? What skills can you think of to teach her so that she can be more self-directed?
4. What reactions do you have to my lack of interest in exploring the past? Do you think that Ruth's present personal issues can best be taken care of by focusing on learning coping skills? Do you think that for change to occur in her current situations she must go back to her past and work out unfinished business?
5. Using other behavioral techniques, show how you might proceed with Ruth if you were working with her. Use whatever you know about her so far, as well as what

you know about behavior-therapy approaches to show in what directions you would move with her.

6. What specific behavioral changes do you want to make in your life? What behaviors would you like to eliminate or decrease? acquire or increase? Applying behavioral methods to yourself, which specific techniques would be most helpful to you in making these changes?
7. How would you go about designing a self-management program in your own life? Identify some behaviors that you want to control or modify, and then describe the specific steps in a behavioral self-management program aimed at your goals. Knowing what you do of yourself, how would you cooperate and follow through with the program? What problems and obstacles would you encounter?
8. Do you see any possibilities of integrating some of the feeling dimensions from the experiential therapies (Gestalt, person-centered, and existential therapy) with the focus on behavior and cognition in this approach? How might you integrate several of these approaches?

Sally: Afraid of Interpersonal Situations

Sally comes to her college counseling center because of various fears that interfere with her life. On meeting the counselor, she lists many of the fears she would like to conquer.

Sally's Self-Presentation

"It seems like I'm afraid of *everything!* I'm very afraid of being in this office now, and my fear of coming to the counseling center almost kept me from doing it. A good friend who's been to counseling here gave me the push I needed. Actually, she practically forced me to come, at least for one session. I'm afraid of new situations, because I have no idea how I'll react. I'm afraid to go to my classes, because I just don't know how to act with other students. I'm deathly afraid of talking out in class and expressing my opinions on a subject. All those eyes looking at me just make me freeze up. I can't even bring myself to ask a simple question, because I'm afraid I'll sound dumb. I'm tight during the entire time when I'm in classes where discussion is expected. It's better when I can sit there and just listen and take notes—that I can handle. I panic at the thought of going to parties or going on a date. I just don't know how to act around people. I break out in a cold sweat just thinking about being in a social situation. Most of my fears have to do with not knowing what's appropriate or expected of me when I'm with people—especially when I'm with men."

My Way of Working with Sally as a Behavior Therapist

I view the therapeutic relationship as a collaborative one. I do not view therapy as merely a matter of my being the all-knowing expert who makes decisions for a passive client. Instead, from our first until our final session, Sally and I will work together toward goals that we have agreed will guide our sessions—if, in fact, Sally decides to enter counseling with me. At the outset my procedures will include the following:

- I will explain the nature and purpose of counseling goals, as well as talking about the importance of making those goals specific and concrete.
- Sally will decide on the specific changes or goals desired as a result of her relationship with me.
- Together we will explore the feasibility of her stated goals.
- Both of us will identify and discuss any risks associated with these goals.
- Together we will discuss the possible advantages of counseling as a way of meeting these stated goals.
- By the end of the initial session, I hope, Sally and I will have made one of the following decisions: to continue counseling for a specified number of sessions, to reconsider her goals, to evaluate whether counseling is appropriate at this time and whether she is willing to actively work at achieving her goals (both in the sessions and in her daily life), or to seek a referral to another therapist or another agency.

Goal setting and deciding on a course of action. As I have indicated, our first task is to develop clear and specific goals, so that we are able to determine what kind of *treatment plan* we will design. This plan includes the possible procedures and techniques we will use, as well as the criteria for determining how well the procedures are accomplishing Sally's stated goals.

Sally and I work at narrowing down her goals. Like many other clients, she is approaching her therapy with global and fuzzy aims. It is my task to help her formulate clear and concrete goals, so that she and I will know what we are working toward and will have a basis for determining how well the therapy is working. When I ask her what she wants from therapy, for example, Sally replies with statements such as these: "I want to learn to communicate better. I want to be able to state my opinions without being afraid. I don't do very well in social situations. I'd like to get over feeling scared all the time." Although her goals are general, they do relate to becoming more effective in social situations. I can facilitate her moving from global to specific goals by asking her: "Who in your life do you have trouble talking to? Are there any particular people to whom you find it difficult to say what you'd like to say? What are some situations where you have problems in being assertive? In what social situations don't you do well? How would you like to change in these situations? Would you tell me about a few specific fears you experience? When you are frightened, what do you tell yourself? And what do you do at these times? What would you like to do differently?" My line of questioning is aimed at helping her translate fuzzy goals into clear statements pertaining to what she is thinking, doing, and feeling (and ways that she would like to think, behave, and feel differently).

Eventually, Sally and I draw up a contract that is geared to helping her develop a course of action to attain her goals. We determine that the basis of her contract will be the following goals: She will work on *identifying* and *lessening* (or, ideally, removing) her unrealistic fears. She will identify specific manifestations of unassertive behaviors on her part, which include her difficulty in stating her opinions, in making contacts with people, in turning down others when that is what she wants to do, and in making her wants and needs clearly known to others. She will experiment with new behaviors, both in the therapy sessions and in daily life. Practicing these behaviors will lead to *increasing* her repertoire of social skills, especially increasing *assertive behavior*.

Because it will take some time to learn and practice skills related to Sally's stated goals, we discuss a realistic time frame for therapy. She decides to commit herself to a series of six one-hour individual counseling sessions. This kind of structuring will encourage her to evaluate her progress after each session and will serve to keep her focused.

Suggestions for outside readings and self-monitorings. I explain to Sally that behavior therapy is an approach that stresses *teaching* and *learning* processes. I tell her at our first session of my conviction that she is likely to get more from our sessions if she is willing to prepare herself during the week. This preparation should include reading selected books as a way of learning new interpersonal skills. I suggest books that deal with assertion training, relating to others, coping with fears, and learning methods of relaxation. We use some session time to discuss how the ideas Sally gets from her readings can be applied to her attempt to make the behavioral changes she most desires.

Besides her reading, Sally can profit from her counseling by reviewing each session during the week, monitoring her behavior in various social situations, and keeping a journal as a record of her thoughts, feelings, and behaviors (in and outside of sessions). I tell her that together we will be assessing how well therapy is working for her—mainly by looking at the results that both of us can clearly see. If progress is slow, we can reevaluate and revise our treatment plan.

Sally learns systematic desensitization. Sally initiates a discussion about dealing with her fears relating to men. She tends to avoid men, mainly because she is frightened of them. She is both put off by men and attracted to them, and she has the dual fears of being rejected by them and being accepted. She thinks that she can handle rejection easier than acceptance; she wonders what she would do if a man actually liked and desired her and if he wanted an intimate relationship.

At this point I work with Sally on clarifying her values. Before using behavioral techniques, I believe, it is essential that she become clear about what she wants, so that she is freely deciding on her behavioral goals. After examining her values, she says clearly that she wants to explore her fears of men. She would like to be free enough to go to parties, to accept dates, and to initiate social contacts with selected men. She hopes to learn how to assertively state what she wants and does not want. Although she is now frightened over the possibility of a man's making a sexual advance or even an offer, she would like to learn to avoid being panic stricken over this prospect.

We then proceed with systematic-desensitization procedures, which start with a behavioral analysis of situations that evoke anxiety in her. We then construct a hierarchy of her anxieties by ranking them in order beginning with the situation that evokes the least anxiety and ending with the worst situation she can imagine. The following is her hierarchy of fears:

1. She sees a man across the room whom she is attracted to.
2. They are sitting together in a room.
3. They are sitting together, and he initiates a conversation with her.
4. He invites her to go on a date.
5. She accepts the date.
6. She goes on a date.
7. He asks her to go to his apartment after a party.
8. They are in his apartment kissing and embracing.
9. They have sex, and she leaves and never hears from him again.
10. They have sex, and he *accepts her*, saying that he hopes this is only the beginning of an intense relationship.

I then teach Sally some basic relaxations procedures, which she practices until she is completely relaxed in the session. I ask her to select a peaceful scene where she would like to be. She picks a lake in the forest. We proceed with the relaxation exercise until she is fully relaxed, has her eyes closed, and has the peaceful scene in her mind.

I describe a series of scenes to Sally and ask her to imagine herself in each of them. I present a neutral scene first. If she remains relaxed, I then ask her to imagine the *least anxiety-arousing* scene she set up in her hierarchy (seeing a man whom she found pleasant on the far side of a classroom). I move progressively up the hierarchy until she signals by raising her index finger that she is experiencing anxiety, at which time I ask her to switch off that scene and become very relaxed and imagine herself at her lake. We continue until we progress to the *most anxiety-arousing* scene she set up in her hierarchy (imagining a sexual relationship with a man who accepts her and wants to continue the relationship).

In our therapy sessions we continue the desensitization procedure until Sally is able to imagine this "worst" scene without experiencing anxiety. (Basically this procedure consists of combining an incompatible stimulus and response. We pair the relaxation exercises and the imagining of a pleasant scene with scenes that evoke anxiety, until gradually the anxiety-provoking stimuli lose their potency.) Now that we have successfully desensitized her of her fears of relating to a man she perceives as attractive on an imaginary level, we hope that she is ready to try new behavior in a real-life situation.

Sally Goes on a Date

As a behavior therapist I believe in the value of *homework assignments*. These are not activities that I pick out as good for Sally. Rather, *she* decides on some new behaviors she would like to experiment with outside of our sessions. Then she applies what she has learned in therapy to a social situation in the hope of acquiring new social skills and overcoming her inhibitions and negative self-talk. She tells me that she has decided to ask Julio, a classmate, to the upcoming Christmas party.

Before she actually carries out this assignment, we examine what she is telling herself before inviting him. She recognizes that she is setting herself up for failure by telling herself that he probably will not want to go and that, if he does accept, it is only because he feels sorry for her. So we do some additional cognitive work that will lead to positive expectancies on her part. Before she asks Julio to the party, she practices her relaxation exercises and calms herself so that anxiety does not interfere with what she wants to do.

When Sally returns to her session the next week, she is smiling and reports that all went *very* well, although the subject of going to his apartment did not come up. She is feeling an increased sense of confidence and is willing to tackle new social situations that are more difficult.

A Commentary

Sally's therapy began with assessment, and at our last session we assess the degree to which she has met her goals. We also review what she has learned in these sessions, as well as what she has done in various situations at school, at work, and at home. Our focus now is on consolidating what she has learned and helping her translate it into future real-life situations. I suggest that she continue reading self-help books, doing her daily relaxation exercises, giving herself behavioral assignments, monitoring and assessing her behaviors, and keeping a behavioral log in her journal. Finally, she agrees to join a ten-week assertion-training group designed to help students improve social skills. In this way she is able to continue what we have begun in these sessions.

Follow-Up: You Continue as Sally's Therapist

After my six individual sessions with Sally, she enters the ten-week assertion-training group. Assume that she has now finished this group and consults you for further counseling.

1. Might you be willing to work with Sally? How do you see her? Do you see any of yourself in her? How might your answers to these questions determine both how and how well you work with her?
2. What are your reactions to the very structured approach I used with Sally? To what degree would you be comfortable using such an approach, and how effective do you think you would be?
3. What are your reactions to the specific techniques that I employed with Sally? What other (behavioral) techniques can you think of that you might use? What general direction do you see yourself taking with Sally?
4. What are a few statements that you would *most* want to make to her? Why?
5. What factors in yourself do you see that might contribute to or detract from your effectiveness in working as Sally's therapist?

Recommended Supplementary Readings

Your Perfect Right: A Guide to Assertive Behavior (fourth edition, 1982) by R. E. Alberti and M. L. Emmons (San Luis Obispo, Calif.: Impact) is my recommendation for those who want a single book on the principles and techniques of assertion training.

The Relaxation Response (1976) by H. Benson (New York: Avon) was a national best-seller. It is a readable and useful guide to developing simple meditative and other relaxation procedures. Particularly helpful are the author's summaries of the basic elements of meditation (pages 110–111) and methods of inducing the relaxation response (pages 158–166).

Clinical Behavior Therapy (1976) by M. R. Goldfield and G. C. Davison (New York: Holt, Rinehart & Winston) is an exceptionally well-written account of behavioral techniques used in clinical practice. The authors provide clear examples of how behavioral methods work.

Helping People Change (2nd ed., 1980) edited by F. H. Kanfer and A. P. Goldstein (New York: Pergamon Press) is a collection of major behavioral strategies in current use.

The Practice of Multimodal Therapy (1981) by A. A. Lazarus (New York: McGraw-Hill) is interesting, easy to read, and highly informative. A wide variety of behavioral techniques is described, and the author shows how such diverse techniques can be integrated into an eclectic framework.

Self-Directed Behavior: Self-Modification for Personal Adjustment (fourth edition, 1985) by D. L. Watson and R. G. Tharp (Monterey, Calif.: Brooks/Cole) is aimed at assisting readers to achieve control over their life. Specific steps are described for setting up behavioral self-management programs.

Toward a Self-Managed Life-Style (3rd ed., 1983) by R. Williams and J. Long (Boston: Houghton Mifflin) is a useful and easy-to-read book. It presents a model for self-control methods in such diverse areas as weight control, smoking and drinking control, study skills, career planning, personal problems, and interpersonal relationships.

Suggested Readings

Belkin, G. S. (1984). *Introduction to counseling* (2nd ed.). Dubuque, Iowa: William C. Brown (Chapter 10).

Corey, G. (1986). *Theory and practice of counseling and psychotherapy* (3rd ed.). Monterey, Calif.: Brooks/Cole (Chapter 8).

Corsini, R. (1984). *Current psychotherapies* (3rd ed.). Itasca, Ill.: Peacock (Chapter 7).

Gilliland, B., James, R., Roberts, G., & Bowman, J. (1984). *Theories and strategies in counseling and psychotherapy*. Englewood Cliffs, N.J.: Prentice-Hall (Chapter 7).

Hansen, J., Stevic, R., & Warner, R. (1986). *Counseling: Theory and process* (4th ed.). Boston: Allyn & Bacon (Chapter 8).

Patterson, C. H. (1986). *Theories of counseling and psychotherapy* (4th ed.). New York: Harper & Row (Chapter 5).

Prochaska, J. O. (1984). *Systems of psychotherapy: A transtheoretical analysis* (2nd ed.). Homewood, Ill.: Dorsey Press (Chapter 10).

Shilling, L. E. (1984). *Perspectives on counseling theories*. Englewood Cliffs, N.J.: Prentice-Hall (Chapter 7).

CHAPTER NINE

A Case Approach to Rational-Emotive Therapy

A Rational-Emotive Therapist's Perspective on Ruth

Basic Assumptions

Rational-emotive therapy is a highly didactic, cognitive, behavior-oriented approach that stresses the role of action and practice in combating irrational, self-indoctrinated ideas. RET and the other cognitive-behavioral therapies focus on the role that thinking and belief systems play as the root of personal problems.

RET is grounded in the philosophy that individuals are born with the potential for rational thinking but tend to fall victim to the uncritical acceptance of irrational beliefs that are perpetuated through self-reindoctrination. It assumes that thinking, evaluating, analyzing, questioning, doing, practicing, and redeciding are at the base of behavior change. RET is a method of personality change that quickly and effectively helps people resist their tendencies to constantly put themselves down with irrational notions. It is a system that is both *disputational* and *reeducational*, in that it teaches clients how to dispute their irrational and perfectionistic *shoulds*, *oughts*, and *musts* and also how to replace self-defeating ideologies with a rational philosophy of life. I draw on a range of cognitive, emotive, and behavioral techniques to demonstrate to my clients that they cause their own emotional disturbances by the beliefs they have uncritically accepted. As a cognitive therapist I operate on the assumption that it is not an event or a situation in life that actually causes negative emotions such as guilt, depression, hostility, and so forth. Rather, it is the evaluation of the event and the beliefs people hold about these events that get them into trouble.

Initial Assessment of Ruth

As I review Ruth's intake form and her autobiography, it becomes evident that the majority of her problems are self-induced and self-maintained. True, as a child she was subjected to many absolutistic and moralistic beliefs, some of which were irrational. Yet she is still clinging to these beliefs and living by them as though they were tested and proven values. The trouble is that she uncritically and unthinkingly accepts these values, many of which rely on guilt as a main motivation to control behavior. So she is not actually making clear decisions based on self-derived values; rather, she is listening to archaic and intimidating voices in her head that tell her what she should and ought to do. In short, she is the victim of *must*urbatory thinking. Her life is ruled by *musts*.

A basic and underlying irrational belief of Ruth's is that she must be perfect in all that she attempts. If she is not perfect, the results are horrible, for this means that she is a rotten person who deserves to suffer and feel guilty. She is continually rating her performances, and she gives herself low ratings because of her unrealistically high standards. I do not see her problems as stemming from the adverse situations that she writes about in her childhood. Instead, it is her evaluation of these events that directly contributes to her emotional disturbances. Therefore, what she needs is to learn practical ways of critically thinking and reevaluating her experiences as she changes her behavior. This will be the focus of my therapy with her.

Goals of the Therapy

The basic goal of RET is to eliminate a self-defeating outlook on life and acquire a rational and tolerant philosophy. Thus, I will teach Ruth how to uproot her faulty beliefs and replace them with constructive beliefs. To do so, I will teach her the A-B-C theory of personality. This theory is based on the premise that A (the activating events) do not cause C (emotional consequences); rather, it is B (her beliefs about activating events) that are the source of her problems.

Therapeutic Procedures

In working with Ruth, therefore, I expect to employ a very directive and action-oriented approach. I will function as a teacher, focusing on what she can learn that will lead to a change in her thinking and also to changes in her behavior. I will stress the value of applying logical analysis to evaluating the assumptions and beliefs that she lives by. It will help if she reads rational-emotive literature as an adjunct to these sessions. Furthermore, like any other form of learning, therapy is *hard work*. This means that, if she expects to successfully change her beliefs and thus change her behavior, it will be necessary to practice what she is learning in therapy in real-life situations. I will stress completing of homework assignments. And I will ask her to fill out a self-help form that has her analyze activating events, her beliefs about these events, the consequences of those beliefs, her disputing and debating of her irrational beliefs, and the effects of such disputing. I teach this A-B-C method of understanding problems to all my clients in anywhere from one to ten sessions.

Ruth's *real* work, then, consists of doing homework in everyday situations and then bringing the results of these assignments into our sessions for analysis and evaluation. I am concerned that she not only recognize her irrational thoughts and feelings but also take steps to abandon them. My main function is to confront her if I see her clinging to these deeply engrained beliefs. Ultimately, my goal is to challenge her to develop a rational view of life so that she can avoid becoming a victim of future irrational thinking.

Therapeutic Process

To accomplish the goal of assisting Ruth in achieving a rational philosophy of life, I perform several tasks as her therapist. First of all, I challenge her to evaluate the self-defeating propaganda that she originally accepted without questioning. I also urge her to give up her irrational ideas and then to incorporate sound beliefs that will work for her. Throughout the therapeutic process my attempt is to actively teach her that self-condemnation is the basis of emotional disturbance, that it is possible for her to stop rating herself, and that with hard work, including behavioral homework assignments, she can rid herself of the irrational ideas that have led to disturbances in feeling and behaving.

Elements of the Process

Beginning therapy. We begin by my teaching Ruth some of the basic principles that I think will make for effective therapy. I provide structure and direction from the outset. Ruth hears about how we incorporate irrational beliefs and then continue to indoctrinate ourselves with them. I go through the A-B-C model and explain that her thinking is what is causing her anxiety, guilt, and depression. Then I ask her to think about the beliefs that she lives by and write them down. I also give her the titles of a couple of RET self-help books that will give her some food for thought.

Ruth quickly learns that reading, writing, thinking, and carrying out activity-oriented homework assignments are part and parcel of this therapy approach. She grumbles a bit about being asked to read some books and keep a record of her daily events. She tells me that she already has more school work than she can fit into her overstuffed schedule and so has no more time to read. I do not give her much sympathy at this point, and I clearly let her know that, if she intends to change, therapy means plenty of work and effort. She will not uproot old patterns easily.

Working on Ruth's "musts." Ruth does cooperate and writes a list of some of the beliefs that she is living by. She brings them to the following session, and we work on a few of them.

RUTH: Here's my list. I'll read a few of the *musts* that I came up with during the week. I *must* be perfect in everything I do. I *must* be the perfect mother, the perfect wife, the perfect daughter, the perfect student, the perfect client, and on and on. And I believe that if I'm not perfect, the consequences are going to be very painful. If I'm not the perfect wife, my husband might leave me, and I'm not sure I could stand that. If I'm not the perfect mother, my children will suffer, and I'll feel guilty for failing them. I came up with a few more: I *must* not have sexual desires for other men. I *must* not make wrong decisions. I *must* constantly be striving for more.

JERRY: That's quite some list. Did you encounter any situations during the week where you started thinking about how these *musts* get you into trouble?

RUTH: Yeah! In my speech class I've been putting off giving my impromptu speech for weeks now. In fact, I thought about dropping the class, but once I start something, I hate to quit in the middle.

JERRY: Is that another *must?* That under no circumstances should you change your mind once you make a decision?

RUTH: Well, sorta. At any rate, I'm not dropping speech, but that impromptu assignment is worrying me sick. I can't sleep thinking about it at times. Going to that class is a pain. I worked myself up so much that I got diarrhea.

JERRY: So what are you telling yourself? What do you see as so horrible about giving an impromptu speech?

RUTH: It's only a five-minute speech, but what agony in thinking about it! If I could prepare it and use notes, it wouldn't be so bad. What I'm afraid of is that I'll get up there and forget what I want to say. Then I'll stutter, and I'll make a complete fool of myself.

JERRY: And then, if all that did happen, what would be so horrible? Would you fail the class?

RUTH: Oh, I've got an "A" so far, so that won't hurt me much. What's horrible is that I'd look dumb and be laughed at.

JERRY: I don't know if you're ready for this, but I'd like you to do a homework assignment. In RET we call this a "shame-attacking exercise." What I have in mind is for you to go into a public place—let's say the lobby of a hotel or a store—and I'd like you to deliberately act foolish. Say something dumb. How about "I'm a mental patient, and I've just been released. What day is it?" Well, are you game?

RUTH: Oh, I just don't think I could ever . . .

JERRY: And what would stop you?

We explore how her fear of making a fool of herself stops her from doing so many things. She then says that she would love to square dance but has not because she is afraid of falling and looking like a jerk. She would love to ski but does not for fear that she will fall on the "bunny hill" and break a leg—and then really look like a fool! I explain to her that the purpose of the shame-attacking exercise is to challenge her worst fears and to test them. Chances are, she will survive the embarrassment and will not die of shame.

RUTH [next week]: I hate to say it, but I didn't follow through. I went to the hotel and stood at the lobby door for the longest time, but I just couldn't walk in that door and make a fool of myself.

JERRY: Couldn't? At least say "I would not!" You could have done it, but you chose not to. Any idea why you didn't do it?

RUTH: I was just too afraid of being that far out. But I've decided to go ahead with that impromptu speech this week.

JERRY: Good, let's work on that. But let's talk some about your reactions to standing outside that hotel. [Even though she did not do the assignment, there is plenty of therapeutic potential in what she put herself through. So we explore her thinking, her catastrophic expectations, and what she might do differently. For example, one of her great fears was that people would think she was crazy. Finally, we begin talking about her upcoming speech.]

RUTH: I'm just afraid I'll freak out or, worse yet, chicken out.

JERRY: So let's go through it right now. Close your eyes and imagine that you're giving the speech, and all the worst things you can imagine happen.

After her fantasy with catastrophic expectations we take them one by one and try to demolish them. I am working with her on her evaluation of events and her prediction that she will fail. All the time, I want her to see that, even if she "messes up," she can still stand the outcomes. They may be unpleasant but surely not absolutely horrible.

We continue for a couple of months, with Ruth agreeing to do some reading and also carrying out increasingly difficult homework assignments. Gradually she works up to more risky activity assignments, and she does risk looking foolish several times, only to find that her fantasies were much worse than the outcomes. She gives her speech and is humorous and spontaneous. This gives her an increased sense of confidence to tackle some other difficult areas she has been avoiding.

Dealing with Ruth's beliefs about herself as a mother. Ruth is feeling very guilty about letting one of her daughters down. Jennifer is having troubles at school and is "going off the deep end," according to Ruth. She partially blames herself for Jennifer's problems, telling herself that she must be a better mother to Jennifer than her own mother was to her.

RUTH: I don't want Jennifer to suffer the way I did. But in so many ways I know I'm unloving and critical of her, just as my mother was of me at that age.

JERRY: What are you telling yourself when you think of this? [Again, I want Ruth to see that her self-defeating thoughts are getting her depressed and keeping her feeling guilty. My hope is that she will see that the key to eliminating needless anxiety and guilt lies in modifying her thinking.]

RUTH: I feel guilty that I didn't help Jennifer enough with her schoolwork. If I had tutored her, she would be doing well in school. I tell myself that I'm the cause of Jennifer's problems, that I should have been a better mother, that I could have cared more, and that I've ruined her chances for a good life.

JERRY: Do you see that this absolutistic thinking doesn't make sense? What about Jennifer's role in creating and maintaining her own problems?

RUTH: Yes, but I've made so many mistakes. And now I'm trying to make up for them so she can shape up and change.

JERRY: I agree that you've made mistakes with her, but that doesn't mean it will be the ruination of her. Can you see that if you do so much for her and make yourself totally responsible for her, she doesn't have to do anything for herself? Why should she accept any responsibility for how she is if you're blaming yourself? [My attempt with this debate is to get her to dispute her own destructive thinking. She has continued this pattern for so long that she now automatically blames herself, and then the guilt follows.]

RUTH: Well, I try to think differently, but I just keep coming back to these old thoughts. What would you like me to say to myself?

JERRY: When Jennifer does something wrong, who gets the blame for it?

RUTH: Me, of course. At least most of the time.

JERRY: And those times that Jennifer does well, who gets credit?

RUTH: Not me. Anyway, I dwell so much on what she's not doing that I don't often see that she does much right.

JERRY: How is it that you're so quick to place blame on yourself and just as quick to discount any part you have in Jennifer's accomplishments?

RUTH: Because problems occupy my mind, and I keep thinking that I should have been a better influence on her.

JERRY: I'd just hope that you could stop damning yourself and *should*ing yourself to death. Do you think you can begin to be kinder to yourself? What I'd like you to consider saying to yourself is something like this: "Even though I've made mistakes in the past and will probably continue making mistakes, that doesn't mean I've ruined Jennifer or will. It doesn't mean I'm the same kind of mother to her that mine was to me. I'll lighten up on myself and be more forgiving, because if I don't, I'll drive myself crazy."

RUTH: That sounds pretty good . . . If only I could say those things and mean them—and feel them!

JERRY: Well, if you keep disputing your own thinking and learning to substitute constructive self-statements, then you're likely to be able to say and mean these things—and you'll probably feel different too.

Process Commentary

As can be seen, my major focus with Ruth is on her thinking. I assume that she creates her own miseries by the thoughts and beliefs she holds. Only through learning to apply rigorous self-challenging methods will she succeed in freeing herself from the self-defeating thinking that led to her problems. I place value on behavioral homework assignments that put her in situations where she is forced to confront her irrational beliefs and her self-limiting behavior. I stress to her that she had better challenge herself over and over when she becomes aware of any *musts*, *shoulds*, and *oughts*.

Ruth needs reminders that striving for others' approval will keep her miserable. I consistently challenge her to question her basic assumption that she needs this approval in order to feel adequate. This prodding is supplemented by reading assignments that give her material to think about. Through her reading she continues a process she began in therapy of seeing how she is continually rating herself for her performances. Eventually, she accepts that her self-rating and her blaming are keeping her depressed and anxiety ridden and that, if she hopes to change these negative feelings, she will have to give up her absolutistic thinking. Through her practicing in real-life situations, I expect her to gradually change her thinking and develop effective skills for living.

Toward the conclusion of her therapy, Ruth brings in the following excerpt from her journal, which gives a glimpse of her experience in RET.

> Well, now that six months have passed, my sessions with Jerry are ending. I'm writing a review of what it has been like for me during these past few months, and what I learned from my therapy. My therapist has shown me that I need to rid myself of my anxiety, guilt, and depression by fully accepting myself as a worthwhile human being in spite of my imperfections. I'm acceptable whether or not I succeed at all the tasks and performances in my life and whether or not significant people like Father and Mother do approve of me and love me. I've worked very hard to come to this line of thinking, because all my life I've been programmed to think the opposite. I now see that I have indeed kept alive this indoctrination that my parents began by telling myself that I *had* to be all the ways in which they told me I *should* be.
>
> Jerry told me that I had *childish demands* and that I needed to replace them with *preferences*. I can see that, while I'd still like for my father to approve of me and love me the way I want him to, I can live without this love. Life doesn't have to be exactly the way I demand it to be. I realize that my insistence that life be fair at all times has contributed to my feeling as anxiety ridden as I have. I'm continuing to work in situations in my life on the many irrational notions I have. I did come to respect my therapist. He always accepted me personally, though at the same time he constantly confronted my distortions in thinking.

Questions for Reflection

1. What are your general reactions to my approach? What did you like best? like least? What do you think you might have done differently with Ruth?
2. Contrast the way an RET therapist works with Ruth with the way the psychoanalytic therapist worked with her. What style do you prefer in Ruth's case? What differences do you see between the RET therapist and the person-centered therapist? the existential therapist? Again, which do you prefer in Ruth's case? Why?
3. What does RET have in common with TA and behavior therapy in the ways the therapists view Ruth and the general styles of working with her problems?
4. What common irrational beliefs do you share with Ruth, if any? To what degree have you challenged your own irrational thinking? How do you think that this would affect your ability to effectively work with her?
5. Using RET concepts and procedures, show how you might proceed in counseling Ruth in terms of what you know about her. What would be the focus in your sessions with Ruth?
6. RET assumes that by changing our beliefs about situations we also change our emotional reactions to such events. How valid do you find this assumption to be for you? Can you come up with examples of how changing your beliefs and interpretations of events has changed your ways of feeling and acting?
7. Can you think of possibilities of using the Adlerian life-style questionnaire to detect basic mistakes and then working with them using an RET framework and RET techniques?
8. How comfortable would you be in employing RET techniques in your therapy with Ruth? To what degree do you think you could be confrontive enough to uproot her faulty thinking and encourage her to begin to think in different ways?
9. What ideas do you have for using RET concepts and procedures in conjunction with Gestalt techniques? Can you think of examples from Ruth's case where you could work on her feelings (with Gestalt techniques) and then proceed to work with her faulty thinking (by using RET techniques)?

Marion: A Woman Who Lives by Oughts and Shoulds

Some Background Data

For most of her 43 years Marion has lived by a series of *musts*, *shoulds*, and *oughts*. She is now telling herself that she *must* succeed in her new role as student in a human services program at a university. She equates success with being *the best* in the class. She constantly berates herself for not being able to write better papers, for not earning a higher score on her tests, for not doing *all* the required *and* supplementary reading that she *should* do, for not having more experiences as a counselor, for not having as wide a range of life experiences as she *ought* to have for going into the helping professions, and on and on. She literally *makes herself sick* by her perfectionistic strivings. She experiences migraine headaches, chronic constipation, stomach pains, and dizziness. While her body is sending her clear messages that she is driving herself relentlessly, she keeps forging ahead, thinking that she *must* meet all of her standards. Unfortunately, these standards are unrealistically high, and she will never be able to attain them. No matter what her level of achievement, she persistently puts herself down for not having done better or done more.

Marion rates herself constantly in all areas of her life. She gives herself grades for her performances in life, and typically her grades are low, for she demands so much of herself. Even though her grades at the university are consistently high (mostly "A"s with an occasional "B"), she rates herself as a "C" student. In the area of being a wife she gives herself a low "C" at best. She does not cook fancy meals the way her mother or her husband's mother did. Her husband's clothes need mending, and she feels that she is neglecting him. In her sex life she gives herself an "F." Her husband complains that she is not responsive enough, not playful, and too prudish. She almost never experiences an orgasm, because this was something she always believed she *must* not feel; sexual pleasure was something you should not have. Of course, she sees it as her fault that she is not as sexually responsive as she thinks she ought to be. In her social life she gives herself a "C." She keeps telling herself that she ought to entertain her husband's clients more often, that she ought to have friends over for dinner more often, and that, when she does, she ought to be a far better hostess than she is now.

How I Would Proceed with Marion from the Perspective of RET and Other Cognitive-Behavioral Methods

Marion presents herself voluntarily for therapy, for she recognizes through her academic studies at the university that she is driving herself in self-destructive circles. She says that she wants to break this chain, learn to modify her perfectionism, and begin accepting herself as a worthwhile person in spite of her limitations. She would like very much to be able to enjoy what she is learning and actually doing without telling herself that she should and must do more. She has told herself that she ought to be less judgmental of herself than she is, yet this does little good. She finally seeks professional help.

Exposing her irrational beliefs. In essence, I want to show Marion that it is her *irrational beliefs* that are the direct cause of her psychological and physiological problems. Further, I will show her that *she* is the one who is feeding herself these irrational and unrealistic assumptions and that she alone is the one who can change her misery by learning to uproot and demolish these self-destructive thoughts and attitudes. Finally, I will work with her to create a new set of assumptions and a rational set of attitudes to replace the outmoded values that she has continued indoctrinating herself with.

I begin by teaching her that her absolutistic thinking is the foundation of her problems. Together we identify and actually write down the *musts, shoulds,* and *oughts* that keep her the driven and unhappy person she is.

Drawing on some of Aaron Beck's notions in cognitive therapy, I also focus on

Marion's internal communications. I assume that she monitors her thoughts, wishes, feelings, and actions. In social situations she probably keeps score of how other people are reacting to her. Her thinking is also polarized in many respects. She sees things in terms of good or bad, wonderful or horrible. Further, she engages in some "catastrophizing," whereby she anticipates negative outcomes of her ventures. In sum, Marion is contributing to her emotional problems by what she is telling herself, by the assumptions she is making, and by her belief system. Some of her faulty assumptions, along with the dire consequences that she tells herself will occur unless she follows her *shoulds*, are as follows:

- I *must* perform well sexually so that I can meet my husband's expectations. If I fail, this confirms that I am sexually dead, unattractive, and incapable of giving anyone sexual pleasure. I won't be able to bear this thought.
- I *must* be at the top of my class. I *must* live up to *all* of the expectations of all of my professors—and then I *should* go beyond what they expect! If I fail at this, then this means that I'm basically stupid.
- I *must* do what is necessary to finally get my parents to approve of me and to give me the love and recognition I've been striving for. If I fail to get this, I'll never be able to value myself or feel that I have succeeded. If they won't validate me, then I'll never be able to validate myself. And I simply couldn't *tolerate* living without their love and acceptance.
- I must be *thoroughly competent* in anything and everything I attempt. If I can't, then I must avoid trying anything new. I couldn't *stand* making any mistakes, because this would prove to me and to the world that I'm deficient as a person.

To more clearly identify her faulty cognitions, I use Maxie Maultsby's written *rational self-analysis* procedure, which is a basic part of his rational behavior therapy. First of all, I ask Marion to write down an activating event, such as one of the times she made a mistake. Next she writes down her beliefs about making a mistake. Here I want to have her write down what she thought, what she told herself, and how she reacted internally to the fact that she had made a mistake. The next step consists of her writing down the consequences of her beliefs. What did she feel, and what did she actually do? After she has listed the activating event, her beliefs, and what she felt and did, I ask her to respond to Maultsby's five rational questions, again in writing:

1. Is her thinking based on fact?
2. Will her thinking protect her life and health?
3. Is her thinking likely to lead to the achievement of her short-term and long-term goals?
4. Will her thinking help her avoid conflicts with others?
5. Will her thinking help her feel what she wants to feel?

In the last step, Marion is asked to write down those feelings she would like to experience and how she would like to behave. What I like about the *written* rational self-analysis is that it provides us with a tool for change. Both of us can actually look at the chain of events that typically leads to problems for Marion. If her thinking is faulty and she jumps to false conclusions, it becomes more apparent when we have a written document.

Also borrowing a technique from rational behavior therapy, I employ the rational-emotive imagery procedure, which consists of asking Marion to intensely imagine herself thinking, feeling, and acting exactly as she would like to think, feel, and behave in daily situations. This is a good method for helping her imagine all the specific ways she would like to be different. What feelings would she like to experience more often? What thoughts would she like to decrease? And what are the beliefs and thoughts that she would like to have? How would she like to behave differently? She can be whatever she wants to be in fantasy, and with this imagery procedure she creates an ideal world. Later we can explore what she is doing to thwart her getting what she would like to have.

After Marion and I clearly identify her self-defeating ideology, the next step is to show her that it is *not* her parents, her children, her husband, or her professors who are indoctrinating her with absolutistic thinking. Rather, it is by a process of *self*-indoctrination that she *now* continues to keep herself in a state of emotional and physical misery. Further, it is essential that she learn that these problems stem mainly from irrational beliefs. It is her thinking and the self-talk that goes on with it, *not* the objective situations in her life, that are at the root of her problems. She thinks that her parents' lack of approval has caused her to feel unloved and unappreciated. I show her that it is *her belief* about this real *or* imagined situation that is causing her difficulties (as opposed to actual events). Our work consists of my teaching her ways to dispute these irrational beliefs. She will have to learn the importance of working hard, both in the sessions and on her own. I hope to teach her that by practicing methods of uprooting and changing disturbing thoughts she can eventually free herself from the tyranny she lives under.

A *typical session.* During a typical session we follow through with a critical evaluation of one of Marion's irrational notions. We explore her belief that she must be at the top of her class, that she must go beyond what her professors expect, and that to fail to do so means that she is hopelessly and forever stupid. I ask her to show me the evidence for her illogical conclusion that she will be stupid if she fails to be *the best* (whatever that means and however that can be measured). I confront her on matters such as: "Who is telling you these things now? Why do you burden yourself with *having* to live up to these expectations? What would be so terrible about doing a fine job, without being perfect? And what would be absolutely horrible and devastating about failing a test, or even a class or two?" I hope Marion will come to see that all the catastrophic thinking and expectations of doom are not nearly so unbearable as she thinks. Surely, it might not be pleasant for her to fail, but she could always repeat the course with another professor.

In working with Marion during the particular session under discussion, I draw on a variety of diverse methods of a cognitive, affective, and behavioral nature. I employ an eclectic approach suited to her individual problems. If a technique does not seem to work in a session, I get rid of it and find suitable procedures that will work. As I mentioned earlier, Marion's progress will be determined in large part by her willingness to work hard outside of the sessions. Thus, I ask her to give herself *homework assignments* that help her get practice in confronting her irrational thinking. The aim here is to learn how to deal with anxiety and to challenge herself by putting herself in difficult situations that are anxiety provoking. For example, I suggest that she finally take the initiative and apply for a position as a volunteer worker at a community mental-health center. This is appropriate, because she has mentioned that this is what she would like; yet she has kept herself from actually doing so for fear that she might not be accepted at the first agency she applied to. I get her to question what would be so terrible if this happened. After all, there are many agencies out there, and what would be so horrible if a number of them did not accept her as a volunteer? I hope that she can consider that there are other reasons besides her not being a suitable person that an agency might not accept her. Has she considered that it might have too many volunteers already? Or that it might not want to take on volunteers who were not willing to commit themselves to more time than she cares to devote?

As an adjunct to homework assignments for Marion, I ask her to keep a journal in which she will record her thoughts and feelings in various situations. It will be ideal for her to write down some of the messages she tells herself before going for her interview. By writing down some of the self-statements she makes silently, she can see with increasing clarity how this type of thinking gets in her way—how it stops her from doing many things she would like to do because of a fear of dire consequences. I also ask her to go over a particular irrational belief for at least ten minutes a day until the belief is weakened. Thus, she can apply logical thinking to beliefs associated with a situation such as avoiding interviews for volunteer work lest she be rejected.

In addition to keeping a journal to record her progress during the week, I ask her to devote some time to evaluating her own progress. Questions such as the following are useful: "What are some of the irrational beliefs that I fed myself this week? When I became aware that I was engaged in this self-indoctrination process, what did I actually *do?* How did it feel to be in situations that brought up anxiety? And how did I react to these situations? Did I risk trying new behavior? Or did I stay with old and safe behavior? What gains am I making in uprooting specific attitudes and beliefs that I see as irrational? What new things have I been telling myself this week, and what are the consequences?"

Homework assignments, learning to dispute specific irrational beliefs, keeping a journal, and trying new behavior are a few examples of ways that Marion can get rid of the *shoulds* and *musts* she lives by. Of course, we go over all of the above projects in our sessions. Through various techniques of an active/directive nature (such as didactic teaching, role playing, behavioral rehearsal, coaching, modeling, confrontation, and desensitization, to mention a few), she progresses toward learning how to challenge her thinking and how to incorporate a constructive philosophy of life.

Employing techniques of cognitive behavior modification. Marion continues to monitor her thoughts during a typical week by writing down specific situations that produce stress for her. She is getting better at noticing those factors that induce stress, and she is also improving her ability to detect statements she tells herself that increase her level of stress. As a part of her homework she records what she *tells* herself in problematic situations, what she then *does*, and how she *feels*. During her sessions we go over her written analysis of her thinking, behaving, and feeling patterns in various situations. We then discuss alternative statements that she could make to herself, as well as ways that she could actually behave differently.

A *bibliotherapy* program, which is a supplement to Marion's sessions, is helping her to become a more astute observer of her own experience. I suggest that she read books such as *A New Guide to Rational Living* (by Ellis and Harper) and *Rational Behavior Therapy* (by Maultsby). As she begins to apply to herself what she is learning from her readings, she also takes a more active role in her sessions with me. At this time I introduce Marion to more of the techniques of cognitive behavior modification, including describing to her how her self-talk, or inner dialogue, influences her behavior. I draw on the work of Donald Meichenbaum, as set forth in his book *Cognitive Behavior Modification*.

I let Marion know that I am interested in teaching her how to change what she is thinking in order to change how she is behaving. She hears about how she is actually creating her own psychological problems (her fears) and her specific symptoms by the way she interprets events and situations. Her perception of herself in social situations influences her emotional reactions to them. I operate on the assumption that reorganizing her *cognitive structures* (her thoughts and self-statements) will result in a corresponding reorganization of her *behavior* in interpersonal situations. The following is a summary of how we work at changing these cognitive processes.

The beginning step in Marion's changing consists of continued observation of her behavior in interpersonal situations. Thus, we go over her week as she recorded it to see what we can learn about the ways she is contributing to her fears in social situations through her negative thoughts. Marion reports that she became aware of how many times in various social situations she set herself up for failure by telling herself that people would not be interested in her.

The second step in changing Marion's cognitive processes involves my teaching her how to substitute *adaptive behavioral* responses for the maladaptive behaviors she now displays. If she hopes to change, what she says to herself must initiate a new behavioral chain, one that is incompatible with her maladaptive behaviors. Thus, we look at positive self-talk that can generate new expectations for her. She considers saying to herself: "Even though I'm nervous about meeting new people, I will challenge my assumption that people find me boring. I can learn to relax, and I can tell myself that I *do* have something to say." She is beginning to learn some new internal dialogues, and she is learning how to create positive expectations to guide new behavior.

The third phase of Marion's cognitive modification consists of learning more effective coping skills, which can be practiced in real-life situations. In this case, I teach her a standard *relaxation exercise* used in cognitive-behavioral therapy and rational-emotive therapy. I ask her to practice it two times a day for about 20 minutes each session. I teach her some training procedures in breathing and deep-muscle relaxation, ones that she can apply to many of the situations she encounters that bring about anxiety. During this phase she is also learning more effective coping skills, which she practices in real-life situations. As she behaves differently, she notices that she is getting different reactions from others, which reinforces her to continue with new patterns of behavior.

A Commentary

By using a combination of rational-emotive techniques and other cognitive-behavioral methods, Marion gradually develops a conceptual framework that helps her understand the ways in which she responds to a variety of stressful situations. First, through Socratic questioning she learns to become astute at monitoring maladaptive behaviors that flow from her inner dialogue. Second, she learns a variety of behavioral and cognitive coping techniques that she can apply in difficult situations. She acquires and rehearses a new set of self-statements. Eventually, she makes fewer negative and self-defeating statements to herself and substitutes positive and reinforcing self-statements. Third, she learns that merely learning to say new things to herself is not enough to result in behavioral change. It is necessary for her to practice these self-statements in real-life situations that present actual threats. Having become proficient in some cognitive and behavioral coping skills, she practices behavioral assignments on a graded level. As she experiences some success in carrying out these assignments in daily life, the assignments become increasingly demanding.

The basic goal of therapy with Marion consists in teaching her self-help strategies that she can employ to deal effectively with current problems and with future problems as they arise. By teaching her a method of thinking *and* behaving differently, I make the assumption that she will begin to feel better about herself.

Follow-Up: You Continue as Marion's Therapist

Consider the concepts and techniques I drew on and the style in which I did so as you think about how you might work with Marion further. What would you do differently?

1. Do any of Marion's *shoulds*, *oughts*, and *musts* remind you of messages you tell yourself? How successful do you see yourself in identifying and working through some of your major irrational beliefs?
2. How do you imagine it would be for you to work with Marion? What might you do if she persisted in clinging to certain self-defeating notions and refused to see the irrationality of some of her beliefs?
3. How comfortable would you be using RET methods? How effective do you imagine you would be?
4. Most of Marion's work with me consisted of identifying irrational notions and learning to dispute them—both in the session and through activity-oriented homework assignments. What do you think of this approach? Do you think it is sufficient to produce lasting change? If not, what else do you think might be needed?

5. To what degree do you find it helpful to integrate the cognitive-behavioral perspective (of Beck, Maultsby, and Meichenbaum) with the RET approach?
6. What are some cognitive-behavioral methods that you'd want to employ with clients?

Recommended Supplementary Readings

Cognitive Therapy and the Emotional Disorders (1976) by A. Beck (New York: New American Library [Meridian]) is a very useful book illustrating how emotional disorders often have roots in faulty thinking. Beck clearly outlines the principles and techniques of cognitive therapy, giving many clinical examples of how the internal dialogue of clients results in various emotional and behavioral problems.

Growth through Reason: Verbatim Cases in Rational-Emotive Therapy (1973) by A. Ellis (Hollywood, Calif.: Wilshire Books) is a recording of actual cases in RET. It gives the reader a good grasp of how the rational-emotive therapist actually works with a wide range of clients.

Handbook of Rational-Emotive Therapy (1977) edited by A. Ellis and R. Grieger (New York: Springer) is one of the most comprehensive, up-to-date overviews of RET theory and practice. It is especially good on the application of RET principles to sex therapy, education, group work, assertion training, depression, and work with children.

A New Guide to Rational Living (rev. ed., 1975) by A. Ellis and R. Harper (Hollywood, Calif.: Wilshire Books) shows how to apply the principles of RET to problems of everyday living. An easy-to-read and interesting book.

Theoretical and Empirical Foundations of Rational-Emotive Therapy (1979) edited by A. Ellis and J. Whiteley (Monterey, Calif.: Brooks/Cole) is a series of articles presenting a comprehensive overview of RET, both as a theory of therapy and as a theory of personality. The first four chapters, by Ellis, represent an excellent summary of his updated thinking as it applies to clinical practice.

Rational Behavior Therapy (1984) by M. Maultsby (Englewood Cliffs, N.J.: Prentice-Hall) describes strategies and techniques of RBT, which is a form of cognitive-behavior therapy. Maultsby discusses his extension of rational-emotive therapy in chapters on written rational self-analysis and rational-emotive imagery. Both of these techniques can be used to make many of the RET concepts alive and concrete for clients.

Cognitive Behavior Modification: An Integrative Approach (1977) by D. Meichenbaum (New York: Plenum) is an excellent source for learning about cognitive-behavioral techniques such as cognitive restructuring, stress-inoculation training, and self-instructional training. The author does a good job of discussing how cognitive factors are related to behavior. He develops the theme that clients have the power and freedom to change by observing their behavior, telling themselves new sentences, and restructuring their belief system.

A Practitioner's Guide to Rational-Emotive Therapy (1980) by S. Walen, R. DiGiuseppe, and R. L. Wessler (New York: Oxford University Press) is a practical manual describing specific methods for teaching clients the basics of RET. It shows ways to design homework for clients, and it presents a variety of different styles of practicing RET.

The Principles and Practice of Rational-Emotive Therapy (1980) by R. A. Wessler and R. L. Wessler (San Francisco: Jossey-Bass) is a useful book designed for practitioners. It contains an expansion of the A-B-C model, RET's clinical theories and findings, and an inventory for evaluating one's own rational therapy skills.

Suggested Readings

Belkin, G. S. (1984). *Introduction to counseling* (2nd ed.). Dubuque, Iowa: William C. Brown (Chapter 9).

Corey, G. (1986). *Theory and practice of counseling and psychotherapy* (3rd ed.). Monterey, Calif.: Brooks/Cole (Chapter 9).

Corsini, R. (1984). *Current psychotherapies* (3rd ed.). Itasca, Ill.: Peacock (Chapter 6).

Gilliland, B., James, R., Roberts, G., & Bowman, J. (1984). *Theories and strategies in counseling and psychotherapy*. Englewood Cliffs, N.J.: Prentice-Hall (Chapter 8).

Hansen, J., Stevic, R., & Warner, R. (1986). *Counseling: Theory and process* (4th ed.). Boston: Allyn & Bacon (Chapter 10).

Patterson, C. H. (1986). *Theories of counseling and psychotherapy* (4th ed.). New York: Harper & Row (Chapters 1, 2, & 8).

Prochaska, J. O. (1984). *Systems of psychotherapy: A transtheoretical analysis* (2nd ed.). Homewood, Ill.: Dorsey Press (Chapter 7).

Shilling, L. E. (1984). *Perspectives on counseling theories*. Englewood Cliffs, N.J.: Prentice-Hall (Chapter 5).

CHAPTER TEN

A Case Approach to Reality Therapy

A Reality Therapist's Perspective on Ruth

Basic Assumptions

Reality therapy is active, directive, practical, didactic, and behavioral. As a reality therapist I employ the contract method to encourage my clients to translate their intention to change into actual behavior that results in change. I see my basic job as establishing a personal relationship with my clients that will give them the impetus to make an honest evaluation of how well their current behavior is working for them. Thus, the focus of reality therapy is behavior, not attitudes, insight, feelings, one's past, or unconscious motivation.

I hold a number of basic assumptions that will guide my intervention strategies with Ruth. One is that people have a striving toward developing a "success identity." Those who achieve this kind of identity see themselves as being able to give and accept love, feel that they are significant to others, experience a sense of self-worth, get involved in a caring way, and meet their needs in ways that are not at the expense of others. By contrast, people who seek therapy often have a "failure identity": they see themselves as unloved, believe they are incompetent to make and stick with commitments, and feel powerless to change their life. Because reality therapy assumes that people are largely able to shape their destiny by what they choose to do, its focus is on helping clients learn behavior that will lead to a success identity.

Another basic premise underlying the practice of reality therapy is that *behavior* controls our perceptions. Although we may not be able to control what actually is in the real world, we do attempt to control our perceptions to meet our own needs. Applied to Ruth, this means that she creates her own inner world. Her behavior has three components: doing, thinking, and feeling. Because I make the assumption that controlling feelings and thoughts is more difficult than controlling actions, the focus of therapy is on what she is doing—behaviors that are observable. She will find that it is typically easier to force herself to *do* something different than to feel or think something different.

Initial Assessment of Ruth

Rather than merely focusing on Ruth's deficits, problems, and failures, I am interested in looking at her assets, accomplishments, and successes. Initially I ask her questions such as these: "What do you consider to be your major strengths? What are the qualities that you most like about yourself? What have you done that you are proud of? What resources can you build on?" From what I know of Ruth from her autobiography and intake form, she has several apparent strengths. She has graduated from college and is in a teacher-education program at the graduate level. She has done this against many odds. Her parents could see no real reason why she should get a college degree. In her current situation her husband and children have not been supportive of her efforts to complete her education. She has been involved in numerous community groups and made some contributions there, she has managed to keep up her family life and still have time for her education, and she has set some career goals that are meaningful to her. Now she needs to develop a clear plan for attaining her *personal* objectives.

Goals of the Therapy

As implied above, the basic goals of reality therapy are to guide clients toward making value judgments about their present behavior and to assist them in deciding on a constructive plan of responsible behavior change that will lead to taking effective control of their life. From Ruth's perspective it appears that her present behavior is not working as well as it might. Her focus is not really helping her meet her goals. Ruth is unproductively dwelling on unfortunate events from her past, and she is paying too much attention to feelings of guilt and anxiety and not enough to those things that she is doing that actually create these feelings. In short, she is making herself anxious and guilty by what she is doing and not doing in everyday life. I will try to direct her attention toward what she is doing, challenging her to make an honest assessment of how well her current behavior is getting her what she wants. Then I will help her make plans to bring about change.

Therapeutic Procedures

As a reality therapist I focus on what clients can do and are willing to do in the present situation to change their *behavior*. I think that it is a mistake to focus on feelings, on attitudes and beliefs, on past mistakes, on unconscious factors, and on childhood experiences. Unlike many other therapists, who dwell on what clients have done wrong and the mistakes they have made, I will focus on what Ruth can *do* now to start living in a responsible manner and thus working toward a "success identity." I work on the assumption that it is the evasion of reality and the failure to live in a responsible way that is the cause of human problems.

I will ask Ruth to develop plans to change failure behavior into success behavior. I will expect her to make a commitment to carry out these plans, for if she hopes to change, then *action* is necessary. It is essential that she stick with her commitment to change and not blame others for the way she is or give excuses for not meeting her commitments. Thus, we will work with a therapeutic contract, one that spells out what she wants from therapy as well as the means by which she will attain her goals.

If Ruth says that she is depressed, I will not ask *why* she is depressed, nor will I ask her to dwell on feelings of depression. Instead, I will ask what she has *done* that day to contribute to her depression. We do not think that changes in behavior depend on changing one's attitudes or gaining insights. On the contrary, we hold that attitudes may change, as well as feelings, once clients begin to change their behavior. I am also concerned about Ruth's *present*, not her past. Why should I dwell on the unsuccessful person that she has been? I would rather focus on the successful person that she can be. Also, I do not pay heed to psychoanalytic factors such as transference, unconscious dynamics, dreams, and early memories. Through my real involvement with Ruth I hope to show her the benefits of facing reality and living in this reality.

Therapeutic Process

Ruth's therapeutic journey consists of my applying the eight steps of reality therapy to help her meet her goals. Although the eight principles may sound simple, they must be adapted creatively to the therapeutic process. It should be noted that, although these principles are applied progressively in stages, they should not be thought of as discrete and rigid categories. Each phase builds on the previous stage, there is a considerable degree of interdependence among these principles, and taken together they contribute to the total process that is reality therapy. These steps are (1) establishing a therapeutic relationship with Ruth and getting involved; (2) asking her to examine what she is doing now; (3) getting her to evaluate the degree to which her present behavior is helping her; (4) developing plans to improve her life; (5) getting a commitment from her to carry out and stick with her plans; (6) refusing to accept excuses; (7) refusing to use punishment; and (8) refusing to give up. We will now look at a few of the highlights and turning points in Ruth's therapy.

Elements of the Process

Establishing the relationship. During our initial sessions my main concern is to develop therapeutic involvement with Ruth. I obtain involvement by attempting to understand her, affirming a belief that she can experience success, and communicating an attitude of caring. At this time I listen carefully to her to get a sense of why she is seeking therapy and what she wants from me. Without pushing her I try to discover as much as possible about her inner world. She seems relatively open and appears sincere in wanting more from life and taking more control of her actions. She is also somewhat frightened and tells me that changing seems so difficult, adding that for years she has made firm resolutions to change the course of her life, only to slip back again. I detect some discouragement, so we pursue how this time she might create self-fulfilling prophecies of success rather than of doom.

In some of our early sessions Ruth wants to talk about times she has experienced failure in her childhood and youth. She quickly wants to blame past negative experiences for her fears. She seems a bit stunned when I tell her that I do not want to go over her past failures and that, if we are going to talk about the past at all, I am more interested in hearing what went right for her. From that topic, she jumps to complaining about feeling anxiety, depression, and some physical symptoms. Because it is early in the course of therapy, I let her talk for a while about her depression and anxiety, but I do not encourage her to focus on such feelings or to really experience them. My reaction to what Ruth says is that part of her present problem is that she is already stuck in some negative feelings, and I do not want to reinforce her in continuing this pattern.

Challenging Ruth to evaluate her behavior. After getting a picture of how Ruth sees her world, I encourage her to try something different—to take a hard look at the things she is doing and see if they are working for her. After some debating she agrees with my suggestion that she is depressing herself by what she is doing. Questions that I pose to her are: "What are the things you've done today? What did you do this past week? Do you like what you're doing now? Are there some things you would like to be doing differently? What are some of the things that stop you from doing what you say you want to do? What do you intend to do tomorrow?" Let me stress that I do not bombard her with these questions one after another. The early sessions are, however, geared to getting her to consider this line of questioning. Rather than looking at her past or focusing on her attitudes, beliefs, thoughts, and feelings, I want her to know that we will be zeroing in on what she is doing today and what she will do tomorrow.

I believe that Ruth will not change unless she makes some assessment of the constructiveness or destructiveness of what she is doing. I assume that, if she comes to realize that her behavior is not working for her and that she is not getting what she wants, there is a real possibility that she might choose other alternatives. Here is a brief excerpt of a session:

RUTH: So what do you think I'm doing wrong? There are times I want to give up, because I don't know what to do differently. [She is very much wanting me to make a value judgment for her.]

JERRY: You know how important it is for you to be the one who makes a judgment about your own behavior. It's your job to decide for yourself what is and isn't working. I can't tell what you "should" do. [For me to simply tell her that some of her present ways are ineffective will not be of much value to her.]

RUTH: Well, I do want to go out and get some practice with interviews for part-time or substitute teaching. I often find lots of reasons to keep me from doing that. I keep telling myself that I'm so busy I just don't have time to set up these interviews.

JERRY: And that is something you'd like to change?

RUTH: Yeah, sure I want to change it. I want to be able to arrange for these interviews and then feel confident enough to have what it takes to get a part-time job.

We look at how Ruth stops herself (not why) and explore ways that she might begin to change behavior that she calls "sitting back and waiting to see what happens." She says that she does not like her passivity and that she would like to do more initiating. One of the factors we talk about is how she lets her family get in the way of her taking action in doing some of these things she says she wants to do.

Planning and action. We devote a number of sessions to identifying specific behaviors that Ruth decides are not working for her. A few of these ineffective behaviors are procrastinating in arranging for job interviews; sitting at home feeling depressed and anxious and then increasing these feelings by not doing anything different; allowing her 19-year-old son, Rob, to come home after squandering money and then taking care of him; allowing her daughter Jennifer to control her life by her acting out; and continually taking on projects that she does not want to get involved in. Knowing that we cannot work on all fronts at once, I ask her what areas she wants to do something about.

Ruth decides first to line up some interviews for jobs. She makes it clear that her life is boring, stale, and without much challenge. Then she tries to convince me that everything she has to do for her family makes it next to impossible for her to get out of her boring rut. I reply "If things are as bad as you say, why aren't you doing anything different?" Ruth then tries to explain to me why she has not been able to change this pattern, and I am sorry I asked the question. So I try to cut through her list of reasons by clearly letting her know that I believe that actions speak louder than words. We gradually work out some realistic plans that include her filing an application with school districts and setting up interviews. Interesting enough, after taking these beginning steps she reports that she is already feeling much better.

We also develop some plans to set clear limits with Ruth's family. She has a pattern of doing things for her children and then resenting them and winding up feeling taken advantage of. Part of her plan calls for sitting down with each of her sons and each of her daughters and redefining their relationships. I suggest that it would be a good idea to have at least one session with Ruth and her family. The idea both excites and frightens her. Yet she actually surprises herself when she is successful in getting her four children and husband to come in for a two-hour session of family therapy. At this session we mainly negotiate some changes in roles after Ruth has told each family member specific changes she would like and has been striving for. One of her sons and one of her daughters is not at all excited about some of the proposed changes, and they want to know what is wrong with the way things are. What I had in mind when I suggested this family session was to give Ruth an opportunity to ask for what she wants and to witness her negotiating for these changes. The session helps me see how she relates to her family, and it helps Ruth ask for what is important to her.

Other phases of Ruth's therapy. Most of our work together consists of developing realistic and specific plans and then talking about how Ruth might carry them out in everyday life. When she does not stick with a subgoal or carry out a plan for the week, I do not listen to any excuses that she might want to offer. Instead, I simply say: "Ruth, do you want to do it or not? When will you do it?" In a few cases where she persistently does not follow through with an agreed-on plan, we then discuss whether what she has planned is something she really wants or something she thinks she should want. Several times she returns looking sheepishly at me, almost expecting to be punished or yelled at. I try to get across that, as long as she keeps coming in, I do not intend to give up on her, nor will I get into a punishing stance with her. Instead, I want her to deal with the consequences of her actions and then be her own judge.

Eventually, Ruth gets better at setting smaller goals and makes more realistic plans. She stops and says "Now I wonder if I really want to do this, or am I hearing someone else tell me that I should want it?" Before finishing her therapy she fills out a form evaluating her progress over the months. Her comments are reproduced below.

> After two months of weekly visits with a reality therapist I have a better idea of what I can do to get out of the boring rut I've been in for so long. I've gotten a lot of miles out of complaining and feeling helpless, but I must say this is something that Jerry just would not tolerate. He quickly told me when I whined that if I really were interested in being different, I'd be taking steps to see that I *was* different.
>
> I remember the time I agreed to begin daily exercise and a jogging program as one way of losing weight. For several weeks I had complained to Jerry that I couldn't stand the way I looked. He worked with me to develop a realistic program for losing weight—and then I didn't follow through with the plans. Jerry said he didn't want to listen to my rationalizations for having failed. I tried to convince him that I had gone on another eating binge because my

husband was ignoring me and I got depressed. Then I ate out of defiance. I said to myself "Why should I lose weight for John if he's going to treat me so mean?" When I told Jerry this, he countered with: "Who are you losing weight for—*yourself* or John? Who are you hurting with your eating behavior?" That got me to thinking about how I so often make others responsible instead of putting the responsibility on me, where it belongs. I do see that if I don't like my weight, or anything else in my life, matters won't be different until I get in there and take action.

By the way, I interviewed for the job, and I did get part-time work as a substitute. This shows me that I'll get nothing unless I make an attempt.

Process Commentary

As a reality therapist I do not tell Ruth what she should change but encourage her to look at her own behavior and decide for herself how well it is working for her. Once she makes a value judgment about what she is actually *doing*, she can take some significant steps towards making changes for herself. She has a tendency to complain of feeling victimized and controlled, and my intention is to help her see how her behavior actually contributes to this perceived helplessness. Rather than focusing on her feelings of depression and anxiety, I choose to focus on what she does from the time she wakes up to the time she goes to bed. Through a self-observational process, she gradually assumes more responsibility for her actions. She sees that what she does has a lot to do with the way she feels.

After Ruth becomes clearer about certain patterns of her behavior, I encourage her to develop a specific plan of action that can lead to change—the changes that she desires. Broad and idealistic plans are bound to fail, so we work on a concrete plan for change that she is willing to commit herself to. Once she makes a commitment to a certain course of action, I will accept no excuses if she does not follow through with her program. I simply ask her to look at her plans again to determine what has gone wrong. Through this process, Ruth learns how to evaluate her own behavior to see ways that she might adjust her plans and experience success.

Questions for Reflection

1. What are your general impressions of the way I worked with Ruth? What did you like best about my approach with her? like least? What are some specific things you might have done differently?
2. What are your reactions to my lack of interest in matters such as Ruth's early childhood experiences? her unconscious dynamics? her dreams? her feelings of being bound by her parents' teachings? her feelings of guilt? What are the major differences you see between reality therapy and psychoanalysis? Which do you think is more appropriate for Ruth?
3. What similarities do you see between reality therapy and existential therapy? transactional analysis? behavior therapy? rational-emotive therapy? Adlerian therapy?

4. Assume that you are Ruth's therapist and she wants to present you with the reasons that she has failed in a particular plan for action. How might you respond? What do you think of the reality therapist's view of *not accepting excuses* and of *not blaming the past* for the way one is today?
5. Show how you would proceed with Ruth on the basis of what you know about her, staying within the framework of reality therapy.
6. Apply the eight steps of reality therapy to what you know of Ruth. Systematically show how you would get her to focus on what she is doing, on making an evaluation of her behavior, and on helping her formulate realistic plans.
7. Assume that you are a client in reality therapy. What do you think this experience would be like for you? Review the eight steps of reality therapy in light of your being the client. How would you describe your current behavior? How well is it working for you? Are you getting what you want from life? If not, what specific behaviors do you think you would have to change in order to do so? Can you come up with a plan for changing a particular behavior you really want to change?

Manny: A Loser for Life?

The scene is a U.S. Army base in Germany. The Army has a counseling program for drug and alcohol rehabilitation, consisting of mandatory counseling for addictive personalities.

I am called in as a consultant to work with training the counselors who are a part of this program. I mention that I would like to get some feel for the type of clientele they work with, and I am quickly given an opportunity. They know that my theoretical orientation is reality therapy, and since the Army is very supportive of this approach to rehabilitation programs, I am sent a client to interview for one session.

My Approach with Manny

After Manny and I introduce ourselves, our exchange goes this way:

MANNY: I really don't want to be here, you know. The only reason I'm here is because my commanding officer told me "You will report to Dr. Corey at 1600 hours on 7 July at the health clinic."

JERRY: If you don't want to be here, how come you're here?

MANNY: What do you mean, man, I *had* to show up. The commanding officer didn't give me any choice!

JERRY: Well, you walked through the door by yourself. Nobody brought you here. What would have happened if you hadn't shown up?

MANNY: They gave me one more chance, and then they're booting me out.

JERRY: So you *did* decide to come and see me rather than get kicked out.

MANNY: Look, man—this doesn't make any sense at all! I just know I would rather not be here.

JERRY: Where would you rather be?

MANNY: It's my day off—I'd rather be watching TV at the recreation center.
JERRY: What program would you be watching?
MANNY: The baseball game.
JERRY: Oh, really. I like baseball too. Do you ever play yourself?
MANNY: Oh, I used to.
JERRY: How come you stopped? They have a team at the base here.
MANNY: Ahh—I'm just not good enough.
JERRY: Is it typical for you to give up on things that don't come easy to you?
MANNY: Hell, I've given up on lots of things in my life.
JERRY: Like what?

Initially, Manny does not want to be in the office. Rather than fighting his resistance, I go with it by engaging in what might seem like "small talk." My hope is that he will find it easy enough to talk with me, that I will not appear overly threatening to him, and that I will be able to lay the foundations for more meaningful *involvement* with him. Note that, even though Manny sees himself as an involuntary client, I challenge him a bit on the fact that he indeed chose to come and see me rather than suffering the consequences of not keeping his appointment. Manny could have been more difficult and more resistant by simply saying: "Hey, why am I talking to you? I don't want to talk to you." A facilitative remark would be "And who would you rather talk to?" Again, if I let him lead the way and go with his resistance, he can provide me with useful information about himself that helps me understand his current situation.

At some point Manny will surely remind me again that he does not want to attend therapy sessions. Then I am likely to tell him what we will be doing in the sessions and what he can expect of me. But I will also tell him what I expect of him. I am not willing to see him unconditionally, nor am I willing to sit with him silently or try to pry things out of him. It is probable, for example, that I will see him three times to explore the possibilities of what counseling can offer him. If he agrees to come in for three sessions, the time will be used mainly to teach him about the counseling process, to get him to look at what he is *doing* now, and to decide how well it is working for him. Notice that I am not determining what he will talk about, but I will insist that on some level he address his present behavior. If he agrees to these limited terms, we can then proceed as follows.

JERRY: I'd like to talk more about why you were sent here and what you might get from this one session today. Are you willing?
MANNY: You're calling the shots. Whatever you say. I'm here because the Army thinks I have a big problem with drugs—Big H and all that stuff—and they think you're supposed to put my head on straight. My problem isn't the drugs—it's the Army and all those Mickey Mouse rules.
JERRY: What about the Army and its rules?

I want to give Manny some slack in saying what problems he has, if any. Unless *he* sees that he has a problem—one that is getting in the way of living—he may do nothing to change any of his behavior. It is one thing for his commanding officer to order him to seek counseling for a problem he sees with Manny and quite another matter for Manny to accept that he does indeed have a problem.

MANNY: Sure, I got my share of problems. You'd have some problems if you grew up the way I did. My old man kicked me out of the house when I was a kid, and I had to go and live with an uncle in East L.A. I got in with a gang and started being a loser then. I got kicked out of school for peddling dope and gang activity. Never was able to hold a job. I mean, man, I've had a rough life. If you had all the things happen to you that I've had to go through, you might not have made it as far as I did. I'm a loser, but at least I'm still alive, I mean, Doc, you don't look like the type that's been with gangs and had to put up with the shit that I did. How can you understand what I'm going through?

I need to exert some caution here not to become defensive. Also, I do not want this to become a session in which Manny tells me how he is not to blame for all his woes. In reality therapy we do not want to encourage a pattern of blaming, in which clients absolve themselves of any personal responsibility for the way they are, nor do we want to encourage a recitation of past history as an explanation of current behavior. But another issue is that Manny is again trying to take the focus off of himself and telling me that I am not able to understand what he has been through. I must deal directly with the question of my ability to understand him.

JERRY: You're right, I haven't been through all that you have. I'm not sure I'd have survived the gangs and all. That doesn't mean that I can't understand you. I'd like for you to give me that chance. Even though I've had different life experiences from you, I may still be able to have some of your feelings and see things the way you do. I'd like a chance to make contact with you, even for this single meeting.

MANNY: Well, before you can understand the way I am, you just gotta know about what I've lived through. My old man was never there, I got beat up all the time, I failed at everything I tried—I was a real loser. A loser from the word go. And it's mostly because I never had the things in life most normal kids had.

Again, there are some rich leads here. I can get some idea of what it is like to be Manny if I let him talk in more detail of what his life was like, as well as what he is facing now. But there is the danger that we can lose sight of his *present behavior*—what he is doing now—if we dwell on the adversity he has faced and the loser that he has been in the past. I want to focus him on the present.

JERRY: You know, Manny, the way I work I prefer to look at what you're doing *right now* in your life and what your *behavior* is actually getting you. I think we can easily get sidetracked if we go back into your past with all the details of the negative things that happened to you. I'm not so much interested in hearing about the loser you've been all your life as I am in getting you to think about the winner you can be in your future.

MANNY: But I want to figure out why my head is all messed up the way it is. Don't you need to know about childhood to help me? Don't I need to know what's caused my problems before I can straighten them out?

JERRY: I don't think exploring the past is important. It doesn't have much to do with change in your present behavior. What I'm after is to get you to look at your life to see in what ways it is or isn't working for you *now*. With what time we have left today, I'd be very willing to discuss with you what your present behavior is getting you. Are you willing to take this look?

MANNY: Well, it's not getting me much except heaps of trouble. I've spent time in the military jail because of my drug trip, and things don't look too rosy for the future. There are times when I'd like to be different, but I don't know how to do it. I've been a real loser all my life.

Where I'd Proceed with Manny from Here

Assuming that Manny is willing to at least take a look at the results of his behavior, I will challenge him to make a judgment about the degree to which his current behavior is paying off in terms of constructive outcomes. I may ask him to talk more about some of the ways he has been a failure, but I will emphasize the possibility that he can become a successful person—that his past failures do not have to determine what he will be in the future. Thus, I will be working on the assumption that his behavior is an attempt to fulfill his basic needs to be loved, to love others, and to feel a sense of self-worth. I will talk with him about how I see the evasion of personal responsibility as directly contributing to his identity as a failure. It is essential that I do not make a value judgment about his life *for* him, but rather that I continue to challenge *him* to do so. Thus, my attempts will be directed toward getting him to realistically appraise his behavior.

My major concern at this point is for Manny simply to see that nothing in his life will change unless he sees the need for change. He says that, although there are times when he would like to be different, he does not know how to go about it. This provides an excellent lead for a discussion of specific plans that could lead to constructive changes for him. Therefore, I will at least begin exploring with him some of the things he can do well, some of the things he likes, and some of the ways he would like to be different. My hope is that he will begin to consider possibilities for himself that he has previously ruled out. For example, in our discussion I find out that Manny would like to specialize in electronics, and he even admits having some talent in this area. I ask him to identify any of his talents and interests, and then I pursue those. This entails talking with him about the chances of enrolling in the Army's electronics program. If he agrees to look into the program, this will be a responsible action, for he will not just be moaning about his ill fate but doing something about changing this fate. Before our session ends, I hope to have a commitment from him to at least check out the program—and also to consider what he might get from further counseling.

Follow-Up: You Continue as Manny's Therapist

I saw Manny for one session. Assume that he does do some thinking about his life and that he does decide to give short-term counseling a try. He consults you and asks you to continue where he and I left off, using reality therapy as a base. How might you proceed with him?

1. First of all, how do you perceive Manny? What are your personal reactions to him? Does it make any difference that he has sought counseling with you voluntarily, rather than being sent by his commanding officer? How might you be affected by him differently if he were an involuntary client? Would you want to work with him? Why or why not?
2. What are your general impressions of and reactions to the way I worked with him? What would you do to further this work? What differences can you see in your style from mine in dealing with Manny (still staying in the reality-therapy perspective)?
3. What might you do or say to get a person such as Manny to look at his behavior and make a value judgment about it?
4. To what degree have you had life experiences that would allow you to identify with Manny's drug problem and his failures? If you have not had similar feelings of being "a loser," do you think you could be effective with him?
5. How might you respond to Manny as your client if he reacted to you in a flip and sarcastic manner?
6. Manny wants to talk about his past and the experiences that he thinks contributed to the person he is today. I kept focusing him on the present and on what he might do about his future. What do you think of such an approach? What are its possible merits and demerits?
7. This approach stresses the importance of a concrete plan of action and a commitment from the client to follow the plan. What might you say and do if Manny neither developed a concrete plan for change nor committed himself to the process of behavioral change? How might you attempt to get him to develop such a plan?
8. In my session with Manny I made it clear that I was interested mainly in his *behavior*, not in his feelings, not in changing his attitudes and beliefs, and not in helping him to acquire insight. What do you think of an approach that focuses so exclusively on one domain—in this case, behavior?

Recommended Supplementary Readings

What Are You Doing? How People Are Helped through Reality Therapy (1980) edited by N. Glasser (New York: Harper & Row) is a case book that gives readers a good sense of how reality therapy can be applied to working with a diverse range of clients.

Reality Therapy: A New Approach to Psychiatry (1965) by W. Glasser (New York: Harper & Row) outlines the basic concepts of reality therapy and gives examples of how this theory works in practice with delinquent girls, hospitalized psychotics, private clients, and the public schools.

Stations of the Mind (1981) by W. Glasser (New York: Harper & Row) deals with new directions of reality therapy and expands on Glasser's basic ideas. His thesis is that humans construct a unique personal world and that what happens in the real world has little significance unless it relates to what is already in one's personal world.

Take Effective Control of Your Life (1984) by W. Glasser (New York: Harper & Row) is a useful source for readers wanting an update of Glasser's thinking. The author develops the thesis that we always have control over what we do and that, if we come to understand how our behavior is an attempt to meet our needs, we can then find ways of taking control of our life.

Suggested Readings

Belkin, G. S. (1984). *Introduction to counseling* (2nd ed.). Dubuque, Iowa: William C. Brown (Chapter 9).

Corey, G. (1986). *Theory and practice of counseling and psychotherapy* (3rd ed.). Monterey, Calif.: Brooks/Cole (Chapter 10).

Corsini, R. (1984). *Current psychotherapies* (3rd ed.). Itasca, Ill.: Peacock (Chapter 9).

Gilliland, B., James, R., Roberts, G., & Bowman, J. (1984). *Theories and strategies in counseling and psychotherapy.* Englewood Cliffs, N.J.: Prentice-Hall (Chapter 9).

Hansen, J., Stevic, R., & Warner, R. (1986). *Counseling: Theory and process* (4th ed.). Boston: Allyn & Bacon (Chapter 9).

Prochaska, J. O. (1984). *Systems of psychotherapy: A transtheoretical analysis* (2nd ed.). Homewood, Ill.: Dorsey Press (Chapter 3).

Shilling, L. E. (1984). *Perspectives on counseling theories.* Englewood Cliffs, N.J.: Prentice-Hall (Chapter 6).

CHAPTER ELEVEN

Bringing the Approaches Together and Developing Your Own Therapeutic Style

This chapter focuses on ways to work with the themes of Ruth's life from a variety of therapeutic perspectives. I want to emphasize that one approach does not have a monopoly on the truth. There are many paths to the goal of providing Ruth with insight and mobilizing her resources so that she can take constructive action to give new direction to her life. These therapeutic perspectives can actually complement one another. Before demonstrating my own eclectic style with Ruth, I will review a few of the major themes that have been addressed in her therapy so far. Then I will accentuate some differences in working with these themes from various theoretical orientations. Some brief dialogues, with process commentaries, should give you a sense of the direction each of the therapists is taking. Although this format will highlight contrasts in therapeutic style, look for ways that you might develop your own style by combining the concepts and techniques of the various approaches.

Themes in Ruth's Life

A few of the major themes that have therapeutic potential for further exploration are revealed in the following statements that Ruth made at one time or another:

1. "You seem so distant and removed from me. You're hard to reach."
2. "In spite of my best attempts, I still feel a lot of guilt that I haven't done enough."
3. "I just don't trust myself to find my own answers to life."
4. "I'm afraid to change for fear of breaking up my marriage."
5. "It's hard for me to ask others for what I want."
6. "I feel extremely tense, and I can't sleep at night."
7. "All my life I've tried to get my father's approval."
8. "It's hard for me to have fun. I'm so responsible."
9. "I've always had a weight problem, and I can't seem to do much about it."
10. "I'm afraid to make mistakes and look like a fool."
11. "My daughter and I just don't get along with each other."
12. "I give and give, and they just take and take."
13. "I've lived by the expectations of others for so long that I don't know what I want anymore."
14. "I don't think my marriage is the way it should be, but my husband thinks it's just fine."
15. "I'm afraid to tell my husband what I really want with him, because I'm afraid he'll leave me."
16. "I fear punishment because I've given up my old religious values."
17. "I wear so many hats that sometimes I feel worn out."
18. "There's not enough time for me to be doing all the things I know I should be doing."
19. "I'm afraid of my feelings toward other men."
20. "When my children leave, I'll have nothing to live for."

Look over the list of Ruth's statements above. Select the ones that you find most interesting. Here are several suggestions for working with them: (1) For each of the themes you select, show how you would begin working with Ruth from *each* of the nine perspectives. (2) If you prefer, take only two contrasting approaches and focus on these. (3) You might want to attempt to combine several therapeutic models and work with Ruth using this synthesis.

Attempt to work with a few of Ruth's statements *before* reading about my eclectic way of working with her in this chapter. *After* you have read the examples provided below, and after you have completed the chapter, you could return to a few of her statements and try your hand at working with her again. This would make interesting and lively material for role playing and discussion in small groups. One person can "become" Ruth while others in the group counsel her from the vantage point of several different therapeutic perspectives. Practicing a variety of approaches will assist you in discovering for yourself ways to pull together techniques that you consider to be the best.

Below I select four of Ruth's themes and show how several therapeutic perspectives could be applied to each.

Theme: "I'm Afraid of My Feelings toward Other Men"

Psychoanalytic therapist's perspective

RUTH: I'm afraid of my feelings toward other men.

THERAPIST: What feelings come up as you think about men?

RUTH: Wanting to be close, but afraid of being put down.

THERAPIST: And being close would involve what?

RUTH: Oh, I'd be held, but I have to watch out that it doesn't go too far too fast.

THERAPIST: So you want to have a relationship with a man, but you're afraid of what might happen if you do. You're scared something will go wrong.

RUTH: Yes, and then I would feel as if I had caused it to go bad.

Then the analyst could ask Ruth to identify the roots of the theme embodied in her statement. The therapist will also make appropriate and timely interpretations. In this situation an interpretation could be that her emotions involving other men are resulting in guilt feelings that are related to her feelings toward her father.

TA therapist's perspective

RUTH: I'm afraid of my feelings toward other men.

THERAPIST: When you have feelings such as these, whose voices do you hear?

RUTH: My parents'.

THERAPIST: Whose voice is stronger?

RUTH: My father's.

THERAPIST: Quickly, without rehearsing, what are all the things he tells you?

RUTH: Don't be sexual. Don't feel. Sex is sacred and for marriage only. Don't have fun. Don't let me down. Don't shame the family.

THERAPIST: How old do you feel right now?

The therapist is pursuing early injunctions and helping her identify the ego states in which she is functioning.

Gestalt therapist's perspective

RUTH: I'm afraid of my feelings toward other men.

THERAPIST: I'm a man. How do you feel toward me? [A long silence follows.] Your face is flushed. Your hands are shaking. What are you experiencing now?

RUTH: I want to run and hide.

THERAPIST: Why don't you do that? Where do you want to run to?

RUTH: Behind the couch.

THERAPIST: OK, go over there and talk to me from there.

RUTH: Now I really feel foolish.

THERAPIST: So tell me about that.

The therapist stays in the here and now and goes with what is obvious, and he makes some assumptions. Rather than talking about other men outside, he focuses the attention on the fact that he is a man and makes the assumption that she may have feelings toward him because of their special relationship. He pays attention to her body language, makes no interpretations, and lets her tell him what her body language means. He does not push her to talk about her feelings toward him but goes with the flow of her feelings of foolishness.

Behavior therapist's perspective

RUTH: I'm afraid of my feelings toward other men.

THERAPIST: What feelings?

RUTH: Well, you know! [Silence.]

THERAPIST: No, I don't know.

RUTH: Well, I guess I do know—sexual feelings.

THERAPIST: Can you give an example of some recent sexual feelings?

RUTH: Well, I find one of the men in my class very attractive.

THERAPIST: And what do you do?

RUTH: Nothing—I avoid him.

THERAPIST: What would you like to do?

RUTH: I would like to talk to him, but I'm too scared.

THERAPIST: Close your eyes and imagine you're in that class. He sits in the chair next to you. What are you thinking and what do you want to do? List some of the things that you want to say to him?

RUTH: [She makes a list.]

THERAPIST: Out of this list, is there anything you'd be willing to say to him directly by next week?

RUTH: I'd be willing to say hello.

THERAPIST: Good, that's a start.

The therapist is paying attention to her lack of assertiveness and is establishing levels of fear and avoidance. After formulating specific plans the therapist would help her role-play assertive behaviors to be carried out in the real world.

Rational-emotive therapist's perspective

RUTH: I'm afraid of my feelings toward other men.

THERAPIST: And what are these feelings?

RUTH: Well, ah—sexual ones.

THERAPIST: So what about these sexual feelings?

RUTH: You know—you shouldn't have such feelings, especially if you're married.

THERAPIST: Why not? Where is it written?

RUTH: You shouldn't, because having sexual feelings could lead to something.

THERAPIST: You're *shoulding* on yourself. Where did you get all those *shoulds*?

RUTH: Well, my parents told me all my life . . .

THERAPIST: Just because your parents told you that you shouldn't have sexual feelings doesn't mean they're unquestionably right. I wonder what stops you from examining more closely what they told you and why you don't think and decide for yourself. Do you really accept everything that they told you? How does this affect your life?

Ruth is being challenged to critically evaluate beliefs that she clings to and now reindoctrinates herself with. Specifically, the challenge is to confront the irrational idea that having feelings of sexual attraction will actually lead to having sex, which she is implying. The therapist is likely to instruct Ruth to carry out a homework assignment to confront her fears. She could be asked to approach three men in her classes whom she finds attractive and then proceed to initiate a conversation with them. She is confronting an anxiety-producing situation in the hope that she will discover that her catastrophic expectations are groundless.

Theme: "You seem so distant and removed from me. You're hard to reach"

Person-centered therapist's perspective

RUTH: You seem so distant and removed. . . .

THERAPIST: I hear you saying that it's hard for you to get close to me and that I'm contributing a lot to that.

RUTH: Yeah, and in some ways I just feel removed from you. Like you're way up there, and I can't reach you.

THERAPIST: So I'm above you, and we don't have equal standing.

RUTH: I suppose if I knew more about you I might feel closer to you.

THERAPIST: Somehow knowing me would reduce that distance. I wish you did feel closer to me.

The therapist's rationale is that accurate reflection is assumed to lead to clarification, identification, expression, and deeper self-exploration of feelings. This therapist is likely to engage in relevant self-disclosure as a way to facilitate Ruth's self-exploration.

Existential therapist's perspective

RUTH: You seem so distant and removed. . . .

THERAPIST: I'm surprised to hear you say that, since I like you and feel very open to you.

RUTH: Really? Well, somehow that didn't come across to me.

THERAPIST: I'm a little uncomfortable with the way you see me, but I'm glad you feel free enough to bring this up. I encourage you to go further with this, because I see it as an important issue.

The therapist engages in appropriate self-disclosure and facilitates Ruth's discussion of how she sees and feels about their relationship. This relationship is what is central, not any technique that he might come up with at this point.

Psychoanalytic therapist's perspective

RUTH: You seem so distant and removed. . . .

THERAPIST: Hmm . . . [pausing pensively]

RUTH: See, you don't tell me much. I feel as if you're judging me now.

THERAPIST: Is that a feeling you've had often before?

A noncommital response is fostering the transference. The assumption is that Ruth is in some ways projecting onto the therapist qualities she felt toward other significant people in her life, particularly her father. The therapist will encourage her to express her feelings and then eventually interpret her reactions.

Gestalt therapist's perspective

RUTH: You seem so distant and removed. . . .

THERAPIST: If you were to move me physically right now, where would I be that would express how you see me in relationship to you?

RUTH: You'd be standing on top of your mahogany desk, looking down on me.

THERAPIST [standing on the desk and looking down on Ruth]: And how is it for you to look up at me?

The therapist is going with the clue Ruth has provided and is exaggerating a feeling. He may have her talk to him from below, he may ask her to guess what he is thinking and feeling about her, and so forth. He is likely to follow leads that she provides and ask her to get involved in experiments to see what she can learn about herself. His aim will be for her to take responsibility for her own feelings of distance, rather than making him responsible for how she feels.

Rational-emotive therapist's perspective

RUTH: You seem so distant and removed. . . .

THERAPIST: And what would be so terrible if I didn't feel close to you?

RUTH: Well, I wouldn't like that. I want you to like me and feel close to me. I want your approval.

THERAPIST: This is just the type of thinking that's getting and keeping you in trouble. You think others must like and approve of you.

The therapist will show Ruth how her irrational beliefs about the necessity of being liked and approved of are now contributing to the negative feelings she has and how such beliefs stop her from taking many actions in the real world. The challenge will be for her to risk being not liked and not approved of.

Theme: "When My Children Leave, I'll Have Nothing to Live For"

For this theme, the probable approach of therapists from all nine disciplines is summarized in Table 11–1.

Adlerian therapist's perspective

RUTH: When my children leave, I'll have nothing to live for.

THERAPIST: How did you get to the point that you would make such a statement? What does making such a statement do for you?

RUTH: Well, all my life I've lived for my children.

THERAPIST: How have you done this?

RUTH: I've always been more interested in them than myself. I've worked very hard to make life better for them than I had it. I've never made time for myself.

THERAPIST: It sounds to me as if once your children leave, you'll have a lot of time for yourself.

RUTH [unenthusiastically]: Yeah, I know.

THERAPIST: How is it that having more time for yourself in the future is making you sad rather than excited?

RUTH: When they're gone, I'm afraid there will be a void.

THERAPIST: So together let's be creative and see how we can fill this void. As a starter, how would you finish this sentence? "Something I always wanted to do and never had time for is . . ." [This therapist is interested in Ruth's goals for her future. Rather than going with her sense of discouragement, the emphasis is on creating new goals that will give meaning to life. The encouragement process helps her formulate new purposes to replace values that are no longer functional.]

RUTH: Something I always wanted to do and never had time for is going hiking and camping in the Smoky Mountains with friends.

THERAPIST: A while back, I saw seven out of ten waterfalls in the Smokies on a one-day hike I took with a friend. So this sounds good to me. I'm wondering what has stopped you from doing this.

RUTH: Hmm—I don't even know if I have any friends who would want to do that with me.

THERAPIST: Do you have any idea how you could find out?

RUTH: I suppose I could ask them.

THERAPIST: When are you going to do so, and whom will you ask?

The therapist is pursuing the importance of *social interest*, which Ruth has neglected. This would be a good place to continue discussing ways that she could become reacquainted with old friends, make new friends, and broaden her interests.

Reality therapist's perspective

RUTH: When my children leave, I'll have nothing to live for.

THERAPIST: What are you living for now?

RUTH: My children, of course. For years I've lived for them and done everything I could for them. [Ruth then goes on, with much energy, listing all the ways in which she has been a devoted mother.]

THERAPIST: Stop, Ruth. It's not very helpful to you to talk about how you've been in the past. What's more important is for you to take a look at what you're *doing now*. If your behavior isn't bringing about the results you want, we can talk about how you'll change.

RUTH: But I don't know what to do differently.

THERAPIST: Well, first of all, do you really want to change the way things are?

The therapist does not let Ruth bemoan the past but quickly gets her to look at how well her present behavior is working for her. Once she makes the decision that her life is not the way she wants it, therapy can begin. She first determines what she wants to change, and then together they make realistic plans pertaining to the *what*, *how*, and *when* of these changes. It is essential that she make a commitment to follow through with her plans.

Existential therapist's perspective

RUTH: When my children leave, I'll have nothing to live for.

THERAPIST: I know what you mean. I myself have had to struggle with finding a new purpose to life after having lost someone.

RUTH: They're not even gone yet, and I'm already missing them.

THERAPIST: Tell me some of the ways in which you'll miss them.

RUTH: I'll miss hearing about their ups and downs. Even my sons come to me with their problems and want my advice. And when they're gone . . . [After a heavy silence she tearfully continues.] It's so hard to let them go.

THERAPIST: I know, it never is easy.

RUTH: It feels good that you understand.

THERAPIST: And I'm glad I can be with you.

The therapist here offers the gift of presence and understanding and engages in selected self-disclosure.

TA therapist's perspective

RUTH: When my children leave, I'll have nothing to live for.

THERAPIST: What tape are you playing now?

RUTH: Without my kids I'm nothing.

THERAPIST: How is this tape working for you?

RUTH: Not very well. It's just that I feel as if I want to die when I think of them gone from my life. Who will I be without them?

THERAPIST: You say your decision to live for your children isn't paying off for you. Do you want to make a different tape?

RUTH: It just seems so hard. I'm not sure I can get rid of these voices in my head. Sometimes I get so down I just don't want to be alive any more.

THERAPIST: Can you tell me more?

RUTH: It's hard for me to talk about, because some of my thoughts scare me. You know, sometimes it seems that life is so complicated, and I wonder what it would be like if I didn't have to struggle any more.

THERAPIST: Have you thought about ways you would end your life?

RUTH: Not really. It's just a fleeting thought. You know, I would never actually take my own life.

The therapist attempts to establish if she is seriously suicidal by asking further questions pertaining to her fantasies as well as any previous suicidal plans or attempts.

Theme: "I Had a Dream Last Week That I Want to Share"

Rational-emotive therapist's perspective

RUTH: I had a dream last week that I want to share. I was in San Francisco. I think I was with my brother-in-law. There were some other people in the dream. I think my kids were there. I was walking up a very steep street. It was very dangerous. I was afraid I was going to fall. I kept on going up. Nobody else seemed to be scared. The street ended at the top of the hill against a house. The only way I could cross the street was to hold onto holes and handles on the house wall. It was very scary. The handles seemed to come loose, and there were things in the holes. One time I thought I saw a snake, but I'm not sure. I think there were spiders. I was afraid and I wondered why I was putting myself through this. I was looking inside a window, and I saw a man in there reading. I wondered if he would be mad at me for intruding on his privacy. But he didn't look at me, and I didn't know who it was. When I finally crossed the street, I realized that I had left my purse on the other side. I again walked across to get my purse. I wondered why I was all alone and where everyone else had gone. There was something else about a funeral procession that I was going to watch, but I don't remember any more.

THERAPIST: Well, for the life of me, I don't know why you're telling me all this. Is this the way you want to spend your money in here?

RUTH: That makes me mad. Why did you listen to my dream if you weren't interested in it?

THERAPIST: Well, frankly I wasn't really listening, but *you* seemed to enjoy it. [It is obvious that this therapist is not therapeutically interested in listening to her dreams and is willing to let her know about his lack of interest and boredom.]

RUTH: Now I feel horrible. I shouldn't have gotten mad at you.

THERAPIST: Why not?

RUTH: You know what you're doing. And besides, I feel foolish.

THERAPIST: You mean you have no right to get angry at me? And what's so bad about feeling foolish? I know you don't feel great right now, but is the world going to end because of what just happened?

The therapist changes direction away from the dream and toward her beliefs about expressing anger and feeling foolish.

Gestalt therapist's perspective

RUTH: I had a dream . . .

THERAPIST: Ruth, continue telling me the dream, but speak as if it were happening right now.

Table 11–1. How nine therapists might deal with Ruth's concern about her children's leaving

Theory	*Therapist's General Direction*
Psychoanalytic therapy	Therapist may focus on unconscious meanings of children in Ruth's life. What are her fears of being without her children? How does taking care of her children ward off anxiety?
Adlerian therapy	Therapist may work with Ruth's general purpose in life. What are her goals? What are her strivings? How has she made a life-style of taking care of and serving others? Focus could also be on what Ruth learned in her parents' family.
Existential therapy	Therapist may be willing to share his or her own experiences and views with Ruth. They will engage in dialogue, as the relationship between client and therapist is central in helping her search for a meaning in life. How will she create meaning without children?
Person-centered therapy	Therapist trusts that Ruth can find her own direction, that she will be able to establish a new meaning in her life once her children leave. This approach will stress listening and understanding as she shares her struggles and fears.
Gestalt therapy	Therapist is likely to ask what Ruth is experiencing now as she reports that she will have nothing to live for when her children are gone. Direction depends on the verbal and nonverbal clues that Ruth provides. If she begins to cry, therapist may ask her to stay with her tears and feel fully whatever she is experiencing.
Transactional analysis	Therapist is likely to explore messages that Ruth has accepted about being a mother. What early decisions did she make about her worth as a person apart from serving others? How is taking care of her children fitting into her life script? Does she want to make a new decision? What kind of contract is Ruth willing to make?
Behavior therapy	Therapist may zero in more carefully on what it specifically means to Ruth that she "will have nothing to live for" when her children are gone. Concrete goals need to be established, and only then can treatment proceed.
Rational-emotive therapy	Therapist is likely to challenge Ruth's beliefs about having no purpose in living. What assumptions is she making? Are they rational and realistic? Focus will be on how her thinking influences her feelings, not just on dealing with the children's leaving.
Reality therapy	Therapist may get Ruth to look at what rewards she receives from living for children. She will be helped to determine if such behavior is working well for her. If Ruth determines that she would like to find meaning apart from her children, therapist will work with her to develop plan that will lead to doing something else.

The therapist listens to the dream, paying close attention to Ruth's nonverbals. She notices that Ruth shows the most emotion on realizing that everyone has gone and that she is all alone. The therapist brings her back to that moment and asks her to relive it. She instructs Ruth to talk out loud to the people who have left her, telling them how she feels. Later on, she asks Ruth to "become" those people who are not there and let them speak to Ruth. The therapist is tuned in to Ruth's emotional energy as a place to explore the dream. She goes not only with Ruth's energy but also with her own interest. None of the directions is right or wrong, for all aspects of Ruth's dream are a projection of herself. Ruth can learn a lot from giving voice to and "becoming" the people and the inanimate objects in the dream. The purse, the steep street, the holes, the handles, the things that she does not remember, the blocked-out funeral—all of these parts have significance. She will learn the meanings of her dream by becoming all these parts and acting them out. She discovers the meaning of her own dream, not the therapist's interpretation of it.

Psychoanalytic therapist's perspective

RUTH: [She recites the dream.]

THERAPIST: Ruth, you said something about a funeral in your dream, but you don't remember. Close your eyes and say whatever comes to mind.

The therapist encourages her to ramble without censoring while he pays close attention to any hesitancy on her part, changes in her voice, repetition of themes, and blockings. He is likely to be interested in the parts in her dream that she is not sure about or has forgotten, for to him, these indicate resistance. The focus may be on the unknown man in the room or her fear of having interrupted him, the lack of certainty about her children and brother-in-law having been there, the snake and spiders that she thinks were there, the vague memory of the funeral, and so forth. He is likely to make interpretations about the symbolism of her dream, which will foster her insight into her unconscious fears and wishes. It is the therapist who points out parallels and meanings in Ruth's dream, rather than her.

Adlerian therapist's perspective

RUTH: I had a dream last week that I want to share . . .

THERAPIST: Does this dream fit into any of your other dreams?

RUTH: Yeah, I often have the feeling that I'm in dangerous situations, but I'm the only one who feels scared. Other people don't seem to think the situation is so dangerous.

THERAPIST: Are there any other patterns here that reoccur in your other dreams?

RUTH: I often forget parts of my dreams. There are many times that I feel left alone in my dreams. And I often wake up crying and scared.

THERAPIST: So there is some consistency with this and other dreams. Let's talk more about how your dream might be connected to the present course of your life.

The therapist sees dreams as purposeful, as reminders of what the person is about and what the person expects to do. Dreams are seen as valuable in that they are rehearsals for future behavior, and they express the unity and consistency of the individual. It is assumed that, if Ruth wants to postpone action, she will forget the dream. Thus, attention could be directed to what actions she is hesitating over and what she is afraid of in her future. Identifying her dreams could serve the purpose of bringing problems to the surface and pointing to her movement in therapy.

My Approach to Working with Ruth

I will now work toward an integration of concepts and techniques from the various schools of therapy by demonstrating the progression of Ruth's counseling. I will then ask you to work with Ruth by drawing particular aspects from each of the models and applying them to her.

Each therapy approach has something unique to offer in understanding Ruth. My attempt will be to use a combination of approaches by working with her on a *feeling*, *thinking*, and *behaving* basis. Table 11–2 shows what I am likely to borrow from each of the therapies as I conceptualize Ruth's case. As I describe how I imagine I would proceed with her, based on the information presented in her autobiography and the additional data from the nine theory chapters, I will make parenthetical comments that indicate from what theoretical orientations I am borrowing concepts and techniques in any given piece of work. Thus, in addition to seeing a sample of my style of working with Ruth, you will have a running commentary on what I am doing, why I am using particular techniques, and what directions I am going in. As you read, think about what you might do that is similar to or different from my approach.

Initial Stages of Work with Ruth

I often feel somewhat anxious as I think about meeting a new client. I wonder what the experience will be like, for both of us. I wonder to what degree I will be present for the person and how I might be instrumental in helping him or her become aware of the choices that are possible. I imagine that, if I had read Ruth's autobiography before our initial session, I would feel excited about working with her. I like her ability to pinpoint many of her concerns, and the data she provides are rich with possibilities. From these data alone, I do not have a clear idea of where our journey together will take us, for a lot will depend on *how far* she wants to go and *what* she is willing to explore. From the data alone, though, I do have many ideas of how I want to proceed.

Our beginning. I assume that Ruth, too, has some anxiety about initiating therapy. I want to provide her with the opportunity to talk about what it is like for her to come to the office today. That in itself provides the direction for part of our session. I surely want to get an idea of what has brought her to therapy. What is going on in her life that motivates her to seek therapy? What does she most hope for as a result of this venture? I structure the initial session so that she can talk about her expectations and about her fears, hopes, ambivalent feelings, and so forth. Because I will be an important part of the therapy process, I give her the chance to ask me personally and professionally how I will work with her. I do not believe in making therapy into a mysterious adventure. I think that clients have a right to know about the process that they are about to become involved with. Further, I think that Ruth will get more from her therapy if she knows how it works, if she knows the nature of her responsibilities and mine, and if she is clear on what she wants from this process. (This way of thinking is typical of models such as transactional analysis, Adlerian therapy, behavior therapy, rational-emotive therapy, and reality therapy.)

The contract. Again drawing on the above-mentioned models, I begin formulating a working contract, one that will give some direction to our sessions. As a part of this contract, I discuss what I see as my main responsibilities and functions, as well as

Table 11–2. Major areas of focus in Ruth's therapy

Orientation	*Areas of focus*
Psychoanalytic therapy	My focus will be on ways that Ruth is repeating her early past in her present relationships. I have a particular interest in how she brings her experiences with her father into the session with me. I will concentrate on her feelings for me, because working with transference is a major way to produce insight. I am also interested in her dreams, any resistance that shows up in the sessions, and other clues to her unconscious processes. One of my main goals is to assist her in bringing to awareness buried memories and experiences, which I assume have a current influence on her.
Adlerian therapy	My focus is on determining what Ruth's life-style is. To do this, I will examine her early childhood experiences through her early recollections and family constellation. My main interest is in determining what her goals and priorities in life are. I assume that what she is striving toward is equally as valid as her past dynamics. Therapy will consist of doing a comprehensive assessment, helping her understand her dynamics, and then helping her define new goals.
Existential therapy	My focus is on challenging the meaning in Ruth's life. What does she want in her life? I am interested in the anxiety she feels, her emptiness, and the ways in which she has allowed others to choose for her. How can she begin to exercise her freedom? I assume that our relationship will be a key factor in helping her take actual risks in changing.
Person-centered therapy	I will avoid planning and structuring the sessions, because I trust Ruth to initiate a direction for therapy. If I listen, reflect, empathize, and respond to her, she will be able to clarify her struggles. Although she may be only dimly aware of her feelings at the beginning of therapy, she will move toward increased clarity as I accept her fully, without judgment. My main focus is on creating a climate of openness, trust, caring, understanding, and acceptance. Then Ruth can use this relationship to move forward and grow.

Table 11–2. Major areas of focus in Ruth's therapy (*continued*)

Orientation	*Areas of focus*
Gestalt therapy	My focus will be on noticing signs of unfinished business for Ruth, as evidenced by ways in which she reaches impasses in her therapy. If she has never worked through her feelings of not being accepted, then it is likely that these issues will appear in her therapy. I will ask her to bring these unfinished issues into the present by reliving them, rather than by merely talking about past events. I am mainly interested in helping her to experience her feelings fully, instead of developing insight or speculating about why she behaves as she does. The key focus is on *how* she is behaving and *what* she is experiencing.
Transactional analysis	My focus will be on reviewing with Ruth the messages she received and the early decisions she made in response to those parental injunctions. I hope she will be able to understand the life script that was written for her by others, so that she can begin to write this script anew.
Behavior therapy	My initial focus is on doing a thorough assessment of Ruth's current behavior. I will ask her to monitor what she is doing so that we can have baseline data. We will then develop concrete goals to guide our work, and I will draw on a wide range of cognitive and behavioral techniques to help her achieve her goals—for example, stress-reduction techniques, assertion training, role rehearsals, modeling, coaching, systematic desensitization, and relaxation methods. I will stress learning new coping behaviors that she can use in everyday situations. She will practice these in our sessions and elsewhere.
Rational-emotive therapy	My interest will be focused on Ruth's internal dialogue and her thinking processes. I will uncover the ways in which she is creating her own misery through self-indoctrination and retention of beliefs that are not rational or functional. By use of Socratic dialogue, I will try to get her to spot her faulty thinking, to learn ways of correcting her distortions, and to substitute more effective self-statements and beliefs. I would be willing to use a wide range of cognitive, behavioral, and emotive techniques to accomplish our goals.
Reality therapy	Our focus will be guided by the eight steps in reality therapy. First we will become friends, or work on our relationship. Key questions are "What are you doing now?" and "Is this behavior helping you?" Once Ruth has made a value judgment about her own current behavior, we will make plans. I will get a commitment from her to follow through with these plans and will never accept excuses.

Ruth's responsibilities in the process. I want her to know at the outset that I expect her to be an *active* party in this relationship, and I tell her that I function in an active and directive way (which is characteristic of most of the cognition/behavior/action-oriented therapies).

I see therapy as a significant project—an investment in self, if you will—and I think that Ruth has a right to know what she can expect to gain as well as some of the potential risks. I begin by getting some sense of her goals, and though they are vague at first, I work with her to get them as specific and concrete as possible. (This process is especially important in TA, Adlerian therapy, behavior therapy, rational-emotive therapy, and reality therapy.) I will come back to goals in a bit.

Letting Ruth tell her story. I do *not* begin with a gathering of life-history data, though I do think this is important. I see value in first letting Ruth tell her story in the way she chooses. The way in which she walks into the office, her nonverbal language, her mannerisms, her style of speech, the details that she chooses to go into, and what she decides to relate and not to relate provide me with a valuable perspective from which to understand her. I am interested in how she perceives the events in her life and how she feels in her subjective world. (This is especially important in the existential and person-centered models.) If I do too much structuring initially, I interfere with her typical style of presenting herself. So I give everything to listening and letting her know what I am hearing (something that person-centered therapists put a premium on, and something I especially value in the initial stages of therapy). I want to avoid the tendency to talk too much during this initial session. It is not easy paying full attention to Ruth, yet doing so will pay rich dividends in terms of the potential for therapy. If I listen well, I will get a good sense of what she is coming to therapy for. If I fail to listen accurately and sensitively, then there is a risk of going with the first problem she states instead of waiting and listening to discover the depth of her experience.

Gathering data. I mentioned earlier that I would not begin the session by asking Ruth a series of questions pertaining to her life history. After letting her tell her story in her way, I ask questions to fill in the gaps. This method gives a more comprehensive picture of how she views her life now, as well as events that she considers significant in her past. Rather than making it a question-and-answer session, I like the idea of using an *autobiographical approach*, in which she writes about the critical turning points in her life, events from her childhood and adolescent years, relationships with parents and siblings, school experiences, current struggles, and future goals and aspirations, to mention a few. I ask her what she thinks would be useful for her to recall and focus on and what she imagines would be useful to me in gaining a better picture of her subjective world. In this way, she does some reflecting and sorting out of life experiences outside of the session; she takes an active role in deciding what her personal goals will be for therapy; and I have access to rich material that will give me ideas of where and how to proceed with her. (This unstructured, or open-ended, autobiography could fit into the existential and the person-centered models, in which the emphasis is on the subjective world of the client. Also, psychoanalytic practitioners would want to know a lot about her developmental history.)

In addition to asking Ruth to write an autobiography, I find value in a structured questionnaire in which she can complete sentences about the course of her life. (For such an exercise I use a modified version of the life-script questionnaire used in transactional analysis.) I suggest that Ruth do both the autobiography and the life-script questionnaire *at home*. Then, as a follow-up procedure, we discuss what this was like for her and anything that it brought up in her. This helps her clarify issues that face her, and it gives me a clear picture of the life forces that have influenced her.

From the Adlerian perspective I am interested in getting background information of Ruth's experiences in her family. Of special interest are her early memories and her perceptions of her family life. I pay attention to the factors that shaped her style of life. We focus on her life goals and how she has sought ways to compensate for her perceived inferiority as a child. Together we summarize the material from her life-style assessment, interpret her basic mistakes, and discuss her assets as well as her limitations. Then we develop a contract to guide our work.

Therapy Proceeds

I favor integrating cognitive work into therapy sessions, and because I see therapy as a *learning* experience, I recommend some books to Ruth to supplement her therapy. These may include novels, books that deal with central areas of concern to her personally, and something on the nature of therapy. For example, I suggest that she read some books about women (and men) facing mid-life crises, about parent/child relationships, about enhancing one's marriage, about sex, and about special topics related to her concerns. (This is consistent with approaches such as TA, behavior therapy, reality therapy, and, especially, rational-emotive therapy.) I find that this type of reading provides a good catalyst for self-examination, especially if these books are read in a *personal way*—meaning that Ruth would apply their themes to her life.

Clarifying therapy goals. During the beginning stages I assist Ruth in getting a clearer grasp of what she most wants from therapy, as well as seeing some steps she can begin to take in attaining her objectives. Like most clients she is rather global in stating her goals in her autobiography, so I work with her on becoming more concrete. When she looks in the mirror, Ruth says, she does not like what she sees. She would like to have a better self-image and be more confident. I am interested in knowing specifically *what* she does not like, the ways in which she now lacks confidence, and what it feels like for her to confront herself by looking at herself and talking to me about what she sees.

Ruth reports that she is unassertive and would like to be more assertive. She can be helped to pinpoint specific instances in which she is not assertive and to describe what she actually does or does not do in such circumstances and how she feels at these times. We consistently move from general to specific, for the more concrete she is, the greater are her chances for attaining what she wants. (It is from the behavior-therapy approach that I have learned the value of specifying goals for therapy. Also, TA stresses the necessity of a contract, which includes a clear statement of what the client wants from therapy.) I do not hold rigidly to the idea of a contract, although I do think that this is a good place to begin with Ruth. As therapy proceeds, then, we both have a frame of reference for evaluating the degree to which she is getting what she came to therapy for.

Importance of the client/therapist relationship. I am convinced that one of the most significant factors determining the degree to which Ruth will attain her goals in therapy is the therapeutic relationship that she and I will create. (This element is given primary emphasis in the person-centered, existential, Adlerian, and Gestalt approaches. Therapy is not seen as something that the therapist *does to* a passive client. It is much more than implementing skills and techniques. It is a deeply *personal* relationship that Ruth can use for her learning.) Thus, I think that the person who I am is just as important as my knowledge of counseling theory and the level of my skill development. Although I see it as essential that I am able to use techniques effectively—and that I have a theoretical base from which to draw a range of techniques—this becomes meaningless in the absence of a relationship between Ruth and myself that is characterized by a mutual respect and trust. (I am influenced by the person-centered approach, which emphasizes the personal characteristics and attitudes of the therapist. Some questions I see as vital are the following: To what degree can I be real with Ruth? To what degree can I hear what she says and accept her in a nonjudgmental way? To what degree can I respect and care for her? To what degree can I allow myself to enter her subjective world? To what degree am I aware of my own experiencing as I am with Ruth, and how willing am I to share my feelings and thoughts with her?) I can help Ruth to the degree that I am authentic myself with her. This relationship is vital at the initial stages of therapy, but it must be maintained during all stages if therapy is to be effective.

Working with Ruth in Cognitive, Emotive, and Behavioral Ways

As I mentioned earlier, my eclectic style is a blend of concepts and techniques from many therapeutic approaches. As a basis for selecting techniques to employ with Ruth, I look at her as a *feeling, thinking,* and *behaving* person. Although for purposes of teaching in this illustration I may have to describe the various aspects of what I am doing separately, do keep in mind that I tend to work in an integrated fashion. Thus, I would *not* work with Ruth's feelings, then move ahead to her cognitions, and finally proceed to behaviors and specific action programs. All of these dimensions would be interrelated. When I am working with Ruth on a cognitive level (such as dealing with decisions she has made or one of her values), I am also concerned about the feelings generated in her at the moment and about exploring them with her. And in the background I am thinking of what she might actually *do* about the thoughts and feelings she is expressing. This *doing* would involve new behaviors that she can try in the session to deal with a problem and new skills that she can take outside and apply to problems that she encounters in real-life situations. (As a basis for this eclectic style of working with Ruth I am drawing on the cognitive and emotional insight-oriented approach of psychoanalysis; on the experiential therapies, which stress the expression and experiencing of feelings; on the cognitive therapies, which pay attention to the client's cognitive structures, to thinking processes that affect behavior, and to beliefs;

and to the action-oriented therapies, which stress the importance of creating a plan for behavioral change.)

Exploring Ruth's fears related to therapy. Ruth begins a session by talking about her fears of coming to know herself and by expressing her ambivalent feelings toward therapy. She says: "Before I made the decision to enter therapy, I had worked pretty hard at keeping problems tucked away neatly. I lived by compartmentalizing my life, and that way nothing became so fearsome that I felt overwhelmed. But this reading that I'm doing, writing in my journal, thinking about my life, talking about my feelings and experiences in here—all this is making me uncomfortable. I'm getting more and more anxious. I suppose I'm afraid of what I might find inside of me if I keep searching."

I see this anxiety as something realistic, and I surely do not want to merely reassure Ruth that everything will turn out for the best if she will only trust me and stay in therapy. I want to explore in depth with her the *decision* that she must *now* make. Looking at her life in an honest way *is* potentially frightening. There *are* risks attached to this process. Although Ruth has security now, she pays the price in terms of boredom and low self-respect. Yet her restricted existence is a safe one. The attractions of getting to know herself better and the possibilities for exercising choice and control in her life can be very exciting, yet also frightening. At this point I hope that she will look at this issue and take a stand on how much she wants for herself and the risks that she is willing to take in reaching for more. The following dialogue between Ruth and me will give you a sense of how I pursue this issue.

RUTH: I want to stay in therapy, but I'm wondering if I want to go through all the pain I'm afraid I'll have to face.

JERRY: What is this pain you fear?

RUTH: The pain of feeling empty so much of the time. And the fear that if I take a good look I'm going to find that I'm nothing but a hollow reflection of what everyone expects of me. There will be nothing of *me!*

JERRY: I'd like for you to imagine that what you fear *does* come true. What's the most horrible thing you can imagine you'd find?

RUTH: That what I am is nothing. Like an onion—I keep peeling away layers, only at the center there's no substance. I just keep peeling away layers of pretenses.

JERRY: OK, with your eyes closed let yourself peel away layer after layer of pretenses. Each layer you peel off, say out loud what you're peeling away.

RUTH: I'm peeling away my niceness. I'm polite on the outside, but on the inside I don't feel so nice.

JERRY: Keep peeling away as many layers as you can.

RUTH: Now I'll peel away my "good-girl" mask. I appear so good. I'd never do or say anything to offend or shock anyone. I'll be exactly what Father expects. But that's a mask so you can't see what's inside of me. Next layer—I'm peeling away the "devoted-mother" mask. All my life I've given and sacrificed for the sake of my children, getting nothing from it for myself.

JERRY: How about peeling away more of those masks.

RUTH: I'm peeling away my layers of fat. I hide behind my fat. I'm so fat that you won't look at me.

JERRY: You're smiling. Is that funny?

RUTH: That's another layer. I hide behind my smile. That way people won't see what's inside. I don't want people to see my hurt—so I'll smile.

JERRY: What are you feeling now?

RUTH: I'm scared. I've peeled away some layers, and now you can see me. And I'm scared you won't like what you see.

JERRY: What are you *most* scared of? Will you let yourself talk about your worst fear?

RUTH: I'm most afraid that what's inside of me is ugly—that inside of me is an evil witch, filled with poison.

JERRY: OK, let yourself be that evil witch and hex me. Talk to me from that side. What would you be saying to me?

RUTH: I'm evil—and deadly. If I get near you, I'll put a curse on you. I'll make you think I'm lovely, and when you get near me, then I'll trap you in a web, and I'll strangle you. And I'm afraid of becoming so dependent on you that if you leave or desert me, I'll be left with even more emptiness.

JERRY: Would you open your eyes and look at me and tell me what's going on inside of you now?

RUTH: That's the side of me I'm afraid to show anyone. If I show you what's inside of me, you may hate me. So I work hard at hiding—from you and from me. And I'm so tired of being afraid that you'll discover what I'm really like.

So far I have been working with Ruth to *experience feelings* that she keeps locked up for fear that she will see her own hate and vengeance. At this point we talk over how it feels for her to have come into contact with a part of her that she hides and how it feels to have shown me that side of her. (I have relied heavily on experiential techniques, especially Gestalt ones, as a way of getting her in contact with parts of herself that she represses.) I discuss with her the fact that she does have a choice—to stay in therapy and face those demons, or not to look at them. (I am working within an existential framework that puts choice and responsibility in a central place.)

Ruth decides to continue. Being in therapy is a series of choices. Not only does therapy open Ruth up to new possibilities by expanding her awareness and thus widening the brackets of her freedom to choose, but she makes choices all during the therapy process itself. I respect her choices, and I support her when she is struggling with difficult ones; I also push her gently and invite her to ask for more and take more risks. Ultimately, she is the one who decides many times during our sessions the depth to which she is willing to go. (This is very much an existential concept.)

Ruth works to become free. Assume that Ruth says: "All my life I've felt unfree. I've had to be the person that my parents wanted me to be, I've had to be the wife that John expected me to be, and I've had to be what my kids expected as a mother. I'd like to be free and feel that I can live for me, but so far I don't seem to be able to."

There are any number of ways that I might go further with Ruth's feeling of being unfree. I suggest the following to her:

"Ruth, between now and our next session I'd like to suggest that you do several things. In your journal let yourself imagine all the ways you've felt unfree in your life. Just write down phrases or short sentences. It might help if you could write down messages that you've heard from your parents. What have they said they wanted of you? It might help if you actually imagine that you *are* for a time your father and just write as fast as you can all the things he might say about all he expects. Then let yourself write to Ruth as your mother. Again, without thinking much, just let her words and thoughts come to the paper. If you do that several times this week, we can pursue it more next week."

(Here is the idea of "homework assignments," borrowed from the cognitive and behavioral therapies; only I am stressing the feelings that go with such an exercise. In this way Ruth can review some parental messages, and I hope she will stir up some old feelings associated with these memories.)

At the following session Ruth brings her journal and says she would like to talk about what it was like to write herself letters (as her father and as her mother), saying all that was expected of her. I ask her to share what this was like, and I pay attention to her body as well as her words. (Like the Gestaltist, I think that the truth of one's messages is conveyed in voice inflections, postures, facial features, and the like. If I listen *only* to her words, I am likely to miss a deeper level of meaning. Like the person-centered therapist, I value *listening* to what she is feeling and expressing.) Although I think it is important that I reflect and clarify (a person-centered technique), I deem it crucial that I bring myself into a dialogue with Ruth. If I am having reactions to what she is saying or if she is touching something within me, sharing with her my present experience can facilitate her work. (This is valued in both the existential and the person-centered approaches.) My own disclosure, at timely and appropriate moments, can lead to a deeper self-exploration on Ruth's part. I must take care not to disclose merely for its own sake; nor is it well to take the focus off of Ruth. But even a few words can let her know that I understand her.

Ruth is talking about her mother's messages to her. As I listen to her, I notice that there is a critical tone and a sharpness to her voice, and she makes a pointing gesture with her finger. I get an idea that I want to pursue, and I say:

"Ruth, would you sit in this red rocking chair? Actually rock back and forth, and with a very critical voice—pointing your finger and shaking it—deliver a lecture to Ruth, who is sitting in this other chair."

Ruth does as I ask: "I want you to work hard and never complain. Look at how I've slaved, and look at how moral I've been. Life is hard, girl, and don't forget that. You're put on earth here to see if you can pass the test. This life is merely a testing place. Bear all your burdens well, and you'll be rewarded in the next life—where it counts! Work hard! Keep pure—in mind, spirit, and body. Look what I've done in life—you can too."

There are many possibilities of places to go from here. (So far I have been using a Gestalt technique of asking her to "become" her mother in the hope that she can actually *feel* what this brings up in her as she relives the scene.) I ask her to sit in the other chair and be Ruth and respond to her mother's lecture. The dialogue can continue with an exchange between Mother and Ruth, and finally I ask her to stop and process what has gone on. This can also be done with her father.

We work on Ruth's cognitions. I see Gestalt techniques as very useful for assisting Ruth to get an experiential sense of what might be called "toxic introjects." These are the messages and values that she has swallowed whole without digesting and without making her own. My goal is to help her externalize these introjections so that she can take a critical look at them. If what she has swallowed is toxic, then in doing so she is poisoning herself and killing herself. I have an investment in getting her to look at this process and make her values truly her own. (This is very much an existential notion. Authenticity consists of living by one's own values, not living blindly by values given by others.)

So, I ask Ruth to identify as many messages as she can that she recalls having received as a child. She recollects parental messages such as *Don't think for yourself. Follow the church obediently, and conform your will to God's will. Never question the Bible. Live a moral life. Don't get close to people, especially in sexual ways. Always be proper and appropriate.*

In addition to working with Ruth's feelings, I find it essential to work with her *cognitive structures*, which include her belief systems, her thoughts, her attitudes, and her values. (In transactional analysis attention would be given to "parental tapes," or injunctions, and early decisions; in behavior therapy attention would be given to her cognitive structures—or beliefs and assumptions that have an influence on her behavior; in rational-emotive therapy attention would be paid to irrational beliefs and self-indoctrination; in Adlerian therapy we would look at her basic mistakes; and in reality therapy the focus would be on values.) Whatever terms are used, I tend to focus on the underlying messages that Ruth pays attention to now in her life. I assume that her self-talk is relevant to her behavior.

Ruth brings up her father. As we explore the messages that Ruth was reared with, one theme seems to emerge. She has lived much of her life in ways that were designed to get her father's approval. She feels that, unless she gets her father's acceptance and approval, she will never have "arrived." She reasons that, if the father who conceived her could not love her, then nobody ever could. If *this* man does not show her love, then she is doomed to live a loveless life! I proceed by getting her to look at the conclusions that she has drawn from such limited data. (Here I rely largely on Adlerian, TA, and rational-emotive concepts and techniques to get her to critically evaluate some invalid assumptions she continues to make.)

As much as possible without pushing Ruth away, I challenge and confront her thinking and her value system, which appear to be at the root of much of her conflict. It is not so much a matter of my imposing my values on her; rather, it is a matter of getting her to look at beliefs and values that she has accepted to determine if she still wants to base her life on them. Does she want to spend the rest of her life in a futile attempt to "win over" her father? Does she want to continue making all men into her father? What will it take for her to finally gain her father's acceptance and love—if this is possible? What might she think of the person she had to become to gain his acceptance? I take this line of questioning in an attempt to get her to *think*, to *challenge* herself, and to *decide* for herself her standards for living. (This is an existential concept, and therapies such as rational-emotive therapy and TA are based on this kind of critical evaluation. I want Ruth to see that she does not have to live forever by the decisions she made as a child and by the beliefs that she uncritically accepted out of fear. TA would stress the notion of making new decisions, or the redecision process. Rational-emotive therapy would stress demolishing irrational beliefs, interrupting the self-indoctrination process that keeps them alive now, and replacing them with a sane and rational philosophy of life. In working with Ruth, I am very heavily influenced by such concepts.)

Dealing with Ruth's past in understanding her decisions. I have been talking about some of the early decisions that Ruth made in response to messages that she received from her parents. I very much value the exploration of a client's early-childhood experiences as a basis for understanding and exploring with the client the nature of present pressing issues. (The psychoanalytic approach emphasizes a reconstruction of the past, a working through of early conflicts that have been repressed, and a resolution of these unconscious conflicts.) I accept that Ruth's childhood experiences were influential factors in contributing to her present development, although I do not think that these factors have *determined* her or that she is fixed with certain personality characteristics for life unless she goes through a long-term analytic reconstructive process. (I favor the Gestalt approach to working with her past.) I ask her to bring any unresolved conflicts from her past into the here and now through fantasy exercises and role-playing techniques. In this way her past is being dealt with in a powerful way—as it is being manifested in her current problems.

In Ruth's attempt to face her past I expect some *resistance*—some hesitation, use of defenses against threat, and getting stuck at certain anxiety-provoking points. (Psychoanalysis has resistance as a central concept; Gestalt therapy mentions the "impasse.") In working with resistance, I attempt to respect it. In other words, I see that Ruth's resistance is an inevitable part of how therapy proceeds. To some extent it is healthy to resist. Resistance shows that she is aware of the risks of changing and the anxiety that coming to terms with unknown parts of herself brings up. Thus (in a psychoanalytic view), I do not see resistance necessarily as conscious defiance or unwillingness to cooperate. (Behavior therapists often assume that "resistance" is an excuse on the therapist's part for poor management of techniques. They see it as a function of failure by the therapist to make a correct assessment and apply properly an appropriate treatment plan. I agree with the psychoanalytic concept of resistance as a fundamental part of therapy and as something that needs to be recognized and dealt with as a part of the therapy process.)

Overall, Ruth is a very willing and motivated client. She is insightful, courageous, able to make connections between current behavior and past influences, willing to try risky behaviors both in the session and out of the session, and willing to face difficult issues in her life. Even under such favorable (and almost ideal) circumstances, I still think that she will experience some resistance. She debated about whether to continue therapy; at times she blames her parents for her present problems; and at other times she chooses to stay comfortable because of her fear of plunging into unknown territory. In short, I work with whatever resistance she shows by pointing out its most obvious manifestations first, encouraging her to talk about her fears and explore them. I think an effective way to deal with resistance is to recognize it and deal with it directly. This can be done in a gentle yet confrontational way, along with providing support to face issues that she might otherwise avoid.

Working toward redecisions. As much as possible I structure situations in the therapy session that will facilitate new decisions on Ruth's part. I think that her redecisions have to be made on both the emotional and cognitive levels. It is not enough that she merely intellectually resolve to stop seeking parental approval; it is essential that she make this new decision from the feeling state (as she did when she made her early decision as a child). (In encouraging Ruth to make new decisions, I draw on cognitive, emotive, and behavioral techniques. I use role-playing procedures, fantasy and imagery, assertion-training procedures, and Gestalt techniques, to mention a few. Ruth can spend years in getting insights into the cause of her problems, but what I think is more important is that she commit herself to some course of action: Here I like the Adlerian and reality-therapy emphasis on getting the client to decide on a plan of action and then make a commitment to carrying it out.)

Encouraging Ruth to act. In many ways I look at therapy as a place of safety where clients can experiment with new ways of being to see what behavioral changes they really want to make. The critical point consists of actually taking what is learned in the sessions and applying it to real-life situations. I consistently encourage Ruth to carry out homework assignments geared to having her challenge her fears and inhibitions in a variety of practical situations. Thus, if she says that she is yearning for a weekend alone with her husband yet fears asking for it because she might be turned down and the rejection would hurt, I challenge her: "If you don't bother to ask, chances are you won't have this weekend you say you want with John. You've constantly brought up in here that you don't ask for what you want, suffer in silence, and then end up depressed and unloved. Here's your chance to actually *do* something different instead of what you typically do. What stops you from asking for what you want?"

Ruth has a long list of excuses to justify her lack of willingness to initiate a weekend alone with John. A few of them are that they do not have the money, their children would miss them, John is too busy, and they might find that they are bored with each other's company. In reality-therapy fashion, I tell Ruth that I don't want to settle for excuses. I argue with her on each point, attempting to convince her that, if she does want to change her situation, she has to actually take risks and try new behavior. (This fits into most of the action-oriented behavioral approaches.) I ask Ruth to decide if she *really* wants to make changes in her life or merely *talk about* making changes. Because she sincerely wants to be different, we use session time in much role playing and behavioral rehearsal, and then I ask her to try out her new learning in different life situations. For me, translating what is learned in the sessions into daily life is the essence of what therapy is about.

Evaluating Ruth's Therapy Experience

My style of counseling places emphasis on continuing assessment by both the counselor and the client from the initial to the final session. In my work with Ruth I bring up from time to time the topic of her progress in therapy. We openly discuss the degree to which she is getting what she wants from the process (and from me). If she is not successfully meeting her objectives, we can explore some factors that might be getting in the way of her progress. I could be a restricting factor. This is especially true if I am reacting to her strictly from a technical approach and am withholding my own reactions from her. If I am being inauthentic in any way in the sessions, I am certain that this will show up in a failure on her part to progress to the degree to which she might.

I also explore with Ruth some of the circumstances in her life that might be contributing to what appears to be slow or nonexistent progress. She may have done a lot of changing, which may itself be creating new problems in her home relationships, and she may feel a need to pull back and consolidate her gains. There may be a plateau for a period of time before she is ready to forge ahead with making other major life changes. Still another factor determining her progress or lack of it lies within herself—namely, her own decision and commitment of how far she wants to go in therapy. Is she willing to make some basic changes in her personality and create a new identity for herself? Is she willing to pay the price that changing entails? Does she merely want to solve some pressing problems on the surface, while remaining personally unchanged? These are but a few of the factors that we have to consider in understanding any failure in the therapy process.

How do Ruth and I determine the degree to which she is progressing? What criteria do we use to make this determination? (Behavior therapy is built on the assumption that assessment and evaluation are basic to the therapy process. Techniques must be continually verified to determine if they are working. *Behavior changes* in the client are a major basis for making this evaluation.) From my vantage point, I look at Ruth's work in the sessions and what she is doing outside of them as a measure of the degree to which therapy is working. Another important index is our relationship. If it is one of trust and if she is dealing with difficult personal issues in her therapy and also working on these issues outside of the sessions, then therapy is working. Also, her own evaluation of how much progress she sees and how satisfied she is by the outcomes is a major factor in assessing therapeutic results.

When is it time for Ruth to terminate therapy? This too is a matter that I openly evaluate at appropriate times. Ultimately, I see it as her choice. My hope is that, once she attains a degree of increased self-awareness *and* specific behavioral skills in meeting present and future problems, she might well be encouraged to end formal therapy and begin to become her own therapist. (This is a cognitive-behavioral approach.) To keep her beyond this point could result in needlessly fostering her dependence on me, which is not too unlike the problem she entered therapy for in the first place.

How Would You Work with Ruth Using Your Own Approach?

At this time you are challenged to try your hand at achieving some synthesis among the nine approaches by drawing on each of them in a way that seems meaningful to you—one that fits your own personality and your view of people and the nature of therapy. I am providing some questions to help you organize the elements of your approach.

1. What would you be thinking and feeling as you approached your initial session with Ruth? Use whatever you know about her from the material presented about her and her autobiography in the first chapter, from the nine chapters on her work with various therapists, and from my eclectic approach in working with her in this chapter.
2. Briefly state how you see Ruth, in terms of her current dynamics and most pressing conflicts. How would you feel in working with her as a client? How do you view her capacity to understand herself and to make basic changes?
3. How much direction do you see Ruth needing? To what degree would you take the responsibility for structuring her sessions? Where would you be on a continuum of highly directive to very nondirective?
4. Would you be inclined toward short-term therapy or long-term therapy? Why?
5. What major themes do you imagine that you would focus on in Ruth's life?
6. In what ways might you go about gathering life-history data in order to make an initial assessment of her problems and to determine which therapy procedures to use?
7. How might you help Ruth in clarifying her goals for therapy? How would you help her make her goals concrete? How would you assess the degree to which she was meeting her goals?
8. How much interest would you have in working with Ruth's *past* life experiences? her *current* issues? her *future* aspirations and strivings? Which of these areas do you favor? Why?
9. What value do you place on the quality of your relationship with Ruth? How important is the client/therapist relationship for you as a determinant of therapeutic outcomes?
10. Would you be more inclined to focus on Ruth's *feelings*? her thought processes and other *cognitive factors*? her ability to take action as measured by her *behaviors*?
11. How supportive might you be of Ruth? How confrontational might you be with her? In what areas do you think you would be most supportive? most confrontational?
12. How much might you be inclined to work toward major personality reconstruction? toward specific skill-development and problem-solving strategies?
13. How might you explore Ruth's major fears, both about therapy and about her life?
14. What life experiences have you had that would most help you in working with Ruth? What personal characteristics might hinder your work with her?
15. How might you proceed in dealing with Ruth's parents and the role she feels that they have played in her life? How important would it be to focus on working through her attitudes and feelings toward her parents? Do you think that this can be done symbolically (through role playing), or for her to resolve her problems is it necessary that she deal directly with her parents?
16. How much might you structure outside-of-therapy activities (homework, reading, journal writing, and so forth) for Ruth?

17. What values do you hold that are similar to Ruth's? How do you expect that this similarity would either get in the way of or facilitate the therapy process?
18. What specific techniques and concepts might you draw from the psychoanalytic approach? from the experiential approaches? from the cognition/behavior/action-oriented approaches?
19. To what degree would you view Ruth's therapy as being a didactic and reeducative process? To what degree do you see therapy as being a teaching/learning process?
20. Would you orient Ruth's therapy more toward insight or toward action? What balance might you seek between the cognitive aspects and the feeling aspects? How might you make the determination of when Ruth was ready to end therapy?

Recommended Supplementary Readings

Now that you have studied nine contemporary theories and seen their applications to cases, you may be interested in sources that will help you develop a basis for integrating these diverse approaches.

Eclectic Psychotherapy: A Systematic Approach (1983) by L. E. Beutler (New York: Pergamon Press) is an excellent source for readers who want to develop an integrated approach. The author describes a systematic eclectic psychotherapy that can be applied in a relatively consistent and reliable fashion. He attempts to define the ingredients of effective therapy by matching clients to both therapists and techniques.

Therapeutic Psychology: Fundamentals of Counseling and Psychotherapy (4th ed., 1982) by L. Brammer and E. Shostrom (Englewood Cliffs, N.J.: Prentice-Hall) presents an "actualizing model of counseling." The authors assert that their creative synthesis of various counseling theories goes beyond popular eclecticism. They provide a concise summary of the theoretical foundations of counseling practice. They draw on a combination of theories as they discuss topics such as assessment and diagnosis in counseling, the client/therapist relationship, transference, countertransference, resistance, and the role of values in the therapeutic process.

The Practice of Multimodal Therapy (1981) by A. A. Lazarus (New York: McGraw-Hill) represents a practical approach that is highly readable. The author develops his own systematic and comprehensive therapy and describes a wide variety of techniques. He endorses and expands on the stance he calls "technical eclecticism."

The Counseling Experience: A Theoretical and Practical Approach (1982) by M. E. Cavanagh (Monterey, Calif.: Brooks/Cole) maintains that counselors should use what works and discard what does not work. Endorsing a pragmatic viewpoint, the author explores some of the following topics pertaining to the nature of counseling: stages in the therapeutic process, the personal qualities of both the client and the counselor, cognitive and emotional factors in counseling, communication in counseling, resistance, and problems facing counselors.

CHAPTER TWELVE

Additional Cases for Practice

This chapter is divided into two segments: Cases 1–9, *identified cases*, are designed to be analyzed within the framework of a particular therapy approach. Cases 10–15, *unidentified cases*, are designed to give you some practice in deciding which approach works best for each case, to help you combine approaches, and to give you opportunities to apply what you learned in the previous chapter. There are a number of suggested class activities, including role-playing possibilities and discussion questions. Think creatively about ways of comparing and contrasting the approaches, of integrating several theories, and of borrowing techniques from all of the nine models as you work with these cases. Remember, there are no "right" answers. The real challenge is to think through why you would use certain interventions with different cases and to be able to describe what you see going on in each of these cases.

1. Tim: A Child Molester (Psychoanalytic)

Assume that you are working in a state mental hospital for the rehabilitation of mentally disordered sex offenders. The psychiatrist who is the head of your ward, and also your supervisor, maintains that a psychoanalytic perspective is most useful for understanding the dynamics of the child molesters on the ward. Although she realizes full well that most members of the treatment staff are limited both in time available and skill in using psychoanalytic *techniques*, she also believes that the staff can draw on psychoanalytic *concepts* to guide the therapy with their patients. She contends that you can think in psychoanalytic terms, even though you do not practice in strict psychoanalytic ways. With this in mind, she presents a case study at a staff meeting, giving some summary details of the psychological development of a client named Tim.

Some Background Data

Tim's mother was overprotective and overpossessive and controlled him with guilt. Even now she reminds him of all she gave and sacrificed and of how he was a "difficult child" from birth on. She almost died delivering him, and she tells him that she has been suffering because of him for many years. Tim was the only boy in a family of five children. Psychosexually, he eventually decided to become a neuter in an effort to become what he thought his mother wanted of him. He became quite overweight, developed a very passive and unassertive style (especially with women), and has avoided developing lasting relationships with women for 50 years.

Tim saw his father as being extremely weak and uncaring. He reports that he cannot remember any events in which he and his father did anything together. His father showed no interest in him, and his typical way of dealing with Tim was to ignore him. Tim's father was controlled by Tim's mother and his grandmother (who lived with the family). Tim recalls tension between his mother and his grandmother (the mother of Tim's father), each fighting to run the house in the way she saw fit. They had very different ideas about how the family should be, so conflict was a continual pattern in the home. Things Tim did to please his mother often upset his grandmother, and the reverse happened when he tried to please the older woman.

As a child Tim envied his sisters because he thought they were treated more fairly than he was. Eventually, the discriminatory treatment he felt he was receiving changed his envy to resentment. He grew to fear females who were older than he, for he continually felt that they could and would dominate him. His relationships with others have been inadequate, and he has never been able to form and maintain satisfactory relationships with adults of either sex.

Tim discovered that he felt relatively comfortable around small children, especially boys. They seemed to take a liking to him, they did not make demands on him, and he did not feel inadequate around them. For a while during his early adult life he worked as a teacher's aide in an elementary school. He began his pattern of molesting young boys in this job. He would invite some of these children to climb onto his lap, and he would then stroke their hair and cuddle them. Eventually, he progressed with several boys to the point of touching their genitals; he also encouraged them to touch him. His pattern continued, and eventually he was arrested.

During the rest of his adult life he has been in and out of state hospitals for sex offenders a number of times. When he "finishes his time" as stipulated by the court, he is released, goes into the community, and then reoffends. He feels that he never hurts his victims and that he is typically "very nice and kind" to them. He even rationalizes that they often enjoy the attention and physical affection he demonstrates. Yet at times he also feels that what he does is wrong, and he feels guilty over his deeds. Tim does not think that his actions are normal, yet he worries about how he will deal with the impulses he might feel toward certain children. He has made resolutions to control himself, yet he has often acted on his impulses. Tim says he would like to learn to control his desires and be able to relate well with adults.

Questions for Reflection

By attempting to think psychoanalytically, show how you might proceed in your contacts with Tim by addressing yourself to these questions:

1. What value do you see in knowing Tim's developmental history, family background, experiences as a child and adolescent in school, work history, and other key adult experiences? Do you think that knowing this information will help you be a more effective therapist? How might you proceed differently with him if you had no prior knowledge about his past and instead simply relied on what you could learn about him through your contacts with him on the ward and observing his behavior? What advantages and disadvantages do you see in having prior knowledge about a client?
2. From the summary notes about Tim alone, how might you react to a person like him? What reactions does it evoke in you when you think about a middle-aged man who has a pattern of sexual molestation of children? In what ways can you predict that your own reactions to a person such as Tim could affect your ability to work with him therapeutically? How might you be able to deal with your own feelings so that they would not be a barrier between you and him?

3. Tim says that he feels guilt and sorrow over what he recognizes are his offenses and also that he would like to learn how to control his impulses. How might you be able to tell the degree to which this is so? Might he be saying what he feels he is expected to say so that he will obtain a release from the hospital? How do you think that either your belief or lack of belief in what he is saying will affect your work with him?
4. Do you think that Tim can change (stop his child-molesting behavior) without gaining insight into the causes of his problems? How much importance might you put on factors such as his understanding of his early childhood? his resolution of psychic conflicts with his mother and grandmother? a resolution of his feelings toward his father? If you see value in focusing on the above issues, *how* might you do this within the limited time that you would have to work with him?
5. Do you see Tim as a victim of his early experiences? Or do you see that, even though he has had adverse experiences in growing up, he could do something to change his behavior now? Again, how do your answers to the above questions determine how you will work with him in therapy?
6. As you proceed with Tim, what would be your major goals for him? Merely stopping his antisocial behavior? Changing his basic personality structure? Merely seeing that he has a choice in doing something about the problem that keeps him in the hospital?

2. The Klines: A Family in Turmoil (Adlerian)

Assume that a person in the agency where you work does an intake interview, and you are given the following information.

Some Background Data

The Kline family consists of mother, father, two daughters (Jessie, 10, and Jaimi, 12), and one son (Gary, 16). The father, George Kline, called for the intake interview. He said that his son's high school was considering expelling the boy for habitual truancy and possession of street drugs. George is following the suggestion of the school counselor that the entire family could benefit from family therapy.

The father does not have much hope that therapy will be of any great help. According to him, the one who is responsible for the family's problems is his wife, who he says is an alcoholic. As a businessman who does a great deal of traveling, he is convinced that he is doing all he can to hold the family together. George comments that he is a good provider and that he does not understand why his wife, Gail, insists on drinking. He feels that Gary has gotten everything that he ever wanted, and he maintains that youths of today are "just spoiled rotten." The father says that his elder daughter, Jaimi, is the best one of the bunch, and he has no complaints about her. He sees her as being more responsible than his wife as well as being more attentive to him. He views his younger daughter, Jessie, as pampered and spoiled by her mother, and he has little hope for her.

George is willing to give family counseling a try and says he hopes that the family therapist can straighten them all out. The father says that he, his wife, and the younger daughter are all willing to come in for a family session. Jaimi does not want to attend, however, because she says she has no problems and sees no purpose in therapy for herself. Gary is very reluctant to come in, even for one session, because he feels sure that others in the family will see him as the source of the family's problems.

The person who did the intake interview saw only the father for the initial session. He suggests that you see the entire family for at least one session and then decide how to proceed.

Questions for Reflection

1. What are your initial reactions after reading the intake interview?
2. As an Adlerian therapist how would you proceed in an initial session if you saw the entire family? What kind of contract would you want to make with this family?
3. George does not seem very open to looking at his role in the turmoil within his family. If you were to see George as your client, how would you go about establishing a relationship with him? Can you think of any ways to challenge him to look at the role he is playing in the family's problems? What kind of contract do you envision yourself making with George?
4. If you believed in the value of seeing the family as a unit for one or more sessions, how might you go about getting the entire family to come in? Assume that all agreed to attend one session. What would be your focus, and what would you most want to achieve in this family session?
5. What are the key dynamics of the family as a system? How would you interpret what is going on in this family from an Adlerian perspective?
6. What speculations do you have about the dynamics of George? From the vantage point of an Adlerian how would you explain his behavior?
7. What are the themes that interest you the most in this case? Why?
8. What are the ethical issues, if any, in this case?
9. What referrals, if any, would you consider? Why?
10. Assume that the mother and father wanted to come in for a number of sessions. Would you be inclined to gather life-history data from each of them? Why or why not? In what ways might you utilize this information as an Adlerian therapist?
11. What would your major goals be in working with this family? How would you go about increasing the social interest of each of the members?
12. Show how you would work with this family, and discuss any problems that you might expect to encounter. Say how you would expect to deal with these problems.
13. As an Adlerian, what are some of the techniques that you would draw on in working with the family?
14. Do you see any aspects of yourself in this case? Can you identify with any of the family members? How do you think this similarity or dissimilarity would help or hinder you in working with this family?

3. Pauline: A Young Woman Facing Death (Existential)

The existentialist views death as a reality that gives meaning to life. As humans we do not have forever to actualize ourselves. Thus, the realization of the fact that we will die jolts us into taking the present seriously and evaluating the direction in which we are traveling. We are confronted with the fact that we have only so much time to do the things we most want to do. Thus, we are motivated to take stock of how meaningful our life is. With this existential perspective in mind, assume that a young woman of 20 comes to the center where you are a counselor.

Some Background Data

Pauline has recently found out that she has leukemia. Though she is in a period of remission, her doctors tell her that the disease is terminal. Pauline is seeking counseling to help herself deal with this crisis and at least get the maximum out of the remainder of her life. She is filled with rage over her fate; she keeps asking why this had to happen to her. She tells you that at first she could not believe the diagnosis was correct. When she finally got several more professional opinions that confirmed her leukemia, she began to feel more and more anger—toward God, toward her healthy friends, whom she envied, and generally toward the unfairness of her situation. She tells you that she was just starting to live, that she had a direction she was going in professionally. Now everything will have to change. After she tells you this, she is sitting across from you waiting for your response.

Questions for Reflection

Attempting to stay within the frame of reference of an existential therapist, what direction would you take with her? Think about these questions:

1. What do you imagine your immediate reactions would be if you were faced with counseling this client? What would be some of the things that you would initially say in response to what you know about Pauline?
2. What are your own thoughts and feelings about death? To what degree have you reflected on this reality as it applies to you? Do you avoid thinking about it? In what ways have you accepted the reality of your eventual death? How do you think that the answers to the above questions will affect your ability to be present for Pauline?
3. What goals would you have in counseling with her?
4. In what ways would you deal with the rage that Pauline says she feels?
5. Pauline tells you that one of the reasons that she is coming to see you is because of her desire to accept her fate. How would you work with her to gain this acceptance? What specific things might you do to help her find ways of living the rest of her life to its fullest?
6. Do you see any possibilities for helping Pauline find meaning in her life in the face of death?

4. Doris: Leaving Her Husband and Child (Person-Centered)

Doris comes to a community counseling center at the recommendation of a friend, who expresses concern that Doris intends to leave her child. The friend thinks she is confused and needs professional help.

Some Background Data

Doris was born and reared in Arkansas. Her father is a reformed alcoholic who drank heavily when the client was a child. Both parents are religious, and the father is described as a strict fundamentalist. Doris has a younger brother who is now an enlisted man in the Army and is described as the family favorite. Doris says her parents were stricter with her than with their son and emphasized the importance of marriage as well as the woman's dependent and inferior role in that relationship.

Doris is a "sweet" girl who dropped out of high school in the tenth grade. She worked as a manicurist in Arkansas until marrying and moving to Kentucky three years ago. She then worked as a waitress. Her husband says that they have had no fights or arguments during their three-year marriage, and the client agrees. Six months ago Doris gave birth to a baby boy. There were no medical complications, and Doris maintains that she adjusted well to the baby, but she reports just not being able to feel much of anything except tired. Two months ago Doris and her husband moved to Houston so that he could join an amateur band. She began working as a cashier at a drugstore. In the course of her work she began to have a series of brief sexual affairs with fellow workers as well as customers. At the same time, although her husband is happy with the band, he has not been able to find a steady job. He has asked her to try to find a second job or to take overtime hours at the drugstore.

Doris is considering leaving her husband and her child, although she is uncertain how she would continue to support herself financially. She is also concerned with what would happen to her son, because her husband has no means of support. She insists that she does not want to take the child with her.

Questions for Reflection

1. Would you be inclined to accept Doris as a client? Do you think that you could empathize with her situation? Explain.
2. What is your attitude about her wanting to leave her husband and her child? What are your values on this matter, and how would they influence the way you would work with her?
3. Would you want to see Doris and her husband together? Would you want to see him individually? see her individually? see them on an individual basis and also as a couple? Explain your rationale, showing what you would probably focus on in each instance.
4. Assume that Doris asked you for your advice regarding her plan to leave her husband and child. What would you say? To what degree do you think Doris can function without advice?

5. If you accepted Doris as a client, in what ways do you think you could be of most help to her?
6. Are there feelings about herself and her husband that Doris is currently unwilling to accept? How would a person-centered approach help with acceptance of feelings and with denied parts of the self?
7. By staying with a person-centered framework, do you feel that you could respond to her in a way you would like? Do you feel limited by this theory in any way? If so, how?
8. What are some of the advantages of working with Doris within a person-centered framework?

5. Linda: In Crisis over Her Pregnancy (Gestalt)

Assume that you are a counselor in a community mental-health clinic, that you have a Gestalt orientation, and that the counselor at the local high school tells you about Linda, a 15-year-old client he has seen several times. He feels that she needs further counseling, but he is limited by a school policy that does not permit personal counseling of any duration. He would like for you to see her for at least three months, as she is facing some difficult decisions. Here is what you learn about her from the counselor.

Some Background Data

Linda comes from a close-knit family, and in general she feels that she can seek her parents out when she has problems. But now she says that she just *cannot* turn to them in this time of crisis. Even though she and her boyfriend had been engaging in sexual intercourse for a year without using birth-control measures, she was convinced that she would not get pregnant. When she did learn that she was pregnant, she expected that her 16-year-old boyfriend would agree to get married. He did not agree, and he even questioned whether he was the father. She felt deeply hurt and angry over this. On the advice of a girlfriend she considered an abortion for a time. But she decided against it because she felt that she could not deal with the guilt of terminating a life within her. The possibility of putting her child up for adoption was suggested to her. But she felt this to be totally unacceptable, because she was sure she could not live knowing that she had created a life and then "abandoned" the child. She considered having her baby and becoming a single parent. Yet when the counselor pointed out all the realities involved in this choice, she could see that this option would not work—unless she told her parents and lived with them, which she was *sure* she could not do. Her pregnancy is moving toward the advanced stages, and her panic is mounting.

Questions for Reflection

Linda agrees to work with you for several months, and you will be using Gestalt procedures with her.

1. What do you imagine would be your initial reactions and responses to the counselor's account? What might your first words be to Linda after you were introduced to her? What do you think you would *most* want to say to her?
2. What might be some of your goals in working with Linda? Check any of the following that apply:
   _____ I hope that she will tell her parents about her situation.
   _____ I hope that she will reconsider the possibility of having an abortion, and I might be inclined to push this alternative.
   _____ I hope that she will reconsider the possibility of having the child and then putting it up for adoption, and I might be inclined to push this alternative.
   Can you suggest other goals?
3. What are *your values* as they relate to the above matters, and what role do you see your values playing in the approach you will take with Linda? Might you be inclined to share your values, so that Linda knows where you stand? Might you be inclined to push your values, and thus steer counseling in a particular direction?
4. At some point you might work with Linda's feelings of anger and hurt toward her boyfriend. What Gestalt techniques can you think of to help her explore these feelings? What techniques could you use to work with her feelings of guilt over not having lived up to her parents' high expectations? What other Gestalt approaches might you use (with what expected outcomes) to explore with Linda her other feelings associated with being pregnant?
5. As you proceed with Linda, you become aware of the following body messages:
   - Whenever she talks about having a baby, she puts her hands to her face, almost as though she were hiding it.
   - As she talks about her fear of telling her parents and expresses her guilt over letting them down, her voice changes to a very soft and almost pleading tone.
   - Her mouth is extremely tight when she mentions her boyfriend, and her eyes become moist.
   - She often has teary eyes and a slight smile at the same time.

   Can you think of some Gestalt-oriented techniques that you would build on to work with the body messages you observe in Linda? How might you use her nonverbal clues as a way of helping her experience her feelings more fully?
6. Below are some Gestalt-oriented techniques that you might consider using. Check any of them that you think you would use, and show how you would go about implementing them. What outcomes do you expect from each technique? What do you hope will be achieved through the use of each?
   _____ I will ask her to have a dialogue between *herself* and her *boyfriend*, using the two-chair technique.
   _____ I will ask her to have a similar dialogue with her father.
   _____ I will ask her to have a similar dialogue with her mother.
   _____ I will ask her to fantasize, with her eyes closed, the worst possible situation and describe it, along with what she is experiencing as she does so.
   _____ I will ask her to write a letter to her boyfriend (or to her parents, or to her unborn child) and say anything that comes to her without censoring it—and I will ask her *not* to mail it.

7. How comfortable would you feel in using techniques such as the above with such a client? How would you prepare Linda for such exercises, so that she would be open to experimenting with some Gestalt fantasy work?
8. Some states have a law requiring parental permission for counseling if the minor is pregnant. How do you think this requirement would affect your relationship with Linda?
9. What are the limitations, if any, of staying within a Gestalt framework in this case? Do you feel that you could say and do what you would like within this theory?
10. What are some advantages of using a Gestalt perspective in this case?

6. Harold: A Client in Search of a Friend (TA)

Harold presents himself for treatment at a community mental-health clinic.

Some Background Data

The client is 55 years old and has been a client for six weeks. Harold is divorced, has no children or other family, and has no real social connections in the city. He has been living a very isolated existence in a hotel in the downtown area. The client receives approximately $400 a month in Supplemental Security Income and does not work. He is a chronic alcoholic who passes through various phases of sobriety and inebriation. He appears to be a very alienated, depressed individual.

Harold is in therapy attempting to qualify for more financial aid as a psychiatrically disabled person. Despite the fact that he initiated therapy as a ploy to receive financial support, you sense that a relationship is developing between the two of you in your weekly sessions. He arrives punctually, is animated and communicative, and often seems in good spirits. He reports, however, that he does not have enough money to live in the hotel, that he is out on the street, and that he needs somewhere to stay. He goes so far as to ask if he can use your office. That evening, he is waiting by your car and asks for a ride to a location a few miles away. You suggest that he take a bus. A week later this behavior is repeated. Meanwhile, in therapy he becomes withdrawn and depressed.

Questions for Reflection

1. Initially knowing that Harold wants to "beat the system," would you be willing to see him? To what degree would you cooperate with his goals? What legal or ethical issues, if any, would you want to address?
2. Is there anything about this case that would cause you to take immediate action? If so, what specifically needs to be done?
3. Would you comply with his wish that you become his friend?
4. If you were to establish a contract with Harold, what might it entail? How would you go about developing a contract with him?

5. How, if at all, would you deal with his concerns over living arrangements and financial matters?
6. What limits do you think would be important to establish in this case? To what degree might you have difficulty in enforcing limits?
7. How would you deal with his change in moods?
8. In what ways would you approach working with Harold as a TA therapist? Specifically, what are some therapeutic procedures that you would probably employ?
9. What hunches do you have about the messages Harold received as a child? What early decision might he have made?
10. Do you have any guesses about what life script Harold might be living out? What games does he play? What are the possible payoffs of such games?

7. Kay: Learning to Cope with Anxiety (Behavioral)

Kay comes to the clinic where you are a behaviorally oriented therapist. Assume that this is your initial meeting with her and that you know nothing about her. Also assume that she would very much like to become involved in short-term behavioral counseling, mainly for the purpose of dealing with chronic anxiety that is getting in the way of her personal and professional life.

Some Background Data

During the initial interview Kay tells you: "I've just *got* to learn how to cope with stress. I'm feeling like there's a dark cloud over my head—a constant and nagging feeling of apprehension. I'm so worked up during the day that when I try to go to sleep I just toss and turn most the night, ruminating over everything that happened to me that day. I keep telling myself that I've got to get to sleep or I won't be worth a damn the next day. I just lie there and can't seem to stop thinking of what I did or will do the next day. When I do get up the next morning, I'm like a basket case. I sell real estate, and lately I'm getting more anxious about my future. I'm fearful of contacting people, afraid I'll say the wrong thing and blow the potential sale, and afraid they'll notice my anxiety. I just don't seem to be able to relax at any time. And what's even worse is that I feel less able to cope with stress now than I used to. Stress is getting the best of me, and I'm afraid that unless I can learn to recognize and deal with the situations I'm in, my anxiety will do me in."

Assume that you and Kay agree to several counseling sessions for the purpose of helping her deal with her anxieties. Specifically, she wants guidance in learning skills that she can use on her own to effectively cope with situations she meets. As a behaviorally oriented counselor show how you would view her and how you might proceed for several sessions.

Questions for Reflection

1. How do you view Kay's anxiety? Will you look at it as a problem in itself (and thus deal directly with behavior that seems to produce anxiety)? Or will you look at it as

symbolic of underlying conflicts? How will the way you answer this question have a direct bearing on the manner in which you work with her in your sessions?
2. What are some specific behavioral procedures that you might employ during your sessions? What are some suggestions you would make to Kay for work she can do by herself outside of the sessions?
3. What are some ways you can think of to teach her how to cope with stress? What self-help or self-management techniques could you suggest?
4. How might you deal with Kay's insomnia? What could you suggest to her concerning her ruminating over the events of the day when she is in bed? How might you design a program for her that would help her relax and sleep at night? What would you do during the sessions? What would you ask her to do outside of your sessions?
5. What other directions might you take in your work with Kay?
6. What cognitive factors might be affecting her behavior? How might her thinking patterns, beliefs, and self-statements be increasing her level of stress and leading to sleep disorders?

8. Hal and Pete: A Gay Couple Seek Counseling (RET)

Hal and Pete seek the services of a clinical social worker in private practice.

Some Background Data

Hal and Pete have been living together in a homosexual relationship for several years. In a manner very much the same as a heterosexual couple, they experience conflicts in their relationship. Lately, the situation has taken a turn for the worse, and Hal wants to either resolve certain problems or break up the relationship. Pete is very anxious about being deserted, and he agrees to come for counseling as a couple. Neither of them is troubled with the fact that they are in a gay relationship, and from their perspective this is not the problem. They want you to know at the outset that they are not seeking counseling to "cure" them of their homosexuality. Rather, they seem to be having major problems that they are unable to work out by themselves and that lead them to wonder if they want to continue living together.

Pete feels unappreciated, and he does not feel that Hal cares for him in "the way I would like." He initially tells you the following: "I try so hard to do what I think Hal expects. It's really important that I please him, because I'm afraid that if I don't, he'll get fed up and simply leave. And if he left, I imagine all sorts of terrible things happening. First of all, I feel the constant threat of being left. I need someone to rely on—someone who will listen to me, who I know cares for me and accepts me the way I am, who wants to be with me, and who will approve of what I do. I feel I *must* have this in the person I live with. If I don't, then this just proves that the other person doesn't love me. I need to be loved. My parents didn't love me, they never gave me the approval I needed to have, and I think that this alone is more than enough for me to have to bear. I feel that life often plays dirty tricks on me. For a long time I felt that I could *really* trust Hal and that he'd stay with me and approve of me and care about me, regardless of who I was. Now, after I trust him, he decides to tell me that I'm too demanding and that he's not able to handle all my demands. I don't think I'm demanding—I just want to be loved and accepted by some other significant person. If I can't find this in at least one person, then I can't see much value in living."

Hal responds with the following initial statement, in which he describes how it is for him to be in this relationship: "Frankly, I'm so tired of always feeling that I *must prove myself* and my constant love for Pete. No matter what I do or say, I typically end up feeling that I'm not enough and that regardless of what I do, it just won't measure up. I'm tired of hearing that I don't care. I'm sick of being made to feel that I'm insensitive, I hate being made to feel inadequate, and I don't want to constantly feel that I have to weigh everything I say for fear that I'll offend Pete and make him upset. I just can't stand having people be upset at me—it makes me feel lousy and guilty—like I somehow should be more than I am, that I ought to be better than I am. If I can't get over being made to feel inadequate around Pete, then I want out!"

Questions for Reflection

Assume that Hal and Pete agree to attend six sessions as a couple. By the end of that time they would like to have decided whether they want to stay together. If they do decide to continue living together, they would be open to considering further counseling to continue working on their separate problems and finding ways of improving their relationship.

1. What are your initial reactions to Pete? to Hal? to them as a couple? How do you see them individually and as a couple? Would you want to work with them as a couple? Do you think that you could work with them effectively? Why or why not?
2. Are your feelings toward this gay couple different than they would be if the couple were heterosexual? What are your views toward homosexual relationships? How do you think they would influence your approach and the goals you had in mind? Would you tell them how you felt toward them—both as separate individuals and as a couple? Why or why not? What difference do you think it would make whether you shared your reactions with them?
3. Pete and Hal initially said that they did not consider the fact of their homosexual preferences to be a problem in itself and that they were not asking you to "cure" what they considered a nonexistent problem. Would you avoid attempting to change their sexual orientations? How might your answer to the above question determine the direction you would proceed in counseling this couple?
4. From the perspective of rational-emotive therapy, some of the following could be identified as *Pete's irrational beliefs*. Show how you would demonstrate to him that they are self-defeating attitudes that are the direct cause of his misery:
   - I *must* please Hal, and if I don't he'll leave, and the consequences will be horrible!
   - I *must* have someone to rely on, or else I can't make it on my own!
   - I *must* have someone to show me caring, love, approval—and if I don't get this, then life is hardly worth living!
   - If I don't get what I want from life, then life is damn unfair!

5. Again as an RET therapist, how might you work with *Hal's irrational beliefs?* How would you teach him to dispute them? How would you show him that these beliefs are at the root of his problems?
   - I *must* prove myself, I *must* be able to meet another's expectations of me—and if I don't, I'll feel inadequate, guilty, rotten, and deficient as a person!
   - If I don't meet Pete's needs, then I am *made* to feel inadequate.
6. Show how both Hal's and Pete's beliefs and assumptions are related to the problems they are having in their relationship. In what ways do you imagine that working on their irrational beliefs will affect their relationship?

9. Janet: A Substance Abuser (Reality)

The client, an attractive woman of 33, is in your office at a community mental-health center because it is a requirement of her parole.

Some Background Data

Janet reports that she has always had difficulties handling her family and her personal life. She says that she had a relatively stable marriage until she found out her "old man was running around with other girls." Although she filed for a divorce from him, she never appeared in court, so she is uncertain about her marital status. She reports that after the separation he "disappeared" until quite recently, when he "reappeared out of nowhere" and took their son (now 15) to live with him. She also has two girls, ages 8 and 10, who still live with her. The client says that, once her husband had left, she was forced to resort to stealing to support the family and her drug habit.

Janet has been addicted to cocaine for four years. During this period she has had behavioral problems with her two daughters, as well as the son. Eventually she moved in with her current boyfriend, and the behavioral problems with the children escalated. She reports that she is on parole for a theft charge and is afraid that she will have to go back to prison for parole violation because of her drug use.

Janet lets her parole officer know that she has seen you and that she wants to get some help "to get her life together." A few days later her parole officer calls and says that her urine test is "dirty," showing traces of several drugs. The parole officer asks about your treatment plan for therapy and requests that you write your opinion on whether the client should be back in prison.

Questions for Reflection

1. What ethical and legal implications does this case have?
2. What referrals might you need to make?
3. What type of information would you provide to the parole officer?
4. If Janet wanted to remain in therapy, what goals would you see as being important?

5. How would you apply the steps of reality therapy to this case?
6. What interventions would you make, and why?
7. How would you work with Janet if she avoided making an evaluation of her behavior?
8. Do you think you could work with her effectively given the fact that she has come to you as a stipulation of her parole? Why or why not? How could you tie this requirement into a reality-therapy perspective?
9. Besides reality therapy, what theoretical framework would be helpful to you in this case? Are there any theoretical approaches that you think would *not* be particularly helpful?
10. Show how your approach in working with Janet from a reality-therapy perspective would differ from your work with her from a person-centered framework.
11. How might you deal with possible manipulation by the client? What would you do if you suspected that she was using you simply to meet the requirement for parole and that she was not really involved in her therapy?
12. Do you see her as a candidate for hospitalization? In your opinion, is Janet a suitable candidate for conventional psychotherapy? Explain.

Cases 10–15 are unidentified, so that you can practice selecting the theory (or theories) that you think would be most appropriate for them. I have several suggestions for working with these cases. First of all, you can try your hand at working with them without restricting yourself to any theory. You can also compare and contrast a theory, showing how you might work very differently with one theory than another or how you might blend two theories. For each of these six cases I suggest that you attempt to answer the following general questions, in addition to the questions that are raised after each case.

1. If you selected a particular theory, why did you do so?
2. As you approach each client, what basic assumptions are you making?
3. What is your initial assessment of each client? What are the major themes you would be likely to focus on in therapy with each person? Why?
4. What specific goals might you have in each case? How would you proceed with the client? How would you evaluate therapeutic progress?

10. Luis: Struggling with a Sexual Problem

The client, a computer technician at a large corporation who earns approximately $30,000 a year, appeared at a public-health clinic asking for help with sexual difficulties he was experiencing with his wife. When questioned why he was not seeking private help, he said that he did not want anyone at work to find out and that he had come to this particular clinic because it was noted for its treatment of sexual disorders. He said that except for the problems with his sex life he felt that his life was under control.

Some Background Data

Luis is 35 years old and has been married three years to a woman 12 years his junior. She does not work. He is of Hispanic background, and his wife is Caucasian. Although they are planning to have a family, he says that his wife does not willingly engage in sexual relations at any time. He is forced to initiate all sexual interaction, and they have intercourse approximately one or two times a month. In the past three months sexual activities have decreased even more. Luis says that his wife is unwilling to attend therapy and is completely closed to the idea of either or both of them seeking help. She is not aware that he has made an appointment at the public-health clinic. When questioned about other aspects of their relationship that might be problematic, the client insists that everything is fine and that he merely desires help with his sexual problem.

Questions for Reflection

1. Are there any key words that Luis uses that you would pay particular attention to?
2. Would you be inclined to provide Luis with a referral to a sex therapist? Why or why not?
3. What is your hunch about the validity of his assertion that besides this sex problem everything is fine with him?
4. Would you be inclined to refer him to a physician for a comprehensive physical? Why or why not?
5. If you did work with him, would you encourage him to persuade his wife to attend any of these sessions? Give your reasons.
6. Do you see it as important to explore the cultural backgrounds of this couple? What might you be looking for if you did?
7. What theoretical framework(s) would guide your interventions with Luis? In what direction would you proceed with him?

11. Wilma: A Depressed Adolescent

Wilma, a 17-year-old high school senior, was referred by her teacher for counseling because of severe bouts of depression. The counselor who did the intake interview gathered some of the following information about her.

Some Background Data

Wilma has never had a father. While her mother was pregnant with her, he decided to leave the family, saying he did not want to be burdened with any more children or responsibilities. Wilma's mother never remarried, and she attempted to keep a job and at the same time rear her children. During childhood Wilma was frequently left with different sitters, many of whom did not pay much attention to her.

Wilma recalls that as a child she suffered from frequent illnesses and was often absent from school. She developed extreme fears of school, and she was referred to the psychologist in her elementary school for therapy to deal with her "school phobia."

According to the school nurse, Wilma's mother was indulgent and overpermissive; the mother also talked about her guilt feelings over not being able to provide a "normal home" for her children. Wilma describes her home situation as having been far from a "closely knit family." Rather, she feels that her mother was permissive and did not care about the children. She remembers that her mother became extremely defensive whenever Wilma brought up the subject of her father. Her mother took many opportunities to describe what a miserable man he was and how they were much better off without him. Nevertheless, Wilma persisted in her interest in her father. But whenever she attempted to find out where he was, her mother reacted with anger and told Wilma to "forget he ever existed."

Wilma's school adjustment during all of her school years left a lot to be desired. She had very few friends and reports that the children picked on her and teased her. She had a pattern of being somewhat withdrawn, sensitive, and timid. Her teachers reported on her cumulative record that she was a "good girl" who was conforming, conscientious, and hard working. It is clear that Wilma was handicapped by a weak ego development. Out of her basic insecurities, she attempted to please and win the approval of teachers, yet she typically felt inadequate and inferior to most of her peers.

The school psychologist who worked with Wilma when she was in the eighth grade gave her a battery of psychological tests with her mother's permission. Intellectually, she was functioning within the average range. She was also given several projective tests of personality that were designed to assess unconscious psychodynamics. The results indicated severe conflicts with her mother, with strong hostility directed toward her; feelings of rejection, inadequacy, and inferiority; sexual conflicts—a desire for sex and a fear of the desire; deep feelings of depression, loneliness, emptiness, and isolation from others; severe difficulties with interpersonal relations; sibling rivalry; weak and unhealthy self-concept; and masochistic and self-punishing tendencies. To the question "Who am I," to which the school psychologist asked her to give 20 answers, some of her replies were "a bunch of molecules," "empty and vacant," "lost," "a person without a purpose for living," and "confused."

In her notes the school psychologist made a summary statement to the effect that Wilma appeared to very much want contact with others, yet she was both frightened of doing so and seemed severely lacking in interpersonal skills. Thus, she surrounded herself with high walls so that people could not hurt her.

Questions for Reflection

Assume that you would be Wilma's therapist for at least several months, and show how you would proceed with her, using these questions as a guide:

1. How do you see Wilma? How do you feel about working with her? To what degree do you think you could understand her and also help her to understand herself?
2. In considering her history, what hypotheses do you have concerning the causes of her present problems?

3. How much value do you place on knowing the data summarized above? Do you think that you can effectively work with a person like Wilma without such background data? How much might you rely on psychological tests to give you some information about her current state of functioning? How might you use these test results in your therapy sessions with her?
4. How might you deal with her resistance to therapy? For example, if she were withdrawn in the sessions and said little, how might you work therapeutically with her resistance?
5. In your estimation, what impact did the absence of a father figure in her life have on her development and adjustment?
6. Is parental consent necessary? Explain.
7. Would you utilize any other sources of care, such as a psychiatrist or hospitalization? Explain. At what point might you turn to these sources?
8. Wilma indicates that she would like to be able to *accept affection*, although she finds this difficult to do. What is your hypothesis concerning the origins of her limited capacity to accept affection, when you consider her psychosexual development pattern? What guesses would you venture about the early experiences she had in both receiving and giving love?

12. Raymond: Afraid of Women

A friend of the client's suggested that he approach you for counseling. Raymond, who is 39, appears rather depressed and does not hold too much hope that therapy will help him feel better. He says that he does not have much purpose in life, that he is without direction, and that about all he feels is anger over the way his life is going.

Some Background Data

What follows is the essence of what Raymond tells you in the first session: "As I walk into the therapist's office, I ask myself 'Why did I come here?' All I know is that I am feeling unhappy and empty in my life. I don't seem to be able to establish a meaningful relationship with a woman, and I feel angry and frustrated with myself. Every time I get with a woman I feel very self-conscious and unsure of myself. I always go away feeling that I've been controlled by them and that I can't do or say what I want around them. Although I have relationships with women, they are generally unsatisfying and unhappy experiences for me. I also feel stifled in my personal life. My life seems sometimes to be nothing more than a set of routines and patterns. It seems that, no matter what I do, I can always find something wrong with everything. I'm constantly getting down on myself and telling myself that what I do is not enough. It's very hard for me to just feel good about the things that I do. It seems that I'm always feeling bad about something.

"I also feel closed in around people. When I get into a group of people, I become very quiet and anxious and feel that I can't say or do anything. I find it hard to let go and have fun. I spend most of my time thinking about how self-conscious and closed in I feel.

"I live with my father and find myself getting very angry with him almost constantly, and yet I'm always holding myself away from him for fear of controlling his life too much. My mother is dead, but when she was alive she was the dominant one in our family. I used to feel very controlled by her. No matter what I did, she would always tell me that I didn't love her, and I would always have to explain things to her. She always came to me to tell her problems.

"Anyway, all I know is that I feel very unhappy, empty, and unfulfilled in my life. I've got to find something to help me make it, because sometimes I just feel as if it's not worth all this struggle. Sometimes I feel helpless to do anything."

Questions for Reflection

1. What possible cause do you see of Raymond's inability to "establish a meaningful relationship with a woman"?
2. How does the continuing influence of Raymond's mother control and dominate him? How might her domination be connected to his current state of being "self-conscious and unsure" of himself when he is with a woman?
3. Raymond constantly "gets down on" himself, and he feels that what he does is "not enough." How might you explain this feeling? What do you see as the underlying psychological factors associated with his self-critical attitude and his guilt over not being "enough"?
4. What do you think is the meaning of his feeling of being "closed in around people"?
5. If Raymond were your client, what else would you want to know about him? What aspects of his case would you choose to focus on, and what would be your therapeutic goals and procedures as you worked with him?

13. The Winterses: A Family in Conflict

Assume that you are a counselor in a community clinic, and that you are assigned to initiate family-counseling sessions with the Winters family. Your supervisor tells you the following about the family you are about to meet.

Some Background Data

The principal of the high school where the two Winters teenagers are enrolled called Mr. and Mrs. Winters and encouraged them to come to school to talk with the school counselor about their son (Doug, 15) and their daughter (Debbie, 17). Doug has been expelled for aggressive behavior, including participating in gang fights at school.

Debbie has a record of habitual truancy, is failing all of her subjects, and has been caught using drugs on campus several times.

In talking with the parents, the school counselor concluded that the problems of Doug and Debbie seemed to grow out of a troubled family situation. At this session Mrs. Winters said that she simply did not know where to turn and that she had long felt that their entire family should get involved in family counseling. Her position was:

"I have completely lost control of both Debbie and Doug. They will simply not listen to any rules my husband and I set down. We've threatened them, punished them, and done everything possible to get them to behave, yet nothing works. We don't communicate with one another. My husband is so involved in his work that he ignores all of us, and he becomes very defensive whenever I try to talk to him about our family situation. I'd like to get to the bottom of our problems and have us begin to talk with one another."

Mr. Winters was quiet for the most part. When the school counselor asked him for his perspective on the situation, he had this to say:

"Frankly, I don't see what good it will do for the four of us to have some outsider come in and tell us how to change our family. I've always been a good provider, and I've worked very hard to give my kids and wife everything I think they should have in a material sense. I'm just basically a quiet guy who likes to keep his feelings to himself. I don't know what my wife means when she says we don't communicate. What does she want, anyway? Let me tell you that I don't like the idea of us hanging out our dirty laundry for everyone to see!"

Reluctantly, under pressure from Mrs. Winters, he agrees to accept a referral to the local community clinic for at least one family session. Both Doug and Debbie react very strongly against the idea, because they are convinced that their parents and the therapist will zero in on them. They fear that they will be the scapegoats. The family is, however, scheduled for an intake session, and you have been assigned to see them for this initial session.

Questions for Reflection

1. What might you say and do at the outset to establish a climate of acceptance, one that would encourage each member of the family to express his or her feelings?
2. What are some of the things you might say to Mr. Winters, who seems convinced that family therapy will not do any good, that these sessions are an invasion of family privacy, and that he has done all he can to provide for his family's welfare? How do you think you might respond to him if he reacted very defensively?
3. What are some ways that you might invite Doug and Debbie to express their views and feelings during the session, assuming both of them were fairly quiet?
4. What would you want to say to Mrs. Winters, based on what little you know about her?
5. What goals would you have for this session? If you were not sure whether you would see this family again, what would you realistically hope to accomplish in this single session?

6. What ideas do you have to facilitate some degree of open communication within this family during the session? Do you have any suggestions of ways they might work on improving their communication?
7. What would you do if the children did not show up for the session?
8. What theoretical perspectives would you tend to draw from in working with this family?

14. Carl: An Adolescent in Search of an Identity

Adolescence is a time when the identity issue is particularly critical, for there is the possibility of losing any sense of personal identity in the desperate search to be approved of by everyone and to belong. By submerging themselves in a group, young people can easily lose any sense of uniqueness. Thus, in counseling adolescents it is well to be aware that the identity issue will often have to be worked through in difficult sessions. Assume that Carl, a 16-year-old, is sent to you by his parents because of their concern that he is becoming more and more defiant.

Some Background Data

What you know about Carl is the following: He did not particularly want to come to counseling but very reluctantly agreed. He does not think it will do any good, and he thinks that his parents are the ones who should go to therapy, not him. They are the ones who are really messed up, according to Carl. He managed to get himself expelled from a private school for using drugs, and he did not finish school that year. Instead, he cut classes at a public high school, ran around with a gang of older adolescents, and generally did a lot to get attention. He is willing to give you a try for a few sessions, because he realizes that he does not know who he is. Carl says that he has spent most of his time being everything his folks did not want him to be. He sees his father as a phony—a businessman who does not know how to live, who is searching for the top but will not know what to do when he finally gets there. Carl does not want to be like his father. He generally rebels against most of his parents' values.

What is important in Carl's world right now is to be liked by the gang he associates with, to fix up his car, to date lots of girls, and to have fun. He tells you that he is tired of hearing about the "responsibility trip" and that he does not want lectures from you on how he should live and what he should be.

Questions for Reflection

Think about ways that you might begin and how you might work with Carl if both of you agreed that he would come in for three sessions.

1. What are your initial reactions to Carl? Which of these reactions would you share with him? keep to yourself?
2. Do you think that an "involuntary client" and counseling mix?

3. Where might you begin? What direction would you take, given that you may see Carl for only three sessions?
4. Carl did mention that he does not know who he is, that he is fighting the image of what his parents want for him, and that he is searching for approval. How would you work with him on the issue of his identity struggle?
5. In what ways would you use who you are in your work with Carl? Do you think he will respond to your confrontation? to your disclosures about yourself?
6. What struggles did you have in your own adolescence? Do you believe that the way you resolved (or failed to resolve) your own issues in those years is vitally related to your ability now to make a significant impact on Carl? Can you identify with any parts of Carl's experience? If so, what aspects? If you have a hard time identifying with Carl, do you think that you could effectively work with him for these limited sessions?

15. Ralph: He Feels Trapped in His Job

Ralph is a 47-year-old married man with four children (all of whom are adolescents or older). He says that he is coming to you for counseling in order to find a way to free himself from feeling trapped by meaningless work. He was referred to you by a friend, and he tells you the following at the intake session.

Some Background Data

"I feel a need to take some action at this point in my life—I suppose you could say I'm going through a late identity crisis. By now, you'd expect that a guy of my age should know where he's going in life, but all I know is that I feel blah. Just sorta like a zombie!

"I attribute most of my problems to my job. I've worked with this department store chain for more years than I can remember. I'm the manager of a store with quite a few people under me. But how I've come to hate that job! There's nothing to look forward to anymore. It's no challenge. Part of me wants to junk the entire thing, even though I'm not that far away from retirement with a nice pension and many fringe benefits. So the conservative part of me says stay and put up with what you've got! Then another side of me says leave and find something else more challenging. Don't *die* living for a stinking pension plan!

"So I'm really torn whether I should stay or leave. I keep thinking of my kids. I feel I should support them and see them through college—and if I go to another job I'll have to take a big pay cut. I feel guilty about even thinking of letting my kids down when they expect me to see them through. And then my wife tells me I should just accept that what I'm feeling is normal for my age—a mid-life crisis, she calls it. She says I should get rid of foolish notions about making a job change at my age. Then there's always the fear that I'll get out there and make that big change and then get fired. What would I do without a job? Who would I be if I couldn't work? I just feel as though there are heavy rocks on my shoulders weighing me down every time I think about being stuck in my job. I sure hope you'll help me get rid of this burden and help me make a decision about what to do with this work situation."

Questions for Reflection

1. Based on his story, what are your impressions of Ralph? Would you like to work with him? Why or why not? Would you share with him any of your initial reactions and thoughts from the intake session? If so, what do you think you would tell him?
2. How might you work with the two sides of Ralph: the part of him that wants to stay in his job versus the part that wants to leave? How many techniques can you think of that might be appropriate in working with this conflict?
3. Check what your goals might be in working with Ralph:
   _____ to provide him with information about the job market
   _____ to give him advice about whether he should remain in his job or look for a new career in life
   _____ to encourage him to work with his feelings of "blahness" and guilt over not providing for his children
   _____ to help him deal with his fear of changing jobs and then failing
   _____ to help him look at what he would be without his work
   _____ to challenge him to deal with his feelings toward his wife
4. Depending on which of the above goals you see as being most pressing, how do you think you would work differently with him?
5. Do you have any ideas about how to work with his burden of carrying heavy rocks on his shoulders?
6. What ideas do you have about helping him explore his feeling of being trapped?
7. What other specific techniques might you be inclined to use, with what expected outcomes?

POSTSCRIPT

The process of beginning to develop a counseling style that fits you is truly a challenge. It entails far more than picking bits and pieces from theories in a random and fragmented manner. As you take steps to develop an integrated perspective, you might ask: Which theories provide a basis for understanding the *feeling* dimension? Which theories help you understand the *cognitive* dimension? And what about the *behavioral* dimension? As you are aware, most of the nine therapies you have studied focus primarily on one of these dimensions of human experience. The task is to wisely and creatively select therapeutic procedures that you can employ in working with a diverse population. Knowing the unique needs of your clients, your own values and personality, and the theories themselves is a good basis for beginning to develop a theory that is an expression of yourself.

By now, I am sure, it is evident that it requires skill, knowledge, art, and experience to be able to determine what techniques work best with particular clients and with certain problems. It is also an art to know *when* and *how* to use a particular therapeutic intervention. Because building your personalized theory of counseling is a long-term venture, I do hope that you will be patient with yourself as you continue to grow through your reading, thinking, experience in working with clients, and your own personal struggles and life experiences.

TO THE OWNER OF THIS BOOK:

I hope that you have found *Case Approach to Counseling and Psychotherapy* (Second Edition) useful. So that this book can be improved in a future edition, would you take the time to complete this sheet and return it? Thanks.

School and address: ______________________________

Department: ____________________ Instructor's name: ____________________

1. What I like *most* about this casebook is: ______________________________

2. What I like *least* about this casebook is: ______________________________

3. How we used this book in class was: ______________________________

4. My general reactions to Ruth's case are: ______________________________

5. Other specific cases in the book I found most helpful are: ______________________________

6. Specific cases I found least useful or would suggest deleting in future editions are: ______________________________

7. The kinds of cases I would like to see added are: ______________________________

8. My general reaction to this book is: ______________________________

9. The name of the course in which I used this book is: ______________________________

10. On a separate sheet of paper, please write specific suggestions for improving this book and anything else you'd care to share about your experience in using the book.

Optional:

Your Name: ______________________________ Date: ______________

May Brooks/Cole quote you, either in promotion for *Case Approach to Counseling and Psychotherapy* or in future publishing ventures?

Yes ____________ No ____________

Sincerely,

Gerald Corey

CUT PAGE OUT AND
FOLD HERE

NO POSTAGE
NECESSARY
IF MAILED
IN THE
UNITED STATES

BUSINESS REPLY MAIL

FIRST CLASS PERMIT NO. 84 MONTEREY, CALIF.

POSTAGE WILL BE PAID BY ADDRESSEE

DR. GERALD COREY
BROOKS/COLE PUBLISHING COMPANY
MONTEREY, CA 93940